Repentance at Qumran

Repentance at Qumran

The Penitential Framework of Religious Experience in the Dead Sea Scrolls

Mark A. Jason

Fortress Press
Minneapolis

REPENTANCE AT QUMRAN

The Penitential Framework of Religious Experience in the Dead Sea Scrolls

Cover design: Alisha Lofgren

Library of Congress Cataloging-in-Publication Data is available

Print ISBN: 978-1-4514-8530-1

eBook ISBN: 978-1-4514-9427-3

The paper used in this publication meets the minimum requirements of American National Standard for Information Sciences — Permanence of Paper for Printed Library Materials, ANSI Z329.48-1984.

Manufactured in the U.S.A.

This book was produced using PressBooks.com, and PDF rendering was done by PrinceXML.

Contents

Abbreviations

AB	Anchor Bible
ACNT	Augsburg Commentaries on the New Testament
APOT	*The Apocrypha and Pseudepigrapha of the Old Testament*. Edited by R. H. Charles. 2 vols. Oxford: Clarendon, 1913.
BBR	*Bulletin of Biblical Research*
Bib	*Biblica*
BI	*Biblical Interpretation*
BN	*Biblischer Notizen. Beiträge zur Exegetischen Diskussion*
CBQ	*Catholic Biblical Quarterly*
CBQMS	Catholic Biblical Quarterly Monograph Series
CCWJCW	Cambridge Commentaries on Writings of the Jewish and Christian World 200 BC to AD 200
DBI	*Dictionary of Biblical Interpretation*
DJD	Discoveries in the Judaean Desert
DSD	*Dead Sea Discoveries*
DSSSE	García Martínez and E. Tigchelaar, eds. *The Dead Sea Scrolls: Study Edition*. 2 vols. Leiden: Brill, 1997–1998.
DSSNT	Wise, M. Abegg, and E. Cook, eds. *The Dead Sea Scrolls: A New Translation*. San Francisco: HarperSanFrancisco, 1999.
EvQ	*Evangelical Quarterly*
ExpT	*Expository Times*

EBC	*Expositor's Bible Commentary*
EI	*Eretz Israel*
EJ	*Encyclopaedia Judaica*
GAP	Guides to the Apocrypha and Pseudepigrapha
HB	Hebrew Bible
HSM	Harvard Semitic Monographs
HTR	*Harvard Theological Review*
IBC	Interpretation: A Bible Commentary for Teaching and Preaching
ICC	International Critical Commentary
IDB	*The Interpreter's Dictionary of the Bible*
IEJ	*Israel Exploration Journal*
JBL	*Journal of Biblical Literature*
JJS	*Journal of Jewish Studies*
JQR	*Jewish Quarterly Review*
JSNTSup	Journal for the Study of the New Testament: Supplement Series
JSPSup	Journal for the Study of the Pseudepigrapha: Supplement Series
JSOTSup	Journal for the Study of the Old Testament: Supplement Series
JSJ	*Journal for the Study of Judaism*
JSS	*Journal of Semitic Studies*
JSSSup	Journal of Semitic Studies: Supplement Series
JSHRZ	*Jüdische Schriften aus hellenistisch-römischer Zeit*
JTS	*Journal of Theological Studies*
KAT	Kommentar zum Alten Testament
LAB	Pseudo-Philo, *Liber Antiquitatum Biblicarum*
LNTS	Library of New Testament Studies
LXX	The Septuagint
MS	Manuscript
MT	Masoretic Text

NBD	*The New Bible Dictionary*
NIB	*The New Interpreter's Bible*
NICNT	New International Commentary on the New Testament
NICOT	New International Commentary on the Old Testament
NovT	*Novum Testamentum*
NTS	*New Testament Studies*
OTL	Old Testament Library
OTP	H. Charlesworth, ed. *The Old Testament Pseudepigrapha*. 2 vols. London: Darton, Longman & Todd, 1983–1985.
PTSDSSP	Princeton Theological Seminary Dead Sea Scrolls Project
RB	*Revue biblique*
RevQ	*Revue de Qumrân*
SBL	Society of Biblical Literature
SBLDS	Society of Biblical Literature Dissertation Series
SBLMS	Society of Biblical Literature Monograph Series
SCSS	Septuagint and Cognate Studies Series
SNTMS	Society for New Testament Studies Monograph Series
STDJ	Studies on the Text of the Desert of Judah
TB	*Tyndale Bulletin*
TDOT	*Theological Dictionary of the Old Testament*. 15 vols. Edited by G. Johannes Botterweck, Helmer Ringgren, and Heinz-Josef Fabry. Translated by David E. Green and Douglas W. Stott. Grand Rapids: Eerdmans, 1974–1995.
ThZ	*Theologische Zeitschrift*
TWAT	Theologische Wörterbuch Altes Testaments
TWOT	Laird Harris, Gleason L. Archer, and Bruce K. Waltke, eds. *Theological Wordbook of the Old Testament*. Chicago: Moody Press, 1980.
VT	*Vetus Testamentum*
VTSup	Supplements to Vetus Testamentum
WBC	Word Biblical Commentary

WUNT	Wissenschaftliche Untersuchungen zum Neuen Testament
Apoc. Zeph.	*Apocalypse of Zephaniah*
Jos. Asen.	*Joseph and Aseneth*
J.W.	Josephus, *Jewish War*
Let. Aris.	*Letter of Aristeas*
T. Ab.	*Testament of Abraham*
T. Gad	*Testament of Gad*
T. Jud.	*Testament of Judah*
T. Naph.	*Testament of Naphtali*
T. Lev.	*Testament of Levi*
T. Jos.	*Testament of Joseph*
T. Zeb.	*Testament of Zebulun*
T. Dan	*Testament of Dan*
T. Reu.	*Testament of Reuben*
T. Sim.	*Testament of Simeon*
T. Zeb.	*Testament of Zebulun*

Acknowledgments

My acknowledgments are a bit like the scrolls themselves, replete with lacuna thereby lacking in vital information; however, like the scrolls, what is preserved is of great importance. What is missing is no less significant . . .

This project came together in two stages, first as doctoral dissertation and then in a revised form, as book. At every stage of this somewhat lengthy process, I am indebted to various academics for their insightful comments and input that enabled this book to come to fruition. Dr. Simon Gathercole, University of Cambridge, stands out. Right from the earliest stages of my research while this work was developing into a dissertation, Dr. Gathercole was my supervisor, and it was he who encouraged me to embark on a journey of discovery into the world of the Dead Sea Scrolls. Back then (as is still the case now) he has always been available and approachable; his valuable input always enabled me to stretch my mind beyond my own imagination. Another scholar to whom I am sincerely grateful is Prof. Bilhah Nitzan (Tel Aviv University) whose article "Repentance in the Dead Sea Scrolls" (1999) proved to be the starting point of my own fascinating engagement with the scrolls. She has always responded to my queries, offered comments, and made suggestions. As a novice in the fraternity of scrolls scholars, I was indeed privileged to have a scholar of her caliber read and comment on a draft of chapter 7 in its dissertation form and, more recently, the conclusion in its present form.

The churches I have served during the writing both of the dissertation and the book have always served as a constant reminder for me that all scholarly research and biblical scholarship is ultimately for the edification of the church. My ministry in these churches constantly challenges me to bridge the gap between *academia* and *pastoralia*.

Sincere thanks is due to the team at Fortress Press, who so smoothly facilitated the whole publication process, transforming what appeared to be daunting (for a first-time author!) into a highly enjoyable task. Two persons at Fortress deserve particular mention. Dr. Neil Elliot, acquiring editor in biblical studies, always willingly and promptly responded to my barrage of questions throughout the project. Ms. Marissa Wold, senior project manager, patiently, skillfully, helpfully, and cheerfully guided me through the production process. Any errors that may have slipped through are purely my responsibility.

Lastly, but by no means the least, I wish to thank my wife Sarah for her unflagging support, friendship, encouragement, and prayers that enabled me to complete this project. I am grateful to her for her love and companionship that has always strengthened and enriched me. It is to her that I dedicate this book.

Introduction

Whoever would have thought that the retrieval of a lost goat would have led to one of the greatest archaeological discoveries of the twentieth century, namely, the discovery of the Dead Sea Scrolls? The story has often been told of the goat that strayed away, unwittingly leading its owner, Muhammad El Dibh, past the many caves that dotted the cliff face along the western shore of the Dead Sea. Exploring one of these caves, he found found several rolls of leather and brought out seven of them. This was the start of an incredible journey, which took these seven leather scrolls from the Judean wilderness to a Bethlehem market, to St. Mark's Monastery in Jerusalem, the Hebrew University, and finally to the American Schools of Archaeological Research, until they ultimately became known to the world. This initial discovery led to renewed archaeological interest in the caves on the northwestern shores of the Dead Sea, which yielded roughly 850 scrolls from eleven caves. Shrouded in mystery and secrecy for many decades, it wasn't until the early 1990s that all the scrolls came into public domain. The initial discovery of the scrolls themselves led to the production of a vast amount of literature; the publication of the entire collection of scrolls led to renewed literary activity in the world and content of the scrolls. At the closing session of the Jerusalem Congress on the

Dead Sea Scrolls (July 20–25, 1997) H. Stegemann said: "There are already more than ten thousand books and scholarly articles written on Qumran evidence over the last fifty years. The present stage of Qumran research seems to cover almost every topic that could be isolated, with the main findings discussed from every point of view at least several hundred times."[1]

While the early phase of scrolls scholarship was focused on piecing together the fragments and consisted largely of reconstruction and some comparatively general synthetic work, the next phase of research arose from the foundation that these reconstructed texts provided. As a result, there have been countless studies on various themes and concepts arising out of individual texts.[2] The abundance of research, which has greatly enhanced our understanding of the scrolls and their authors, testifies to this. In this scenario, the obvious question at the very outset is: Why another study on the scrolls? or What new dimension is this study going to bring to existing Qumran scholarship?

Direction of Travel

In the following chapters, we will embark on journey entailing a detailed investigation into the role and function of repentance in the religious experience of the Qumran community. We will do this through the evidence provided by the Dead Sea Scrolls against the backdrop of contemporaneous Second Temple literature. The

---

1. H. Stegemann, "Qumran Challenges for the Next Century," in *The Dead Sea Scrolls: Fifty Years after Their Discovery*, ed. L. Schiffman, E. Tov, and J. VanderKam (Jerusalem: Israel Exploration Society, 2000), 944–50 (944).

2. G. Nickelsburg says: "We should recognize and celebrate the fact that the first decade and a half of Qumran scholarship produced a great deal of intelligent and even brilliant work on the scrolls and their context, and we should acknowledge that this pioneering work was foundational for what followed and that will continue to inform further studies." G. Nickelsburg, "Currents in Qumran Scholarship: The Interplay of Data and Agendas, and Methodology," in *The Dead Sea Scrolls At Fifty*, ed. R. Kugler and E. M. Schuller (Atlanta: Scholars Press, 1999), 79–99 (80).

purpose of such an exercise is to show that repentance was the very basis of the community's existence and a key factor that shaped its religious self-identity. In doing so, it establishes the Qumran community as an important penitential movement within Second Temple Judaism. Our focus then is to explore how this penitential worldview dominated and permeated every level of the community's religious experience and existence.

Our guiding principle is that motifs, language, and images elucidating "repentance" as a vital theological-soteriological concept at Qumran can be used as an analytical tool to reconstruct how repentance functioned within the belief system at Qumran, and to what extent. That is to say, repentance never occurred in a vacuum; it was an integral part of the religious experience of a real, historical community. In other words, our hope is that at the end of this journey, the study of repentance texts in the Dead Sea Scrolls will help postulate how such texts might have been translated into daily life at Qumran.

As hinted at above, I will do this by interacting with repentance motifs in other Second Temple literature. This will show that despite the shared theological and ideological climate of the scrolls, the Apocrypha, and Pseudepigrapha, and their similarities in the understanding of repentance, the emergent and distinctive features regarding the role and function of repentance in the scrolls present the Qumran community as an important penitential movement in Second Temple Judaism. Furthermore, this Second Temple material can "provide us with important information about the development of Jewish religious thought."[3] The use of this additional material serves a twofold purpose: First, against the backdrop of contemporaneous sources, we will be able to discover any features

---

3. A. Tomasino, *Judaism Before Jesus: The Events and Ideas that Shaped the New Testament World* (Downers Grove, IL: InterVarsity Press, 2003), 32.

particularly emphasized or distinctive regarding the concept of repentance in the scrolls; second, we will use any such picture of repentance that might emerge from our comparison as a "tool" to reconstruct the function of repentance in the Qumran community.

How will we do this? Beginning with the question of how repentance justified the community's separated existence in the Judean wilderness and reshaped their understanding of covenant, we will explore how repentance determined who was "in" and who was "out" of God's plan, how repentance featured prominently in daily governance and cultic activities, and how it authenticated their view of the end times. This panoramic sweep, which covers the place of repentance from entry into the community through existence within the community right up to the eschatological expectations of the community, will firmly establish an overriding penitential worldview that prevailed at Qumran.

This detailed study of the concept of repentance in the Dead Sea Scrolls addresses a significant lacuna in Qumran scholarship. To date, this subject has not received sufficient scholarly attention, as repentance at Qumran is usually taken for granted and thus relegated to a peripheral position. As such, it has never received any comprehensive or systematic investigation. Our study addresses this lack by attempting to establish the importance of the penitential framework of religious experience at Qumran.

Scrolls and Caves: The Qumran Community

Up to now, I have been talking about the Qumran community and the Dead Sea Scrolls as documents that offer us an insight into this community. This necessarily assumes that there was indeed a link between the remains of a community dwelling that was excavated on the northwestern shores of the Dead Sea and the large cache of scrolls discovered in the caves nearby. However, we cannot take this link for granted (as this connection between the community and the scrolls is vital to the scope of this book), and therefore it warrants a brief mention. Once this is done, we can get on with our journey and begin to explore how this isolated desert community saw repentance as an integral part of their religious experience.

The site at Qumran might have been the "City of Salt" (Josh. 15:62), in around the eighth to seventh centuries BCE.[4] If this was the case, after remaining unoccupied for a few centuries there was a period of reoccupation beginning around 140 BCE (Phase 1a). In 134–104 BCE (Phase 1b), there was an expansion of buildings. Phase 1b ended abruptly because of an earthquake and a fire, occurring around 31 BCE, after which the site was abandoned. Reoccupation began after the death of Herod in 4 BCE (Phase 2) and lasted until the settlement was possibly destroyed by a Roman army in 68 CE.[5] Activity began again when Roman troops stationed at Qumran built some barracks (Phase 3). Judging by the coins belonging to this period, this phase possibly ended around 90 CE.

More recently, J. Magness has argued for a revised chronology for Qumran, attributing a later date to the beginning of the community. She argues that there is insufficient archaeological evidence to maintain Phase 1a as theorized by French archaeologist and biblical scholar R. de Vaux.[6] Further, Magness subdivides de Vaux's Phase 1b into a pre-31-BCE and post-31-BCE period[7] and concludes that the sectarian settlement at Qumran began around the first half of the first century BCE (c. 100–50 BCE).[8]

---

4. See R. de Vaux *The Archaeology of Qumran* (London: Oxford University Press,1973).
5. It is generally believed that the Essenes almost certainly perished with this attack. For the continuing existence of the Essenes, see A. Negoïtsa, "Did the Essenes Survive the 66–71 War?," *RevQ* 6 (1969), 517–30.
6. J. Magness, *The Archaeology of Qumran and the Dead Sea Scrolls* (Grand Rapids: Eerdmans, 2002), 63–69.
7. This enables us here to confine Phase 1a remains to the pre-31-BCE period of Phase 1b. Magness, *Archaeology of Qumran*, 64.

De Vaux's theory that there was a relationship between the community that deposited the documents found in the eleven caves and the site excavated nearby at Khirbet Qumran still enjoys scholarly consensus.[9] The best evidence for a connection between the scrolls caves and the settlement at Qumran is the fact that pottery found in both places is virtually unique to Qumran.[10] J. Magness comments that "Qumran provides the unique opportunity to use archaeological evidence combined with the information from ancient historical sources and scrolls to reconstruct and understand the life of a community."[11]

This leads to the natural question: What was the identity of this community that lived at Qumran and deposited the scrolls into the eleven caves? In the early days of scrolls scholarship, the Essene connection was taken for granted. In 1956, B. J. Roberts said: "Khirbet Qumrân is now generally acknowledged to be the remains of an Essene convent, and consequentially the Qumrân scrolls should be regarded as Essene literature, because there can be no doubt about the direct connexion between the scrolls and the convent."[12] Scholars are now much more reluctant to assert a priori an Essene identification. F. F. Bruce says that "the Qumran community has been identified in turn with every religious party in Judaism in the later period of the Second Commonwealth—with the Sadducees, Pharisees, Zealots and Essenes."[13]

---

8. Magness, *Archaeology of Qumran*.
9. This connection of the manuscripts with the archaeological discoveries has not gone unchallenged. One theory has it that Qumran was a "country villa" that was taken over by the Essenes. See Jean-Baptiste Humbert, "L'espace sacré à Qumrân" *RB* 101 (1994): 161–214.
10. Magness, *Archaeology of Qumran*, 44. She points out that the type of ceramic of pottery items found in the caves and on the excavated site is identical.
11. Magness, *Archaeology of Qumran*, 13. She confirms that the scrolls provide evidence that complements the archaeology.
12. B. J. Roberts, "The Qumran Scrolls and the Essenes," *NTS* (1956): 58–65 (58).
13. F. F. Bruce, *New Testament History* (London: Oliphants, 1971), 109. The identification of the community with the Pharisees is no longer advocated since it is generally accepted that the Pharisees are criticized in the scrolls. P. R. Davies, G. Brooke, and P. Callaway, *The Complete*

However, despite the various theories, the Essene identification has become "a kind of *opinio communis*."[14] This is chiefly because of the accounts about and descriptions of the Essenes in the classical sources, chiefly in the writings of Pliny,[15] Philo,[16] and Josephus.[17] Although the community at Qumran largely resembles these sources' description of the Essenes, there are considerable differences[18] that have led some scholars to reassess this identification.[19] Still, as Geza Vermes says: "The Essene theory appears not only to be sound but endowed with a high degree of intrinsic probability. To reject it would not render any of the other hypotheses more likely but merely lead to the conclusion that the Qumran relics must belong to a hitherto totally unknown Jewish sect almost identical to the Essenes!"[20] Insofar as our journey is concerned, I accept this view that there was indeed a connection between the scrolls and the

World of the Dead Sea Scrolls, 205. L. H. Schiffman suggests that in its earliest stages, the Qumran community was Sadducean or at least exhibited heavy Sadducean influences on its legal positions. L. Schiffman, *Reclaiming the Dead Sea Scrolls: Their True Meaning for Judaism and Christianity* (Philadelphia: Jewish Publication Society, 1994). C. Roth presses for a Zealot identification based on a fragment of the *Songs* at Masada. C. Roth, "'Qumran and Masadah': A Final Clarification Regarding the Dead Sea Sect," *RevQ* (1964): 81–88. He is convinced that the pacifist Essenes did not participate in the revolt against Rome. C. Roth, "Why the Qumran Sect Cannot Have Been Essenes" *RevQ* (1959): 417–22. N. Golb argues that the scrolls represent the wealth of the libraries of Jerusalem hidden there by people who fled from the approaching Romans around the time of the First Jewish Revolt. For Golb, it is more plausible that so many manuscripts came from a large intellectual center rather than a small group. N. Golb, *Who Wrote the Scrolls? The Search for the Secret of Qumran* (London: Michael O'Mara, 1995).

14. G. Vermes, "The Essenes and History," *JJS* (1981): 18–31 (20).

15. Pliny, *Natural History* 5.15.73. R. Kroft cautions that Pliny "had no first hand knowledge" of this group about which he reports. R. Kroft, "Pliny on Essenes, Pliny on Jews," *DSD* 8, no. 3 (2001): 255–61 (260).

16. Philo, *Apology for the Jews* as preserved in Eusebius, *Praeparatio evangelica*. 8.10.

17. Josephus, *Antiquities of the Jews* 13.5.9 (§§171–73); 18.1.5; *Jewish War* 2.8.2-13 (§§119–61).

18. Despite the differences, the similarities that do exist are striking and appear to fit into the evidence better than the others. Hence, the burden of proof is with those who outrightly reject the Essene theory. See T. Beall, *Josephus' Description of the Essenes Illustrated by the Dead Sea Scrolls* (Cambridge: Cambridge University Press, 1988).

19. Another theory suggests that the Essene movement had two offshoots, the Qumran community and the Therapeutae in Egypt. F. García Martínez and A. S. van der Woude, "A 'Groningen' Hypothesis of Qumran Origins and Early History," *RevQ* (1990): 521–42.

20. Vermes, "Essenes and History," 21.

remains of the community, and assume that the scrolls belonged to the community. A study of these documents, then, could provide a useful window into the lives of the community that used them.

We are now ready to move on and highlight some methodological issues that need to be borne in mind. Given that I have been talking about *repentance* "texts," "concepts," "images," and "motifs," how do we identify them?

Methodological Considerations

Repentance Texts

In any journey, there needs to be a starting point, a sense of 'rooting' that serves as a point of reference. We too need a "rooting point," a working definition that we can return to again and again in order to get our bearing, to check that we are on track. Such a working definition ought to be fluid and general so that we can develop it as we go along. A repentance text therefore should exhibit a general conformity to our working definition, either explicitly or implicitly through language, metaphor, image, or allusion. Before we can proceed further, we need to pin down this "working definition" of repentance and for that, this definition is very helpful:

> Repentance is the radical turning away from anything which hinders one's whole-hearted devotion to God and the corresponding turning to God in love and obedience.[21]

Although this definition is very unspecific, it expresses the bare outlines of what repentance is, thereby allowing us to supplement

---

21. J. Milgrom, "Repentance," in *Encyclopedia Judaica* (Jerusalem: Keter, 1974), 14:74. It may be argued that the reference to "love" in this working definition has Christian overtones and therefore is incompatible to this study on the scrolls. However, it can be pointed out that one of the very purposes of the *Rule of the Community* is stated thus: "in order to love everything which he selects and to hate everything that he rejects" (1QS 1:3b–4a). This maintains the general thrust of our working definition.

and modify it as we go along. A couple of other clarifications are necessary at this point. I have been talking about how to identify "repentance texts" in the "Dead Sea Scrolls." Because of the many archaeological finds around the region of the Dead Sea, this raises the question, which Dead Sea Scrolls? J. Fitzmyer says that the term could denote the scrolls and fragments recovered from the eleven caves in the vicinity of Khirbet Qumran,[22] and texts related to them found either at Masada[23] or in the Cairo Genizah.[24]

Just when we think we have narrowed down our literary corpus, it will be pointed out that the Dead Sea Scrolls (as defined above) are made up of biblical, extrabiblical (apocryphal and pseudipigraphical), and sectarian literature. Of this mix, "sectarian literature"[25] is what we are primarily concerned with, as this corpus provides "information on the beliefs and practices of the sect that used (and in some cases composed) these scrolls and deposited them in the caves at Qumran."[26] Again, further clarification is necessary when talking about this "subcategory" within the scrolls. Scholars have proposed various criteria for describing a particular work as "sectarian." For example, E. Chazon[27] says that in order to determine whether a particular document is of sectarian authorship, one must consider features such as orthography and language; absence of these features

---

22. J. Fitzmyer, *The Dead Sea Scrolls and Christian Origins* (Grand Rapids: Eerdmans, 2000), 2.
23. The single copy of the *Songs of the Sabbath Sacrifice* (Mas 1k).
24. CD A and B.
25. Those works that prior to their discovery were largely unknown but that are distinctive in style and ideology. D. Dimant, "The Qumran Manuscripts: Content and Significance," in *Time to Prepare the Way in the Wilderness*, ed. D. Dimant and L. Schiffman, STDJ 10 (Leiden: Brill, 1995), 25–58 (26).
26. Magness, *Archaeology of Qumran*, 36. S. W. Crawford says that these hitherto unknown documents "betray certain traits and biases that identify them as the property of a particular Jewish group." S. W. Crawford, "Not According to Rule: Women, the Dead Sea Scrolls and Qumran," in *Emanuel: Studies in Hebrew Bible, Septuagint and Dead Sea Scrolls in Honour of Emanuel Tov*, ed. S. Paul, R. Kraft, L. Schiffman, and W. Field (Leiden: Brill, 2003), 127–50 (129).
27. E. Chazon, "Is *Divrei Ha-Me'orot* a Sectarian Prayer," in *The Dead Sea Scrolls: Forty Years of Research*, ed. D. Dimant and U. Rappaport (Leiden: Brill, 1992), 3–17.

suggest a nonsectarian origin.[28] Likewise, if the script of a scroll predates the settlement of Qumran, it is nonsectarian;[29] if it can be positively shown that a particular scroll represented the version of a prayer in general usage at that time, it might indicate a nonsectarian origin. Further, the content of documents that deal with the sect's history and organizational patterns use distinctive ideas and terms. The absence of such language and ideas is indicative of a nonsectarian work.

C. Newsom proposes a wider set of criteria to identify a sectarian work;[30] for her, sectarian material implies that it was written by a member of the sect or that it was read by members of the sect no matter who wrote it. Further, Newsom suggests that the term *sectarian* describes a text with rhetorical purpose and polemic emphasis. While both Chazon's and Newsom's criteria are helpful, Newsom's slightly broader approach should be borne in mind since we are concerned with assessing the larger picture of how repentance may have functioned in the community. Therefore, those documents that were composed at Qumran will not be treated differently from those that were imported to or copied at Qumran. This does not affect our overall emphasis on repentance.

However, that said, this approach presents us with one potential difficulty, and that relates to the development of ideas over a period of time. Not all the scrolls come from the same period. Since our texts have been composed or copied between 150 BCE and 68 CE,

28. See E. Tov, "The Biblical Scrolls Found in the Judean Desert and their Contribution to Textual Criticism," *JJS* 39 (1988): 5–37; Tov, "The Orthography and Language of the Hebrew Scrolls Found at Qumran and the Origin of These Scrolls," *Textus* 13 (1986): 31–57.

29. On the relation between scripts and dating, see F. Cross, "The Development of Jewish Scripts," in *The Bible and the Ancient Near East: Essays in Honour of W. F. Albright*, ed. G. E. Wright (London: Routledge and Kegan Paul, 1961), 133–202.

30. C. Newsom, "'Sectually Explicit' Literature from Qumran," in *The Hebrew Bible and Its Interpreters*, ed. W. Propp, B. Halpern, and D. Freeman (Winona Lake, IN: Eisenbrauns, 1990), 167–87.

the possibility of development and progression in thought and ideas regarding the community's understanding of repentance is very real. We can never be sure whether an idea received the same emphasis throughout the community's various stages of development; the importance of repentance could have waxed and waned over the various periods of the community's existence. This "development" of ideas was noted even in the early days of scrolls research. A. Dupont-Sommer points out that "as far as the Qumran documents are concerned . . . these writings are not all of the same age and can betray, from one document to the next, a certain evolution in institutions and beliefs."[31] Similarly, E. P. Sanders says: "It should be noted that the Qumran material is not perfectly homogenous. In some instances a developmental history can be traced, and the various documents—and parts of documents—represent differences of opinion on individual points as well as differences of overall intention and view point."[32]

As our study of repentance texts proceeds, we will bear this difficulty in mind and take it into consideration when attempting to reconstruct how repentance may have functioned within the community.[33] However, this does not prevent us from approaching these documents as a whole. Unless necessary, we will not confine ourselves to text-critical issues such as deciding whether a text is from an early or later stage of the community. C. Evans and P. Flint acknowledge the diversity of the material that the scrolls represent but also observe that "such a diversity does not preclude the existence

---

31. A. Dupont-Sommer, *The Essene Writings From Qumran* (Oxford: Basil Blackwell, 1961), 66.
32. E. P. Sanders, *Paul and Palestinian Judaism: A Comparison of Patterns of Religion* (London: SCM, 1977), 239n1.
33. A.S. van der Woude warns: "In the first decades of Qumran research, many authors tended in those years to look upon the corpus of texts as reflecting a homogeneous system of thought." A. S. van der Woude, "Fifty Years of Qumran Research," in *The Dead Sea Scrolls after Fifty Years*, ed. P. Flint and J. VanderKam (Leiden: Brill, 1998), 1:1–45. He also mentions that some scholars unfortunately still advocate this approach (ibid., 36).

of central ideas or a common core."[34] It is such a "common core"
regarding repentance that we are attempting to investigate, albeit
keeping in mind the above proviso regarding the development of
ideas.[35] I have highlighted in the next section (below) selected texts
that feature prominently in the subsequent chapters.

Overview of the Scrolls to Be Used

What follows below is a very brief overview of some of the key
sectarian scrolls that we will be interacting with. The purpose of this
overview is merely to serve as a reference point, an aide-mémoire, for
the background of these particular scrolls. It should be remembered
that the list of scrolls below is representative rather than exhaustive of
the key scrolls I have used. I have divided the material purely on the
basis on the caves in which they were discovered. I hope that having
this "reference point"/summary of these scrolls will facilitate a smooth
transition when we read sections of these scrolls as repentance texts.

34. C. Evans and P. Flint, introduction to *Eschatology, Messianism, and the Dead Sea Scrolls*, ed. C.
Evans and P. Flint (Grand Rapids: Eerdmans, 1997), 1–9 (5). On the back cover of *Religion
in the Dead Sea Scrolls*, G. Brooke comments that the collection of essays is the first attempt
after the release of all the unpublished fragments in 1991 "to consider *in a comprehensive way* the
various religious perspectives to be found *in the whole body of evidence*" (emphasis added). Thus
our investigation seeks to consider in a comprehensive way the various aspects of repentance
to be found in the whole body of evidence. In fact, Brooke acknowledges that "though there is
much more yet to be said on the topics raised here, and indeed on others not included, in many
ways these essays will set the agenda for future discussion." Our investigation seek to address
one such topic "not included."
35. The difficulty of tracing the development of ideas in the scrolls is affirmed by G. Brooke: "At
the moment, the texts from Qumran refuse to be arranged in chronological order or presented
as ideologically uniform in any one period." G. Brooke, review of G. S. Oegema, *DSD* 4
(1997): 367.

Cave 1

1QpHab

This document contains thirteen columns of text and is written in a Herodian script. It is the "longest and best preserved of all the Qumran *pesharim*."[36] It also is one of the most important sources "not only for sectarian Bible interpretation but also for the study of the history of Qumran origins."[37] Its importance lies in the fact that the author uses the biblical book as a pattern to understand his own times.[38] Just as the biblical book speaks of the threat posed to Judah by the Babylonians, the author of the pesher reinterpreted it for his own times as the threat posed by the Kittim (in all probability, the Romans); similarly, the internal struggles between the pious worshipers of God and the ungodly of the biblical were understood by the author as the conflict between the Teacher of Righteousness and his opponents (including the wicked Priest). The commentary is based on the first two chapters of the biblical book.[39]

1QS (*The Rule of the Community*)

1QS was among the first scrolls to be discovered and also has the distinction being the "best preserved manuscript from cave one."[40] It throws valuable light on the modus operandi of the community. Despite its composite nature,[41] it is thought to be one of the oldest

---

36. E. Schürer, *The History of the Jewish People in the Age of Jesus Christ (175 B.C.–A.D. 135)*, rev. and ed. G. Vermes, F. Millar, and M. Goodman (Edinburgh: T&T Clark, 1986), vol. 3, pt. 1, 433.
37. Ibid., 434.
38. *DSSNT* 114.
39. The silence regarding the prayer of chapter 3 (in the biblical book) might indicate that the text used by the author of the pesher lacked this prayer; alternatively, it may indicate that this liturgical section did not suit the author's interpretative aims. See E. Ferguson, *Backgrounds of Early Christianity*, 3rd ed. (Grand Rapids: Eerdmans, 2003), 471.
40. G. Vermes, *The Dead Sea Scrolls in English* (Sheffield: JSOT Press, 1987), 61.
41. Ibid. S. Metso, *The Textual Development of the Qumran Community Rule* (Leiden: Brill, 1997); J. Pouilly, *La Règle de la Communauté de Qumrân. Son Évolution Littéraire* (Paris: Gabala, 1976);

documents of the community, its oldest form going back to about 100 BCE.[42] Immediately prior to the publication of the 4QS fragments, G. Vermes predicted: "At a preliminary glance, it can be already surmised that 1QS is more likely to be an expanded edition of the Cave 4 texts rather than 4QS an abridgement of 1QS."[43] The existence of twelve copies shows its popularity and importance in Qumran.[44] Despite the varied nature of its contents, it provides us with the "fullest picture now existing of the actual functioning of the sect."[45] P. S. Alexander notes that 1QS was "not an exhaustive rule-book or code of practice for new members, but an *aide-memoire* for someone well versed in the community's ways."[46]

1QSa (*The Rule of the Congregation*)

1QSa consists of two columns that have been reconstructed from fragments originally part of the scrolls containing 1QS and were most likely to have been copied by the same scribe during the same period of 1QS.[47] This composition sets down regulations for the eschatological integration of the entire "congregation of Israel" into the Zadokite-led community.[48] C. Hempel comments that "most commentators on 1QSa would agree that this so called Messianic Rule reflects the life of an existing earthly community."[49] Although the prevailing consensus is that it is an eschatological rule describing

M. Bockmuehl, "Redaction and Ideology in the Rule of the Community," *RevQ* 72 (1998): 541–60.

42. Vermes, *Dead Sea Scrolls in English*, 61.

43. G. Vermes, "Preliminary Remarks on Unpublished fragments of the Community Rule from Qumran Cave 4," *JJS* 42, no. 2 (1991): 250–55 (255).

44. D. Dimant, "Qumran Sectarian Literature," in *Jewish Writings of the Second Temple Period*, ed. M. Stone (Assen: Van Gorcum, 1984), 483–550 (498).

45. Ibid., 497.

46. P. S. Alexander, "The Redaction History of *Serek ha-Yahad*," *RevQ* 17 (1996): 437–56 (438).

47. Schürer, *History of the Jewish People*, 386.

48. Ibid., 386.

49. C. Hempel, "The Earthly Essene Nucleus of 1QSa," *DSD* 3 (1996): 254.

the life and conduct of the community in the messianic era, H.
Stegemann believes that 1QSa is the oldest rule book of the *yahad* for
the present age.[50]

1QH (*Hodayot*)

It is now an accepted fact that this scroll, written in a Herodian script,
was written at least by two scribes.[51] The fragmentary nature and
frequent lacunae in 1QH make interpretation difficult.[52] From the
eighteen columns and numerous fragments found, there are about
twenty more-or-less complete psalms. The remaining fragments
could possibly make up to about twenty more.[53] The existence of six
other copies of the scroll in Cave 4 hints that it was highly valued and
rated by the community.[54] The collection of hymns in 1QH consists
of spiritual expressions and confessions, adoration of God, expressions
of total submission to his will, sinfulness, hope for eternal bliss, and so
on.

Cave 4

Pesharim

The pesharim[55] are "hermeneutical" compositions comprising two
parts, the sacred text of the Torah and a commentary that follows.
The pesharim reveal the way the community saw their recent past

50. H. Stegemann, "Some Remarks to 1QSa, to 1QSb, and to Qumran Messianism," *RevQ* 17
(1997): 479–505 (495). According to Hempel, 1QSa 1:6-2:11a was "a traditional Essene
communal legislation that was later incorporated into an eschatological setting." Hempel, "The
Earthly Essene Nucleus of 1QSa," 254.
51. S. Holm-Nielsen, *Hodayot: Psalms from Qumran* (Aarhus: Universitetsforlaget, 1960), 9.
52. Dupont-Sommer, *Essene Writings*, 198–99. Dupont-Sommer describes 1QH as "the jewel of all
the mystical literature from Qumran."
53. Ibid., 198.
54. Ibid., 199.
55. This introduction also governs 1QpHab. See M. P. Horgan, *Pesharim: Qumran Interpretations of
Biblical Books* (Washington, DC: Catholic Biblical Association of America, 1979).

by scrutinizing the Scriptures (primarily the prophetic books) and saw the fulfillment of these prophecies in their own life in the community.

4Q171

This scroll, written in a Herodian hand, contains pesher-type commentaries on sections of Psalm 37, 45, and 60.[56] While no clear dating criterion can be discerned from the existing material, it may be assumed that, like other pesharim, this document also originated in the first century BCE.[57] Particularly relevant to our purposes is the treatment of Psalm 37 where a description of the destiny of the righteous and the wicked is applied to the sectarians and their opponents.[58]

4Q174

This document consists of a selection of biblical texts with expository comments, written in an "early Herodian" hand.[59] The section that we are concerned with is 1:14-17 and is introduced as מדרש "implying no doubt an interpretative method whereby the meaning of the text under consideration is derived from other biblical quotations."[60]

4Q186

4Q186 is an unusual document, written from left to right. It also irregularly uses letters of the archaic alphabet mixed with Greek characters.[61] It is written in "Herodian" script and employs

---

56. Schürer, *History of the Jewish People*, 438.
57. Ibid.
58. Ibid.
59. Ibid., 445. Twenty-six fragments were found, of which only the first ten were large enough to be meaningful.
60. Ibid.

physiognomy. P. Popovic describes it thus: "Physiognomics is the means to discern another person's character, disposition or future from his physical features."[62] This text enabled one to draw conclusions regarding the observed person's inner character.

4Q215a

Written in late "Hasmonean" or "early Herodian" script,[63] a Qumran authorship is rejected because of its more universal outlook,[64] although it cannot be completely excluded since it looks forward to the renewal expected after the eschatological war.[65] In fact, the language of 4Q215a creates "a strong sense of 'heightened eschatology.'"[66] Based on the content, it is not difficult to see why the Qumran community might have appropriated and copied this text, even if it was not composed at Qumran.

---

61. Ibid., 464–65. Coded writing was to control the accessibility of the learning contained in the text. See P. Popovic, "Physiognomic Knowledge in Qumran and Babylonia: Form, Interdisciplinarity, and Secrecy," *DSD* 13, no. 2 (2006): 150–76. Delcor points out that such astrological horoscopes were a common contemporary phenomenon especially in the Greco-Roman world. M. Delcor, "Recherches sur un Horoscope en Langue Hébraïque provenant de Qumrân," *RevQ* 5 (1964–1966): 521–42 (534–38).
62. Popovic, "Physiognomic Knowledge," 150–51.
63. E. Chazon and M. Stone, "4QTime of Righteous," in *Qumran Cave 4. XXVI,* ed. S. Pfann et al., DJD 36 (Oxford: Clarendon, 2000), 173.
64. T. Elgvin, "The Eschatological Hope of 4QTime of Righteousness," in *Wisdom and Apocalypticism in the Dead Sea Scrolls and in the Biblical Tradition,* ed. F. García Martínez (Leuven: Leuven University Press, 2003), 89–102. He says that it speaks of "the expected renewal that is for all mankind (and likely all Israel as well), not for a narrow sectarian group" (94).
65. Ibid., 101. Although Elgvin opts for a non-Qumran origin, he notes that the orthography demonstrates that the text was copied and read at Qumran and that the composition "would easily lend itself to a sectarian reading" describing the trials and giving meaning to the struggles of the elect.
66. Chazon and Stone, "Time of Righteous," 174. The eschatological expectations of this composition share many themes with biblical end-of-days' prophecies and with extrabiblical eschatological predictions.

4Q267–273 CD

The "Damascus Document" (CD) is "the only sectarian document to have been found before the discoveries at Qumran."[67] With the discovery of the Qumran documents, scholars observed striking doctrinal, verbal, or organizational parallels between CD and some of the distinctively sectarian material.[68] That the medieval MSS were based on an ancient original was proved by the discovery of fragments of this work in Caves 4, 5, and 6 at Qumran.[69] Unlike caves 5 and 6, however, Cave 4 contained significant amounts of the text along with previously unknown portions of the document.[70] Ever since, the close relation between CD and the 4QD documents has been unquestioningly accepted.[71] The medieval Genizah manuscripts can be divided into two distinct parts: "the admonition," containing exhortations, moral addresses and historical teachings, and "the laws," containing halakic prescriptions and sectarian regulations.[72]

4Q393 (Communal Confession)

The script in this scroll contains a mixture of late Hasmonean and early Herodian formal hands.[73] The fragments belong to a type of postexilic prayers that make up a response to the warning of Lev. 26:40-45, where a confession of one's own sins and the sins of one's ancestors is expected.[74] D. Falk observes that the concept of

---

67. Dimant, "Qumran Sectarian Literature," 490.

68. P. R. Davies, *The Damascus Covenant* (Sheffield: JSOT Press, 1983), 14. See also C. Hempel, *The Damascus Texts* (Sheffield: Sheffield Academic, 2000).

69. 4Q266–4Q273; 5Q12; 6Q15.

70. J. Baumgarten et al., eds., *Qumran Cave 4. XIII. The Damascus Document (4Q266–273)*, DJD 18 (Oxford: Clarendon, 1996).

71. Davies rightly observes, "CD has . . . for all practical purposes been treated as one of the scrolls and included in virtually every edition of Qumran texts and translations." Davies, *The Damascus Covenant*, 14.

72. Dimant, "Qumran Sectarian Literature," 491.

73. D. Falk, "Works of God and Communal Confession," in *Qumran Cave 4. XX. Poetical and Liturgical Texts, Part 2*, ed. E. Chazon et al., DJD 29 (Oxford: Clarendon, 1999), 47.

communal confession was not unique to Qumran. In the Second Temple period, such confessions might have been occasioned by national or community distress, penitential liturgies for specific fast days, annual festivals, covenant renewal, or weekday prayers.[75] In all probability, this work was used as an integral part of the community's worship.

4Q394-399 (4QMMT)

4QMMT is described as one of the most significant documents reconstructed from Cave 4.[76] The original document was discovered in six manuscripts (4Q394–399) reduced to almost one hundred fragments.[77] E. Qimron initially said that 4QMMT represented copies of a letter written by the Teacher of Righteousness to his rival, the wicked priest.[78] However, he later described the work as a "group composition" rather than a personal letter, addressed to an individual leader and his people Israel.[79] Terms typical of, and frequent in standard sectarian works, are absent in MMT, possibly suggesting a dating very early in the organization of the Qumran movement.[80] However, the polemical nature could make it a sectarian work: the editors say that "nowhere else is in the Qumran literature is there any mention of such an effort to convince the leader of Israel of

---

74. D. Falk, "4Q393: A Communal Confession," *JJS* 45, no. 2 (1994): 184–207 (184).
75. Falk, "4Q393," 206.
76. J. Kampen and M. Bernstien, introduction to *Reading 4QMMT: New Perspectives on Qumran Law and History* (Atlanta: Scholars Press, 1996), 1.
77. Because of the poor state of preservation, "some passages remain a matter of conjecture since no reconstruction based on fragmentary evidence can ever be considered for certain to be an exact reproduction of the original text." Qimron, "The Nature of the Reconstructed Composite Text of 4QMMT" in *Reading 4QMMT*, 9.
78. Davies, Brooke, and Callaway, *Complete World of the Dead Sea Scrolls*, 137.
79. E. Qimron and J. Strugnell, "MMT," in *Qumran Cave 4.V. Miqsat Maʿase Ha-Torah*, DJD 10 (Oxford: Clarendon, 1994), 121.
80. Ibid., 113.

the validity of the sect's halakhic views and of the invalidity of those of its opponents."[81]

More recently, S. Fraade has argued that MMT was not a letter, but was addressed to members or potential members of the community. It consisted of a call to study its set of rules with its unique emphases as "a way of reinforcing the process of social separation and religious return that they had begun."[82] The texts in their present forms bear witness to the active intramural employment of the document. Thus Fraade asks: "How would [4QMMT] have functioned intramurally at such a later stage in the community's history?"[83]

M. Grossman[84] uses MMT to show that it is not enough to read sectarian and protosectarian scrolls for their historical content and assume that when they corroborate one another, they reflect historical fact. What they reflect, instead, is an ideological tradition, developed over a course of several generations. In facing new challenges, the members of the community would have written new texts and reread old ones to confirm the truths that have shaped their understanding of their own history.[85]

Thus, by considering a series of possible interpretations, without selecting a unitary, correct reading of the text, we can isolate the range of historical accounts that this text supports.

---

81. Ibid., 5.
82. Ibid.
83. Fraade, "To Whom it May Concern: 4QMMT and Its Addressee(s)," *RevQ* 19 (2000): 507–27 (525). Similarly, J. Høgenhausen suggests that the epistolary form in 4QMMT is a central part of its rhetorical strategy and that it operates on two levels: first, it refers to the historical epistolary situation of the sender and addressee; second, it influences the subsequent reading of the document within the historical community that received and preserved it. J. Høgenhausen, "Rhetorical Devices in 4QMMT," *DSD* 10, no. 2 (2003): 187–204.
84. M. Grossman, "Reading 4QMMT: Genre and History," *RevQ* 77 (2001): 3–22.
85. Ibid., 22.

4Q434–438 (*4QBarkhi Nafshi*)

Based on the opening lines: ברכי נפשי את אדני ("Bless, O my soul, the Lord"), five texts (4Q434–438) have been titled the *Barkhi Nafshi* hymns.[86] Of these, 4Q434 contains the largest section of text.[87] These hymns are praises of thanksgiving to the Lord for his deliverance of his people and for his grace shown to them.[88] The recipients of God's deliverance and grace could be the members of the community.[89] D. Seely sees in these hymns many connections in language, themes, and ideas with explicitly sectarian works and posits a sectarian origin for them.[90] M. Weinfeld says that the *Barkhi Nafshi* collection describe "praise to God for the salvation of the pious and for giving them a pure heart that will keep them away from temptation."[91]

4Q504–506 (4QDibHam)

This liturgical work consists of prayers to be used each day of the week. It is "one of the most informative prayer texts found at Qumran"[92] and offers a glimpse into the "community piety of Qumran."[93] These texts consist of a survey of biblical history from

86. D. R. Seely, "Implanting Pious Qualities as a Theme in the *Barkhi Nafshi* Hymns," in *The Dead Sea Scrolls: Fifty Years after their Discovery*, ed. L. H. Schiffman, E. Tov, and J. VanderKam (Jerusalem: Israel Exploration Society, 2000), 323.

87. M. Weinfeld and D. Seely, "Barkhi Nafshi," in *Qumran Cave 4. XX. Poetical and Liturgical Texts, Part 2*, ed. E. Chazon, DJD 29 (Oxford: Clarendon, 1999), 267.

88. Weinfeld and Seely, "*Barkhi Nafshi*," *DJD 29*, 267.

89. Ibid.

90. Ibid. He says that the *Barkhi Nafshi* hymns "echo sectarian themes and theology" (330). Brooke argues that there is "no explicit sectarian vocabulary in the extant fragments of *Barkhi Nafshi*." Thus their composition probably occurred in nonsectarian circles but were "used" by those responsible for the collection of these manuscripts. The contents 4QBarkhi Nafshi are "entirely consistent with the community's worldview." G. Brooke, "Body Parts in the *Barkhi Nafshi* and the Qualification for Membership of the Worshipping Community," in *Sapiential, Liturgical and Poetical Texts from Qumran*, ed. D. Falk, García Martínez, and E. Schuller (Leiden: Brill, 2000), 80–94.

91. M. Weinfeld, "Grace after Meals in Qumran," *JBL* 111 (1992): 427–40 (427).

92. D. Falk, *Daily, Sabbath, and Festival Prayers in the Dead Sea Scrolls* (Leiden: Brill, 1998), 59.

Adam to the (writer's) present,[94] maintaining a tone of supplication. There are forty-eight fragments of the two, possibly three manuscripts.[95] 4QDibHam provides a rare instance in which the original title has survived.[96] The general pattern followed by the first six prayers consists of a call to God to remember his past acts, a summary of some aspect of Israel's history, a request for God's mercy/deliverance, and a closing benediction.[97] The early date that 4Q504 was copied suggests that it was a presectarian composition adopted by the sectarians and used by them for a very long time.[98] The frequency of use (daily and weekly) points to the fact that the document appealed to the sentiments of the community and was in keeping with their own ideas.

Cave 11

11Q13 (11QMelchizedek)

In this document, written in late Hasmonean or early Herodian book hand, the main theme involves the heavenly prince Melchizedek and final salvation.[99] This document provides interesting information concerning the eschatology of the Qumran community.[100] According to É. Puech, the central figure is clearly considered as the high priest of the heavenly liturgy of the Day of Atonement since he

---

93. J. Charlesworth, ed., *Pseudepigraphic and Non-Masoretic Psalms and Prayers*, PTSDSSP (Tübingen: Mohr Siebeck, 1997), vol. 4A, 107. The piety captured in this document is ancient. Baillet says that "on pourra voir dans ces textes une relique de la piété assidéenne de l'époque des Maccabées." M. Baillet, "Un Recueil Liturgique de Qumrân, Grotte 4: Les Parôles Des Luminaires," *RB* 68 (1961): 195–250 (250).

94. J. Davila, *Liturgical Works*, Eerdmans Commentaries on the Dead Sea Scrolls (Grand Rapids: Eerdmans, 2000), 239.

95. Ibid.

96. Ibid., 240.

97. Ibid., 241

98. Ibid., 242.

99. Schürer, *History of the Jewish People*, 449.

100. M. De Jonge and A. S. van der Woude, "11QMelchizedek and the New Testament," *NTS* 12 (1965): 301–26.

executes divine judgments and makes definitive expiation, which is seen in his divine pardon of the sins committed by those of his lot.[101]

11Q19 (*The Temple Scroll*)

Consisting of nineteen pieces of leather, this is the largest of the scrolls discovered, with a total length of nine meters, consisting of sixty-six columns. Several copies of part of the text have been found. The original date of composition is placed before 100 BCE.[102] It was possibly written by two scribes, with one writing columns 1–5 and the rest of the scroll by the other.[103] Much of the content of the scroll is concerned with the temple itself and is a type of "blueprint for a new temple to be built in the future when the right people were in control."[104] There are also large sections on festivals and sacrifices to be observed at this new temple.[105]

Use of other Second Temple Literature

I mentioned earlier that, from time to time, we will consider some repentance motifs that we identify in the scrolls with material contemporaneous to the scrolls, primarily Second Temple literature. However, in using texts from corpora that have come to be known as "Apocrypha" and "Pseudepigrapha," it will be useful at this stage to clarify how we will understand the terms. "Apocrypha" and "Pseudepigrapha" refer first of all to "categories created in the context of the transmission of the texts in question and refer thus to the

101. É. Puech, "Notes sur le Manuscrit de XIQMelkîsèdeq," *RevQ* 12 (1987): 483–513. See also F. García Martínez, E. Tigchelaar, and A. Van Der Woude, eds., *Qumran Cave 11. II. (11Q2–18, 11Q20–31)*, DJD 23 (Oxford: Clarendon, 1998); and P. J. Kobelski, *Melchizedek and Mechireša'*, CBQMS 10 (Washington, DC: Catholic Biblical Association of America, 1981), 826; J. Maier, *The Temple Scroll: An Introduction, Translation and Commentary* (Sheffield: JSOT Press, 1985), 1.
102. Maier, *Temple Scroll*, 2.
103. Dimant, "Qumran Sectarian Literature," 526.
104. J. C. VanderKam, *The Dead Sea Scrolls Today* (Grand Rapids: Eerdmans, 1994), 59.
105. Ibid.

Christian canonical process in which the texts were preserved and transmitted."[106] F. García Martínez comments, "In spite of their inadequacy these categories are useful shorthand labels that bring together a great variety of different texts, and as such their use seems to me completely justified."[107] I am aware of the anachronistic nature of these terms and that they allude to modern, artificial categories. I understand "Apocrypha" as referring to "Jewish works of the period of the Second Temple not included in the Hebrew Bible but which are to be found in the Greek and Latin Old Testaments."[108] Similarly, "Pseudepigrapha" has been understood in two different ways in recent scholarship. Originally, it referred to texts falsely ascribed to an author (usually of great antiquity) in order to enhance their authority and validity.[109] Later, the connotation of this word was expanded to include a collection of Jewish and Christian writings dating from the last centuries BCE to the first centuries CE that did not become part of the canon in either religion.[110] They are "books written in the age of the Second Temple, and for the most part Jewish"[111] (and generally excluding the Apocrypha). When I talk about Second Temple texts in the subsequent chapters, these are the main two corpora I have in mind. It is acknowledged that this could run the risk of being selective, as I have omitted valuable information from texts by Philo or Josephus or the Septuagint, all of which are more or less contemporaneous to the scrolls. Nevertheless, due the confines of space, such selectivity and omissions are unfortunate but necessary.

---

106. F. García Martínez, "Apocryphal, Pseudepigraphical, and Para-Biblical Texts from Qumran," *RevQ* 83 (2004): 365–77 (370).
107. Ibid.
108. M. Stone, "The Dead Sea Scrolls and the Pseudepigrapha," *DSD* 3, no. 3 (1996): 270–95 (270).
109. J. H. Charlesworth, ed. *The Old Testament Pseudepigrapha.* vol. 1, *Apocalyptic Literature and Testaments.* London: Darton, Longman & Todd, 1983, 1:xxv. [Hereafter, *OTP, 1*]
110. M. Bernstein, "Pseudepigraphy in the Qumran Scrolls: Categories and Functions," in *Pseudepigraphic Perspectives: The Apocrypha and Pseudepigrapha in the Light of the Dead Sea Scrolls,* ed. E. Chazon and M. Stone, STDJ 31 (Leiden: Brill, 1999), 1–26 (1).
111. Stone, "Dead Sea Scrolls and the Pseudepigrapha," 270.

The use of these corpora can be justified by the fact that several texts from the Apocrypha and Pseudepigrapha have been discovered (in different states of preservation—some more fragmentary than others) among the Dead Sea Scrolls. The presence of these texts in the Qumran caves justifies my use of selection of this corpora rather than any other, as there was a fair chance of their having been read at Qumran. For example, fragments of two manuscripts of the Hebrew text of Sirach have been found at Qumran[112] and at Masada,[113] confirming that Sirach was read at Qumran. Five fragmentary manuscripts of Tobit were discovered at Qumran. This attests an early date and a Semitic original as well as the popularity of this work at Qumran.[114] *First Enoch* was also popular at Qumran. Regarding the Cave 4 Aramaic MSS of *Enoch*, five copies of the Book of Watchers were found, none of the Book of Parables; four fragmentary MSS of the Astronomical Book were discovered; the Book of Dreams is also represented by four fragmentary MSS; the Epistle of Enoch was found in two fragmentary Aramaic MSS. J. T. Milik dates the earliest of these Qumran *Enoch* MSS to around early 200 BCE.[115] While the *Testament of the Twelve Patriarchs* as we know it was not found at Qumran, sources for some of the individual testaments have been discovered in Cave 4.[116] Similarly, twelve

---

112. J. van der Ploeg describes Sirach as "part of the devotional reading of Qumran, as the remains of it testify." J. van der Ploeg, *The Excavations at Qumran: A Survey of the Judean Brotherhood and Its Ideas* (London: Longmans, Green, 1958), 115.

113. G. Nickelsburg, *Jewish Literature between the Bible and the Mishnah* (London: SCM, 1981), 64 (2Q18 and 11Q5 21:11-18). G. Sauer says, "Die funde von Qumran und auf Masada konnten für diese Frühzeit die hebräische Textform nachwiesen." G. Sauer, *Jesus Sirach*, in *JSHRZ* 3.5 (Gütersloh: Gütersloher Verlaghaus; Gerd Mohn, 1981), 484.

114. The Qumran Aramaic and Hebrew MSS of Tobit date from between 100 bce to 50 ce. Fitzmyer suggests that these are only possible dates of the *copies* found at Qumran and not the actual date of composition of the book. J. Fitzmyer, *The Dead Sea Scrolls and Christian Origins* (Grand Rapids: Eerdmans, 2000), 12. Two texts are relevant for our purposes (Tob. 13:6; 14:6). Unfortunately both these texts have not survived in the Qumran Tobit fragments. Either the beginning or the ending is lost. The latter part of Tob. 13:6 remains in 4Q196 fr. 17, 2, while the latter part of Tob. 14:6 is found in 4Q198, fr. 1.

115. H. F. D. Sparks, ed., *The Apocryphal Old Testament* (Oxford: Clarendon, 1984), 173–77.

fragmentary Hebrew manuscripts of *Jubilees* have been found at Qumran. G. W. E. Nickelsburg says that "connections between the *Book of Jubilees* and the Qumran community are especially close." He points out that "the religious ideas, theology, and laws in Jubilees closely parallel and are often identical with those in writings unique to composition at Qumran."[117]

Literary Approach

I will adopt a *literary* approach, relying primarily on texts from the scrolls to provide relevant information regarding the function of repentance in the life of the community who used these scrolls. Since I am interested in the examination of the concept itself rather than a word study of "repentance," this investigation will necessarily be inductive. A study of this nature would require a broad textual base in the primary sources. However, a considerable amount of selectivity is employed since we will examine only repentance texts (in, of course, their wider literary, theological, and historical setting in the scrolls).

Repentance never occurred in a vacuum; it was an integral part of the soteriological aspirations of a real, historical community. This approach will attempt to show how such texts might have been translated into daily life at Qumran.[118] Therefore I am not merely attempting to reconstruct from these texts the function of repentance but also to locate it in space and time within the framework of the community.

116. Sources for *T. Naph.* (4Q215), *T. Jud.* (3Q7; 4Q484; 4Q538), *T. Lev.* (Aramaic Levi Document: 4Q213–14,1Q21), and possibly *T. Jos.* (4Q539). VanderKam, *Dead Sea Scrolls Today*, 40.

117. Nickelsburg, *Jewish Literature*, 79.

118. S. Metso's caution is valid: although he is speaking specifically about Rule texts, he remarks that even though a text might originate in a simple, historical occurrence, it could assume a life of its own: "If the text passes through several editorial hands, the resulting text that we read may have been disconnected from its historical moorings and no longer reflects that history but a developed set of thoughts." S. Metso, "Methodological Problems in Reconstructing History from Rule Texts Found at Qumran," *DSD* 11, no. 3 (2004): 315–34 (334).

In light of the literary approach, it should be noted that since I am treating repentance as a concept, I will not deal with minute text-critical issues. Rather, I will adopt a complementary approach to all technical, restoration, and reconstruction studies that have been undertaken until now.[119] Ever since the discovery of the Dead Sea Scrolls, scholars have devoted incredible amounts of time and energy to piecing together the scrolls and restoring and reconstructing damaged fragments or partially erased letters, words, and even sections of texts.[120] We must acknowledge the benefits and advantages of earlier scholarly work in this area and seek to build on the reconstructions of other scholars. Hence, I will not focus on the reconstruction of texts unless it has direct bearing on the interpretation of a repentance text.

Finally, it is worth pointing out some of the limitations of the task at hand. While some scrolls are in a better state of preservation than others, the material is largely of a fragmentary nature. At interesting and key parts of the text, there are gaps and tears or the script is too faint to produce a definitive reading. As a result, a comprehensive and often coherent picture of the contents of many of the scrolls is not possible. Furthermore, because of the fragmentary nature of the texts, one is largely dependent on the reconstruction of texts by scholars. However plausible these might be, at best they are guesses (educated guesses, but nevertheless guesses). But these "scholarly guesses" are invaluable to any research on the scrolls. Further caution is also in order in attempting to locate repentance within the religious experience of the community, for the following reason: "We cannot fully understand a religion—Its preferred attitudes and emotions, its

119. Especially the Discoveries in the Judaean Desert series (I–XXXIX) published by Clarendon Press, Oxford.
120. One may recall photographs from the early days of scrolls research of the first groups of scholars, surrounded by thousands of scraps of leather of different shapes and sizes, intensely poring over their work with magnifying glasses!

prescribed Rituals, its important stories and myths, and it's recommended way of life—by simply looking at it."[121] As in the case of "scholarly guesses" in relation to the texts, the same scenario applies to any reconstruction of the religious experience of a community that existed over a millennium ago.

Now that we have an initial sense of direction, we must further map out the terrain and consider at least briefly the "religious parameters" within which we are trying to locate our discussion of repentance texts: What is religious experience? How did repentance at Qumran fit in with the general religious climate of the day? A survey of the lay of the land is the task of the first chapter.

121. M. Peterson, W. Hasker, B. Reichenbach, and D. Basinger, *Reason and Religious Belief: An Introduction to the Philosophy of Religion* (Oxford: Oxford University Press, 1991), 5.

1

Religious Experience and Repentance

From time immemorial, deepening one's relationship with God has always been a central aspect of human religious experience. It forms and shapes our identity and our outlook or worldview—how we see our place before God and in our relation with others. We will ultimately be exploring how the Qumran community's understanding of repentance influenced their religious experience, how it shaped and formed their religious identity and their worldview. With this overriding purpose in mind, it will be helpful to first of all understand religious experience in very general terms.

Religious Experience in General

William James, in his famous study from the early part of the nineteenth century, understood religious experience as "the feelings, acts and experiences of individual men in their solitude, so far as they apprehend themselves and stand in relation to whatever they may consider the divine."[1] While the experiential dimension of James's understanding stands out, his emphasis on the private and subjective nature of the experience is evident. However, there are those who argue that that for a religious experience to be genuine, it should be rooted in historical facts lest it become "a series of subjective phenomena in which the individual may find contentment in the enjoyment of his own feelings but which can have not secure basis in fact."[2]

For the purposes of this study, we will harmonize these two perspectives and see them as being complementary, thereby taking religion at Qumran as one that is rooted in community and history. Therefore, a fundamental premise of the following chapters is to keep this historical rooting in perspective at all times. In our study of the Dead Sea Scrolls, whatever we may discover about repentance and its impact on the religious experience of the members of the community, this information is not merely a literary construct, or the private and subjective experience of one individual or community. Rather, as I shall argue, the community's religious experience was largely controlled and mediated by the community. Furthermore, this community did not exist in a vacuum, but was itself rooted and grounded in verifiable history.[3] To this historical aspect of religious experience, which is our basis for understanding repentance at Qumran, we may add several other factors that enhance our understanding. Ninian Smart's "dimensions of religion" are helpful. It should be pointed out, however, that all of Smart's dimensions of religion do not necessarily apply to the religious experience of the Qumran community; even if they appear to apply, it may not necessarily be in the way that Smart describes them. I only offer them

---

1. William James, *Varieties of Religious Experience* (New York: Longmans, Green and Co., 1903), 31.

2. H. Dermot McDonald, "What Is Meant by Religious Experience?," *Vox Evangelica 2* (1963): 58–70 (63).

3. This is a premise to which we will return at a later stage in this chapter.

as a general point of reference for understanding religious experience at Qumran.

Smart states that religion tends to express itself through rituals and that even the simplest form of religious service involves *ritual* "in the sense of some form of outer behaviour coordinated to an inner intention to make contact with, or participate in, the invisible world."[4] He talks about the importance of *mythological*, historical events of religious significance in a tradition. This is reiterated in the lives of the worshiping community through the reenactment of a highly important event that once occurred in a particular community. With regard to the Qumran community, we see this aspect in the annual covenant-renewal ceremony that was fundamental to membership in the community, both for new members and for existing ones.[5]

Smart states that *doctrines* are an attempt to give system, clarity, and intellectual power to what is revealed through the mythological and symbolic language of religious faith and ritual.[6] While the term is certainly anachronistic to the scrolls, there is evidence of the existence of such "doctrines" at Qumran. The systematization of the beliefs of the Qumran community are described in texts such as the *Rule of the Community* (1QS).

Many religions incorporate a code of *ethics*, which concerns the behavior of the individual, and to some extent, the code of ethics of the dominant religion controls the community.[7] Again the *Rules* of Qumran could reflect this dimension.

4. N. Smart, *The Religious Experience of Mankind* (London: Collins, 1969), 16. He also grounds these rituals in history when he notes that the "meaning of ritual cannot be understood without reference to the environment of belief in which it is performed" (17).
5. Ibid., 18.
6. Ibid., 19.
7. Ibid.

As I stated above, any aspect of religious experience that we might discover about the Qumran community, repentance included, did not occur in a vacuum or as a literary construct. There was a *social* dimension to it. It occurred within the context of an existing community. Smart points out that "religions are not just a system of belief: they are also organizations . . . [and] have a communal and social significance."[8] The importance of this social dimension of religion is that it indicates the way in which people's lives are shaped by these claims and the way in which religious organizations operate.[9]

That humans can experience the divine is fundamental to any religious experience. Smart identifies as a central dimension of religion the place of *experience*. The basis of any "quest for, contact with or participation in the world is that personal religion involves the hope of, realization of, experience of that world."[10] Whether personal (as Smart notes) or communal (as in the case of the Qumran community—or any religious group for that matter), this experiential dimension is central to the validity of the religious encounter.

Bearing the above general dimensions of religion in mind, we can sharpen our focus and briefly consider the religious scenario of first-century Judaism with a specific emphasis on repentance. Our understanding of how repentance functioned in the religious experience of the Qumran community must be rooted within the religious climate of its time.

8. Ibid. He adds that "the religious and ethical ideals are adapted to existing social conditions and attitudes" (20).
9. Ibid., 20.
10. Ibid., 21.

Religion and Religious experience in First-Century Judaism

Judaism of the first century attempted to bring the entirety of life under the heading "Divine Law."[11] God cared for alls aspects of life, so no part of it was outside "religion."[12] As the first-century Jewish historian Josephus puts it in *Against Apion* 2.170–172: "Religion governs all our actions and occupations and speech; not of these things did our lawgiver leave unexamined or indeterminate. . . . He left nothing, however insignificant, to the discretion and caprice of the individual." First-century Jews sought to discern and follow God's will in very aspect of life. The Jewish people understood that along with their election God was committed to them and would save and protect those who were loyal to him. This conviction gave meaning to their religious identity even in the face of great opposition and the courage and conviction to stand firm in their faith. Further, the fact that God created the world and controlled history was another key factor in Jewish theology. Belief in this all-powerful, Creator God shaped and governed their faith-response and daily life.[13] In other words, it is needless to talk of "religious experience" per se in first-century Judaism because *all experience was religious.*

How, then, does repentance fit and function in such a worldview? Repentance too permeated all spheres of a life that was already deemed to be religious; this probably explains why there appears to be no undue emphasis as such on repentance: T. Hägerland comments: "The fact that few first-century pieces of Jewish literature deal with repentance as their primary topic should not be taken as evidence that the concept was unimportant."[14] In attempting to understand it in

---

11. E. P. Sanders, *Judaism: Practice and Belief 63 BCE–66 CE* (London: SCM, 1992), 5.

12. Ibid., 50.

13. While many scholarly works address this topic in detail, of particular note is E. P. Sanders's *Judaism*, which is an account of Judaism during the turn of the first century; the reader is referred to this comprehensive monograph for further information.

the wider context of repentance in first-century Judaism, Hägerland speaks of the "set of symbolic actions" that first-century Jews normally performed as an integral part of repenting. "Confession and prayer for forgiveness" were at the center of this ritual repentance.[15] These symbolic penitential actions or rites were more or less taken for granted.[16] This underlying penitential emphasis permeating Jewish religious experience is aptly captured by M. Philonenko, who notes:

> La notion [de la repentance] est capitale et son histoire est ancienne. Déjà les prophètes avaient exigé sans relâche que le peuple revienne à Dieu, que le méchant se détourne de l'iniquité et que tous renoncent aux idoles. Toutefois, le mot même de repentance (הבושת/μετάνοια) n'apparaît que tardivement. On le relève dans les apocryphes, les pseudépigraphes, les manuscrits de Qoumrân, chez Philon et Josèphe, dans la literature rabbinique enfin. La repentance devient un element fondamental de la piété.[17]

Regarding this all-pervasive attitude to repentance, Hägerland observes that it was not a sectarian concern that had to be intensely promoted in rivalry with a competing position: "This explains why almost none of our sources treat repentance as their principal concern, while nearly all of them mention the concept with approval."[18] However, he does acknowledge that "this is naturally not to say that all first-century Jews would have shared a common opinion on what it meant to repent."[19] This then becomes the starting

14. He says, "The theme of repentance, the return to a way of life in accordance with God's covenant with Israel, is nearly ubiquitous in first century Judaism." T. Hägerland, "Jesus and the Rites of Repentance," *NTS* 52 (2006) 166–87 (168).

15. Ibid., 174.

16. Ibid., 184. Hägerland asserts that the historical Jesus took a controversial view of repentance: while sharing the common belief that moral improvement was necessary for sinners, Jesus did not require the traditional rites of repentance to be carried out (ibid., 187). If the toll collectors and sinners had really repented through fasting before joining Jesus in table companionship, they would no longer have been sinners.

17. M. Philonenko, *Joseph et Aséneth* (Leiden: Brill, 1968), 53–54.

18. Hägerland, "Jesus and the Rites of Repentance," 169.

19. Ibid.

point of our own investigation, as the above view on repentance gives us the opportunity to test the premise that a distinctive understanding of repentance did indeed exist at Qumran.

Repentance at Qumran: The Journey So Far

Detailed scholarly discussions on repentance at Qumran has been sparse. Up to the late 1980s, any paucity in the attention given to repentance could be explained by the limited number of scrolls published. However, from the early 1990s, with the publication of all remaining scrolls, we have witnessed an abundance of studies on the various themes and concepts in the scrolls. Nevertheless, the concept of repentance has largely been taken for granted and so has never warranted an examination for its own sake. Since a secondary task of this book is to draw attention to and address this lack of attention, it is worthy highlighting this lacuna. Obviously due to limitations of space, I cannot possibly survey all the relevant material to establish my case.[20] Therefore, for the sake of convenience, I will confine myself to representative works that can be divided into two broad categories:

1. Studies produced before the entire collection of the scrolls became available
2. Studies produced after the complete collection became available

Most introductory works on the scrolls normally focus on the faith of the Qumran community in some way or other, and when scholars talk about repentance in Qumran, they speak in relation to a particular text from the *Community Rule* (1QS 3:1-9):

1. He shall not be justified while he maintains the stubbornness of

---

20. A detailed survey of repentance in recent scholarship is not necessary for our study since a brief survey of key works is sufficient to demonstrates this point.

his heart since he regards as darkness paths of light. In the spring of the perfect

2. he shall not be counted. He will not become clean by acts of atonement, nor shall he be purified by the cleansing waters, nor shall he be made holy by seas

3. or rivers, nor shall he be purified by all the waters of ablution. Defiled, defiled, shall be all the days he spurns the decrees

4. of God so that he cannot be instructed within the community of his counsel. For it is by the spirit of the true counsel of God that are atoned the paths of man, all

5. his iniquities, so that he can look at the light of life. And it is by the spirit of holiness of the community, in its truth, that he is cleansed of all

6. his iniquities. And by the spirit of uprightness and of humility his sin is atoned. And by the compliance of his soul with all the laws of God

7. his flesh is cleansed by being sprinkled with cleansing water and being made holy with the waters of repentance.

This text emphasizes the necessity of the correct inward attitude that is to accompany ritual immersion. This "correct inward attitude" can undeniably be equated with repentance. Hence, scholars point out that in order to be effective, these external rituals had to be accompanied by repentance. Thus, from the time of the discovery of the scrolls, if the function of repentance has been mentioned by scholars, it has almost always been in relation to 1QS 3:1-9. The focus of attention on this one text should not be a surprise, considering such an attitude was taken for granted in first-century Judaism. In fact, purification was a standard metaphor in Judaism for the elimination of evil or unworthy thoughts and desires, and we may assume that many pilgrims took the opportunity to purify their hearts as well as their bodies.[21] To confine repentance at Qumran to this one key text, however, reduces the importance of the concept.

Studies Produced before the Entire Collection of the Scrolls Became Available

In the early days of scrolls scholarship, the notable introductory works were those of M. Burrows (1956, 1958), F. M. Cross (1958), and A. Dupont-Sommer (1961). Burrows surveyed the "general beliefs"[22] of the community and concluded that the community's emphasis on "returning to the Law of Moses" did not produce a merely mechanical, external observation of the Law but rather emphasized "the necessity of sincere, wholehearted devotion."[23] Similarly, Cross mentions repentance only in terms of 1QS 3:3-9 (above) denying the "*ex opere operato* nature of the water rites" without inward repentance. This brief mention of repentance is relegated to a footnote.[24] Interestingly, Dupont-Sommer too makes only a passing reference to repentance in a footnote. He speaks of the need for the "correct interior disposition" that accompanies purificatory rites.[25] That both Cross and Dupont-Sommer refer to repentance only in a footnote indicates the low priority devoted to understanding "repentance" in the early days of scrolls scholarship. The scenario did not change much even with the appearance of the first monograph devoted to the

---

21. Sanders, *Judaism*, 252. Philo speaks of this connection when he says: "outer purification brought to mind inner purification" (*Spec. Laws* 1.263–266).

22. M. Burrows, *The Dead Sea Scrolls* (London: Secker & Worburg, 1956).

23. Ibid., 251. However, in his next book in the section titled "Beliefs of the Sect," he comments on the idea of God as the one who pardons those who repent from sin: the "grace of repentance is given only to the elect." M. Burrows, *More Light on the Dead Sea Scrolls: New Scrolls and New Interpretations* (New York: Vikings, 1958), 295. He understands repentance as an integral part of salvation. While this is accurate, Burrows does not discuss it further. He also states that ritual cleansing involves an "inner, moral purification." As in his first book, he does not dwell further on the function of repentance.

24. F. M. Cross, *The Ancient Library of Qumran* (London: Duckworth, 1958), 70n96.

25. Dupont-Sommer, *The Essene Writings from Qumran*, 76n3.

"theology" of the scrolls, by H. Ringgren. One would expect to find here more than in other works a detailed discussion of repentance. Ringgren mentions the relation between repentance and moral purity (p. 125), but apart from these cursory references, repentance does not feature in his "theology" of Qumran.[26]

A monograph that was greatly influential in the late 1970s was E. P. Sanders' monumental work *Paul and Palestinian Judaism*, which provided a detailed analysis of the various "patterns of religion" in Palestinian Judaism.[27] In his section on the Dead Sea Scrolls, he points out that repentance was required to join the covenant in the first place and notes that this basic and initial repentance is "of vital importance."[28] Moreover, one's continuing life in the community is to be characterized by repentance.[29] Sanders thus highlights the need to stay penitent and manifest an ongoing life of repentance. However, his observations are limited by his overall purpose of establishing covenantal nomism. Repentance is therefore only one aspect of his overall scheme and is not singled out as a key theological concept.

We should also note the study of H.-J. Fabry.[30] His work was not connected with repentance per se but focused on the use of the verb שוב at Qumran.[31] Directly related to repentance are his observations

---

26. H. Ringgren, *The Faith of Qumran* (Philadelphia: Fortress, 1963). Almost thirty-five years after Ringgren's study of theology in the scrolls, A. Deasley attempted to compile a "Qumran theology" (A. Deasley, *The Shape of Qumran Theology* [Carlisle: Paternoster, 2000]). Because of the book's popular style, it has not enjoyed great attention in scholarly circles. In his reconstruction of Qumran theology, he observes that the importance of repentance is conveyed through the frequent use of the verb שוב (ibid., 91). Although Deasley attempts to provide a holistic overview of Qumran thought, very little attention is given to "repentance."

27. E. P. Sanders, *Paul and Palestinian Judaism* (London: SCM, 1977).

28. Ibid., 270. He also points out that in rabbinic literature one does not *join* the covenant by repenting of transgression, since one is *born* in it (284).

29. Ibid., 305.

30. H.-J. Fabry, "Die Wurzel שוב in der Qumranliteratur," in *Qumran. Sa piété, sa théologie et son milieu*, ed. M. Delcor (Paris: Gembloux, 1978), 285–93. For an amplified treatment, see H.-J. Fabry, *Die Wurzel שוב in der Qumran-Literatur. Zur Semantik eines Grundbegriffes* (Köln: Hanstein, 1975).

of *Abkehr von der Sünde* ("turning from sin") and *Umkehr zu Gott* ("[re]turn to God"). Fabry's work is primarily a word study, and in highlighting "returning" imagery associated with the word שוב, he mentions in passing the idea of conversion and repentance.[32] Fabry sees repentance as merely another meaning conveyed through שוב and attributes no further importance to the concept. His study is further limited by the fact that in 1975 he had only a small number of scrolls available to him.[33]

Studies Produced after the Complete Collection Became Available

B. Nitzan's article "Repentance in the Dead Sea Scrolls" in the late 1990s is significant since it represented the first and only study at the time entirely focusing on repentance in the scrolls.[34] She shows that repentance in Qumran literature goes beyond biblical tradition since the members of the community saw their repentance as the realization of the eschatological repentance demanded by the prophets. There is thus an emphasis on the "correct repentance" required to validate the covenant.[35] At Qumran, repentance was a "way of life" demanding a complete return to the law of Moses in its unique sectarian interpretation.[36] Sincere repentance was vitally important if one was to remain faithful to the oath taken on entrance.

---

31. Fabry, "Die Wurzel 286 ", שוב.
32. Ibid., 287–88.
33. However, even if he did have more scrolls available to him, it would not have made any impact on the study of repentance apart from recording more texts that employ שוב to refer to repentance.
34. B. Nitzan, "Repentance in the Dead Sea Scrolls" in *The Dead Sea Scrolls After Fifty Years*, ed. P. Flint and J. VanderKam (Leiden: Brill, 1999), 2:145–70.
35. Ibid., 2:146.
36. Ibid., 2:146. E. Condra's study the on the soteriology of the scrolls also reflects this. He notes that the sectarian idea of repentance was not just an initial repentance that placed one graciously into the covenant but also implied an ongoing covenant faithfulness. E. Condra, *Salvation for the Righteous Revealed* (Leiden: Brill, 2002), 141n29. Furthermore, he says that "repentance, and especially, Torah obedience, is what removes God's wrath and provides the entrance into the lot of the righteous saved as well as maintaining one's position therein" (275).

Nitzan speaks of a "ceremony of repentance"[37] where confession becomes "a formal expression of repentance" emphasizing the "moral aspect of repentance."[38] She notes that repentance established the congregation of penitents as the seed of eschatological Israel. Such an understanding of repentance is reflected in several psalms and prayers from Qumran.[39] She underscores the importance of repentance at Qumran, acknowledging that her study needs to be undertaken more intensively.[40]

T. Hägerland's article on repentance is concerned with Jesus' understanding of repentance,[41] but it is noted here because of its overall relevance to our own direction of travel. He attempts to understand repentance in its wider first-century Jewish context. In this regard, Hägerland speaks of the "set of symbolic actions" first-century Jews would normally perform as an integral part of repenting. "Confession and prayer for forgiveness" were at the center of this ritual repentance.[42] Hägerland asserts that the historical Jesus took a controversial view of repentance: while sharing the common belief that moral improvement was necessary for sinners, Jesus did not require the traditional rites of repentance to be carried out.[43]

---

37. Nitzan, "Repentance in the Dead Sea Scrolls," 156.
38. Unlike the priestly ritual of repentance, at Qumran there was no guilt offering. However, 1QS 9:5 describes a perfect life as a "pleasing freewill offering."
39. "The custom of expressing repentance by a recitation of confession had become a prominent factor in Second Temple Jewish liturgy with this phenomenon evident especially in prayers and psalms from the late biblical and Second Temple periods making the motif of repentance characteristic of an entire genre itself." Nitzan, "Repentance in the Dead Sea Scrolls," 160–61.
40. Ibid., 168.
41. Hägerland, "Jesus and the Rites of Repentance," 166–87. Condra's study on the soteriology of the scrolls (*Salvation for the Righteous Revealed*) is a similar sort of work since his concern was with the cultural milieu of Jesus. He notes that the sectarian idea of repentance was not just an initial repentance that placed one graciously into the covenant but implied an ongoing covenant faithfulness (141n29). For Condra, the repentance of all those outside the community (the gentiles included) is the corollary of the community's righteousness (126). Repentance was the necessary requirement to join the community for the continuing observance of the sectarian law. This is "the very nature of repentance" (129).
42. Hägerland, "Jesus and the Rites of Repentance," 174.
43. Ibid., 187.

Thus the accusation against Jesus for his association with sinners resulted from the fact that he did not require any ritual repentance from them.[44] Hägerland comments: "The fact that few first-century pieces of Jewish literature deal with repentance as their primary topic should not be taken as evidence that the concept was unimportant."[45] He observes that repentance was not a sectarian concern that had to be intensely promoted in rivalry with competing positions: "This explains why almost none of our sources treat repentance as their principal concern, while nearly all of them mention the concept with approval."[46]

Regarding repentance at Qumran, Hägerland notes that those outside the community are apostates; a formulaic penitential prayer is necessary for anyone who wants to repent and reenter the covenant.[47] Also, anyone who has renounced the covenant must repent, and repentance entails a public confession of sin.[48] Hägerland's article is helpful in that it paints in broad strokes something of the contextual background of first-century repentance in which to locate my own research.

In an article titled "Repentance and the Qumran Covenant Ceremony,"[49] R. Arnold asserts:

> The concept of repentance, which is centered on the first stage of the initiation of prospective members, is employed to mark clearly the boundary between those who are inside (the repentant) and those who are outside (the wicked). Repentance had a more limited role within

---

44. Ibid., 184. If the toll collectors and sinners had really repented through fasting before joining Jesus in table companionship, they would no longer have been sinners.
45. He says, "the theme of repentance, the return to a way of life in accordance with God's covenant with Israel, is nearly ubiquitous in first century Judaism," ibid., 168.
46. "This is naturally not to say that all first-century Jews would have shared a common opinion on what it meant to repent." Ibid., 169.
47. Ibid., 172.
48. Ibid.
49. R. Arnold "Repentance and the Qumran Covenant Ceremony," in *Seeking the Favour of God*, vol. 2, *The Development of Penitential Prayer in the Second Temple Period*, ed. M. Boda, D. Falk, and R. Werline, SBLEJL 22 (Leiden: Brill, 2007), 159–75

the ongoing life of the community due in part to the community's deterministic world view and expectation of perfection from its members.[50]

While he sees repentance as related to the identity of the community (expressed by the epithets שבי ישראל and שבי פשע), he believes its importance is confined only to those about to become members, since repentance was required for membership. However, once within the community, because of the emphasis on maintaining a life of perfection, "the need for repentance was also essentially obviated."[51] Arnold's description of the limited role of repentance at Qumran arises from his reading of the highly deterministic emphasis of the scrolls. This is a factor that needs to be borne in mind since the determinism of the scrolls and the voluntary aspect that repentance implies appear to be incompatible with each other. A recent article by David Lambert highlights this difficulty.[52]

Lambert talks about the anachronistic challenge when studying religion in the Dead Sea Scrolls. He says that "both rabbinic Judaism and early Christianity made great strides in devising a vocabulary of religious experience that ultimately became the standard for religious discourse in the west."[53] In applying some of these terms to ancient literature, Lambert says: "we run the risk of in appropriately absorbing terminological baggage of later religious systems."[54]

Lambert challenges that the Qumran community was in fact a penitential movement and that Israel's repentance was one of its central tasks. This is because "most religious movements favour

---

50. Ibid., 162. He also says that "in such a deterministic view [as one find's at Qumran], petition [hence repentance] of any kind is of no effect" (171).
51. Ibid., 175.
52. D. Lambert, "Was the Qumran Community a Penitential Movement?," in *The Oxford Handbook of the Dead Sea Scrolls*, ed. T. Lim and J. J. Collins (Oxford: Oxford University Press, 2012), 501–13.
53. Ibid., 502.
54. Ibid.

rejecting one's former way of life, in some fashion, and adopting a new one." As a consequence, the contemporary task is to identify "which *theory* of human change a given movement adopts to account for and instill such transformation."[55]

His underlying concern is that "it is anachronistic to speak of repentance as a concept operative at Qumran." He speaks instead about a notion of "Divine re-creation."[56] For Lambert, this conveys the idea that could be described as repentance but avoids superimposing modern terms (with its related conceptual baggage) on to an ancient concept. For example, regarding ritual immersion, he says the transformation enacted through the initiate's immersion draws its strength not from individual human consciousness but from the 'holy spirit of the community' (1QS 3:7), the power God has invested in the sect. Reconstituted, the initiate is now fit to join in the community."[57] He describes the initiate as being "newly remade."[58] When seen as such, Lambert believes that the "logic of this ritual and its effects fit better with the notion of re-creation with its focus on external agency than with the penitential framework that presently dominates."[59]

For him, a distinction should be drawn between biblical *shuv*, connoting a behavioral change (a turn away from sin) and rabbinic *teshuva*, connoting an internal change (regret over sin). He points out that "the distinction may seem subtle at first but it bears great functional weight, for *teshuva* derives from inside the individual and is, by necessity, an act of free will, whereas *shuv* need not be either." Thus Lambert compares *teshuva* to the Greek *metanoia* and its Latin equivalent *paenitentia*. Repentance understood in such a way is closer

55. Ibid.
56. Ibid.
57. Ibid., 505.
58. Ibid.
59. Ibid.

to Hellenistic philosophical thought than Judaism or Christianity.[60] At Qumran, שוב terminology serves as a technical term for the adoption of sectarian practice, not for the painful internal struggle over one's sins that comes to be known respectively in Hebrew, Greek, and Latin as *teshuva*, *metanoia*, and *paenitentia*.[61]

The thrust of Lambert's article challenges the existence of repentance at Qumran in the way the concept is normally understood; we must conclude that the answer to the question he uses as the title of his article, "Was the Qumran Community a Penitential Movement?," for him was no—at least not in the traditional understanding of the concept of penitence. However, he offers an important caution that is relevant to our own task of identifying the place of repentance in the religious experience of the community. He says: "The religious experience of the sect must be reconstructed from the ground up, using its own language and symbols, rather than on the basis of standard Western vocabularies for depicting spirituality."[62] This is what I intend to do in the rest of this book, as I argue, using repentance-specific language, terms, and concepts, that the Qumran community was indeed a penitential community.

From this brief survey, we can observe an increase in studies related to specific theological themes and concepts after 1990, coinciding with the publication of all remaining scrolls. That said, most works present repentance as a "given" and thus take it for granted, while other works highlight repentance insofar as it fits into their overall argument. This scenario in Qumran scholarship justifies the present investigation; more work needs to be done in further exploring the concept of repentance at Qumran.

60. Ibid., 503.
61. Ibid., 507.
62. Ibid., 510.

Before we actually embark on our journey of exploration of the scrolls themselves, another matter needs to be dealt with to facilitate a more cohesive reading of the scrolls, namely the motivations for repentance. Why is repentance so important in the first place? What motivates an individual or a community to repent? Probing these questions is the task of the next chapter.

2

Motivations for Repentance

As I noted in my working definition, repentance is expressed most commonly by two-dimensional turning language that involved a turning *away* from wickedness (transgression, wickedness, sin, evil, idolatry) and a turning *toward* God. In the Hebrew Bible, repentance is a call to return to God and live in obedience to him and may be "subsumed and summarized by one verb"—שׁוּב.[1] This root combines in itself both requisites of repentance that I highlighted in my working definition: to turn from evil and to turn to the good. In other words, the essence of repentance is turning. The key to life is to be found in the direction one faces; if that direction is wrong, one must turn to see the true direction and walk in that path of life.[2] But why does one repent? What motivates an individual or community to

---

1. W. A. Quanbeck, "Repentance," in *The Interpreter's Dictionary of the Bible*, ed. G. A. Buttrick (New York: Abingdon, 1962), 4:33.
2. P. C. Craigie, Kelley, and J. Drinkard, *Jeremiah 1–25*, WBC 26 (Nashville: Thomas Nelson, 1991), 68.

recognize the error of one's direction and to correct it, thus orienting oneself in the right direction?

While it is not possible to examine every possible motivation for repentance, it will be helpful to be aware of a motivation that frequently recurs both in the Hebrew Bible and in Second Temple literature more or less contemporaneous with the Dead Sea Scrolls. Repentance motivated by destruction/punishment is clearly the most fundamental form of motivation. In some texts, the destruction has happened already and therefore serves as a motivation for repentance; in other cases, it is imminent or threatened, which also serves as a motivation. While it could be said that I am employing a high degree of selectivity here, it quickly becomes evident that this motif is the foundation on which the whole biblical narrative stands since the sinfulness of the people is a theme that runs throughout the Scriptures. The Hebrew Bible makes it clear that in the light of this, an increase of genuine repentance expressed in a wholehearted turning to God was what God required. Repentance was the appropriate response in the face of approaching judgment; as a result, genuine repentance could avert further judgment and lead to restoration and salvation. This teaching spans to the breadth of material and undoubtedly was a key aspect of the people of God's understanding of important events in their history. There are different nuances to this basic premise, and in highlighting representative texts, it is hoped that these nuances will become evident.

Motivations for Repentance in the Hebrew Bible

In Deuteronomy,[3] both at the beginning and the end of the book, we encounter a motivation for repentance, namely, destruction meted out to the unrepentant. Moses, in recapitulating the Lord's goodness to the people (4:20), warns them of the perils that will befall them because of unfaithfulness (4:23-28). Even then, if they sincerely repent, God would be merciful to them and keep the covenant (4:31):

> From there you will seek the Lord your God, and you will find him if you search after him with all your heart and soul. In your distress, when all these things have happened to you in time to come, you will return to the Lord your God and heed him. (Deut. 4:29-30)

Similarly, toward the end of the book, when on the threshold of the promised land, Moses cautions the people of the consequences of being unrepentant.

> But if you will not obey the Lord your God by diligently observing all his commandments and decrees, which I am commanding you today, then all these curses shall come upon you and overtake you. (Deut. 28:15)

He then reminds the people of God's faithfulness in providing for them during the forty years in the desert (29:5) and of their own unfaithfulness to God (29:4). Moses underscores the need to swear allegiance afresh to God before entering into the promised land (29:10,12-13). However, he cautions them that there is only

---

3. We start with Deuteronomy not just because it reflects the self-understanding of postexilic Judaism but also bearing in mind that this document was considered of great importance in the Qumran community, with twenty-nine copies of Deuteronomy being discovered in the caves. Also, most of the penitential motifs in the Qumran literature relate to Deuteronomic or Priestly traditions of repentance that became typical of penitential compositions of Second Temple Judaism in form and content. B. Nitzan, "Traditional and Atypical Motifs in Penitential Prayers from Qumran," in *Seeking the Favor of God*, 187–208 (187).

destruction and devastation for those who enter insincerely (29:19-28). Then he says in 30:1-2:

> When all these things have happened to you, the blessings and the curses that I have set before you, if you call them to mind among all the nations where the Lord your God has driven you, and return to the Lord your God, and you and your children obey him with all your heart and with all your soul, just as I am commanding you today.

In this text, repentance is the outcome of knowledge of punishments (30:1). These punishments act as the motivating factor for repentance and lie at the heart of Israel's turning back to God. It is worth noting that although Deuteronomy is replete with references to spiritual "turning," the majority of occurrences of this turning language are employed primarily *negatively*, a turning *away* from God and his statutes, highlighting the unrepentant attitude of Israel (Deut. 7:4; 9:12, 16; 11:16, 28; 13:5, 10; 17:11, 17, 20; 28:14; 29:18, 26; 30:10, 17; 31:18, 20, 29). In fact, H.-J. Fabry observes that the phrase "return to Yahweh" was not originally a theme of Deuteronomy. The root שוב in the sense of "repent, return" occurs only in these two late Deuteronomistic addenda (4:29-31; 30:1-10), both of which come from postexilic circles.[4] Nevertheless, these texts show that knowledge of divine punishment serves as the motivation for repentance. Furthermore, repentance thus motivated is then coupled with complete obedience to God's commandments. Such repentance will result in great blessings by the Lord.

---

4. Fabry, "שוב" in *TDOT* 14:461–522. Similarly P. Buis and J. Leclercq say: "d'ailleurs l'idée d'une conversion occasion ée par l'exil, d'un recommençement de l'histoire d'Israë l est à l'opposé de l'intention fondamentale du Deutéronome; c'est un théme prophétique." P. Buis and J. Leclercq, *Le Deutéronome* (Paris: Gabala, 1963), 61. G. von Rad notes that in both 4:29-31 and 30:1-10 "the concept of returning to Yahweh is central." He therefore suggests that these two sections are part of the structure of "that great historical and theological work which encloses Deuteronomy as if within a frame." G. Von Rad, *Deuteronomy: A Commentary*, OTL (Philadelphia; Westminster, 1966), 183.

For the Lord will again take delight in prospering you, just as he delighted in prospering your ancestors, when you obey the Lord your God by observing his commandments and decrees that are written in this book of the law, because you turn to the Lord your God with all your heart and with all your soul. (Deut. 30:9-10)

I. Cairns says that the precondition of restoration is genuine repentance.[5] As I noted above, Fabry points out that turning imagery in Deuteronomy is used mainly to describe a turning *away* from God. Deuteronomy 30:1-10 is a pivotal text that corrects the apparent imbalance regarding the unrepentant nature of the people that runs through the book. Thus the realization of these eschatological blessings serves as an important motivation of repentance, as repentance becomes the precondition for God's continued favor.

These two motivations for repentance—the promise of destruction (imminent or current) or the promise of restoration (futuristic)—appear in Leviticus as well. Here, repentance is spoken of against the background of judgment and faithfulness to the covenant. Toward the end of the book the Lord promises wrath and destruction if Israel is unfaithful (26:14-15, 18, 21). He then says: "If in spite of these punishments you have not turned back to me, but continue hostile to me, then I too will continue hostile to you: I myself will strike you sevenfold for your sins" (Lev. 26:23-24). This text thereby refers to the "unrepentant" nature of the people while at the same time implying that imminent judgment is the motivation for repentance (26:23). The overall context states that even if knowledge of such punishment has no effect, then the wrath will be intensified (26:24, 28). Continued punishment will lead to the people's eventual banishment from the land and their dispersion among the nations

5. I. Cairns, *Deuteronomy: Word and Presence* (Grand Rapids: Eerdmans, 1992), 263. H. D. Preuss says: "Das Gericht des Exils soll auch Umkehr bewirken, und diese hat verheißung aufgrund des Erbames Jawhes." H. D. Preuss, *Deuteronomium* (Darmstadt: Wissenschaftliche Buchgesellsschaft, 1982), 161.

(26:33). Although the situation so far appears to be hopeless, the anticipated repentance of the people changes the entire tone.[6]

> But if they confess their iniquity and the iniquity of their ancestors, in that they committed treachery against me and, moreover, that they continued hostile to me—so that I, in turn, continued hostile to them and brought them into the land of their enemies; if then their uncircumcised heart is humbled and they make amends for their iniquity, then will I remember my covenant with Jacob; I will remember also my covenant with Isaac and also my covenant with Abraham, and I will remember the land. (Lev. 26:40-42)

J. Hartley says, "The experience of the exile will humble the Israelite survivors, motivating them to turn back to God in fervent zeal."[7] Confession of their iniquity is equated with admission of their hostility to God and is the starting point for repentance. It is only *after* their repentance that God will remember his covenant with their ancestors (26:49). Repentance is the precondition for God's favor and covenantal faithfulness. In both Deuteronomy and Leviticus, judgment (past, present, or future) is to serve as the motivation for repentance. Furthermore, repentance and faithfulness to God (and the covenant) would result in God's continuing favor on Israel, making repentance the precondition for restoration.

It should not be surprising to find that the "repentance-motivated-by-judgment" motif occurs in the prophetic literature as well. A few random examples from Jeremiah will suffice to highlight the recurrence of this motif.[8] Jeremiah cries out:

---

6. The shift from addressing Israel in second person plural to addressing the remnant (v. 39) in third person plural marks the content of 26:40-45 as a new theme. M. Noth, *Leviticus*, OTL (London: SCM, 1965), 197.

7. J. Hartley, *Leviticus*, WBC 4 (Dallas: Word, 1992), 469.

8. Confines of space make it impossible for us to highlight this motif in detail in the Hebrew Scriptures, but is certainly an underlying theme: Jer. 18:8; 26:3; 36:3,7; Isa. 30:15; Ezek. 18:30b; Amos 4:6, 8-11; Joel 2:12-13; Hag. 2:17; Zech. 1:6; Dan. 9:13; 1 Kgs. 8:47-48; 2 Kgs. 17:13, 15.

Circumcise yourselves to the Lord,
remove the foreskin of your hearts,
O people of Judah and inhabitants of Jerusalem,
or else my wrath will go forth like fire,
and burn with no one to quench it,
because of the evil of your doings. (Jer. 4:4)

Jeremiah uses "circumcision" imagery to speak of repentance. D. P. Volz says: "4:1 sagt vollends deutlich, daß die Wiedergeburt des Volkes nur durch eine Erneuerung der Herzen geschehen kann."[9] Failure to do so would result in destruction. In Jer. 15:7, despite the punishment they suffered at God's hand, Israel remains unmoved and "they did not turn from their ways," thus implying that it was hoped that knowledge of disaster would bring about repentance. This anticipated repentance was the basis for the continual call to repentance (26:3): "It may be [אולי] that they will listen, all of them, and will turn from their evil way, that I may change my mind about the disaster that I intend to bring on them because of their evil doings." Jeremiah's prophecy contains a persistent call to repentance, best summarized in Jer. 25:4, which states: "and though the Lord persistently sent you all his servants the prophets, you have neither listened nor inclined your ears to hear." The content of this call is: "Turn now, everyone of you, from your evil way and wicked doings, and you will remain upon the land that the Lord has given to you and your ancestors from of old and forever" (25:5). A total transformation is demanded through repentance, in order to attain security in the land. In the light of this constant call to repentance, the book of Jeremiah seems to suggest that Israel's unrepentant attitude is one of the main reasons by which they are to understand what has befallen them (44:2-4, 6), thereby highlighting

9. D. P. Volz, *Der Prophet Jeremia*, KAT 10 (Leipzig: A. Deichertsche, 1928), 41.

the motif of destruction, punishment, and judgment in the past and present (or even future) was a key motivation for repentance.

When we look at material from the Second Temple period, we immediately notice that this motif has influenced this literature.

For example, the *Sibylline Oracles*, which consist of the attribution of inspired Jewish and Christian oracles to the pagan Sibyl,[10] predict the woes and disasters that are to come upon humanity and, consequently, the response to these predictions.[11] This imminent disaster is usually an expression of divine wrath and serves as the motivation for repentance: Noah "entreated the people" (1.149), warning them that continuance in their present sinful behavior would surely bring destruction (1.153). They are to "entreat him" (God) (1.159) in order for him to be gracious (1.161). This call to repentance becomes all the more explicit as Noah warns of imminent destruction "unless you propitiate God and repent as from now, and no longer anyone doing anything ill-tempered or evil, lawlessly against one another but be guarded in holy life" (1.167b-169). So also in 3.545–657, for the Greeks, the sin of idolatry will bring destruction. Interestingly, ritualistic sacrifices are offered as a means of repentance. Thus sacrificing at the temple averts destruction, and restores one's relationship with God: "Greece, also by offering the holocausts of oxen and loud-bellowing bulls, which she has sacrificed, at the Temple of the great God, will escape the din of war and the panic and pestilence and will again escape the yoke of slavery" (3.564–657). Such a repentance would not only avert disaster but

10. J. J. Collins, "Sibylline Oracles," in *OTP* 1:317–472. The theological importance of the oracles lies in the attribution of inspired Jewish (and Christian) oracles to the pagan Sibyl (318). The texts highlighted here are from oracles 1, 3, and 4. This is because despite numerous Christian interpolations, the almost completely Jewish character of *Sib. Or.* 1,3, and 4 is generally accepted. Collins suggests these dates: books 1 and 2: 30 BCE–70 CE; book 3: 163–45 BCE; and book 4: 80 CE.

11. Ibid., 1:318. To be noted also is the fact that the oracles are dominated by eschatology, which for the Jewish oracles is mainly concerned with the advent of a glorious kingdom and the transformation of the earth (323).

also bring the Greeks into a relationship with the "Living One" as opposed to idols. Similarly, 4.153–159 contains a description of the impiety in the last times after which God's wrath would be manifested in a "great conflagration" (4.161). To avoid this, there is an exhortation to "change these things" (4.163) and "abandon" violence (4.163c–165). Attached to this process of repentance is the injunction to "stretch out your hand to heaven and ask forgiveness for your previous deeds and make propitiation" (4.166). The result of this transformation, washing, and supplication is described in 4.168b–169a: "God will grant repentance and not destroy." As John J. Collins puts it, "The exhortation to refrain from violence, and the need for ritual washings and supplication gives a concise summary of what is necessary to avert disaster."[12]

In the *Life of Adam and Eve* (*VAE*), we encounter in midrashic form some episodes in the life of Adam and Eve after their expulsion from paradise.[13] *VAE* begins with an account of Adam and Eve's repentance following their banishment from paradise (1.1). This repentance is motivated by the punishment/judgment they are receiving (1.1b),[14] and it is hoped that repentance will lead to a restoration of their previous comforts. Adam says:

> It is just and fitting for us to lament in the sight of God who made us. Let us repent with a great penitence; perhaps the Lord God will be forbearing and pity us and provide for us that we might live. (4.3)

Their acts of penitence involve fasting and standing in neck-deep water (6.1–8.3) in order to gain God's pity (6.3). Satan, in attempting to deceive Eve again (9.1–2), appeals to the sufficiency of her

---

12. Ibid., 1:382.
13. M. D. Johnson, "Life of Adam and Eve," in J. H. Charlesworth, ed. *The Old Testament Pseudepigrapha*, vol. 2, *Expansions of the "Old Testament" and Legends, Wisdom and Philosophical Literature, Prayers, Psalms, and Odes, Fragments of Lost Judeo-Hellenistic Works* (London: Darton, Longman & Todd, 1985), 249. [Hereafter, *OTP* 2.]
14. The inaccessibility to food was part of the punishment.

repentance. He says to her in 9.3a, "The Lord God has heard your sighs and accepted your repentance.

Only the *Apocalypse of Moses* (*Apoc. Mos.*) includes a section on Eve's account of the fall, its consequences (15–31), and her repentance through the confession of sin (*Apoc. Mos.* 32.1–2). The angelic messenger who informs her of Adam's death says: "Rise, Eve, from your repentance" (32.4a). Her confession is perceived as her repentance.[15]

In the Enochic literature, the Book of Watchers (1–36) describes the condemnation of the wicked and the blessings of the righteous run through as a continuous thread.[16] Enoch is sent as an emissary to pronounce judgment on the wicked Watchers (10.4–5, 11, 13), and they call out to Enoch to intercede on their behalf, he reports: "And they begged me to write for them a memorial prayer in order that they may be for them a prayer of forgiveness" (13.4). That this was a form of repentance is seen in 13.6:

> And then I wrote down their memorial prayers and petitions on behalf of their spirits and the deeds of each one of them, on account of the fact that they have prayed in order that there may be for them forgiveness [of sin] and length of days.[17]

Their prayer for forgiveness reveals an awareness of sin and also a conscious bid to turn away from these sins. The context indicates that it was not just the judgment they were already receiving that led them to repent; rather, it was the knowledge of further judgment,

15. Ibid., 2:252. A.-M. Denis says that some scholars postulate an Essene origin for the following reason: "Certains l'ont dit essénien, en raison des usages ascétiques de pénitence et des rites d'ensevelissement." Denis, *Introduction à la littérature religieuse judéo-hellénistique* (Turnhout: Brepols, 2000), 1:25.

16. E. Isaac says of the focus of *1 Enoch* on the last judgment, the coming destruction of the wicked, and the triumph of the righteous: "This eschatological concept is the most prominent and recurring theme throughout the whole book." E. Isaac "1 Enoch," in *OTP* 1:9.

17. Greek text: M. Black, ed., *Apocalypsis Henochi Graece* (Leiden: Brill, 1970).

and knowledge that at a future occasion, they would be denied of the opportunity to repent, as 14.1–2 implies:

> There will not be peace unto you; a grave judgment has come upon you. They will put you in bonds, and you will not have [an opportunity for] rest and supplication and because you have shown to the people deeds of shame, injustice, and sin.

The "grave judgment" motivates the people to repent; however, what is notable here is that their cries for repentance are not heeded.[18]

In the *Apocalypse of Zephaniah*,[19] the theme of judgment and the condemnation of ungodly souls to eternal punishment is prominent.[20] In the Sahidic text, we have a description in which, on seeing the torment of a soul in Hades, the seer asks the accompanying angel about the reason for punishment. Such is the angelic response: "This is [a] soul which was found in its lawlessness, and before it attained to repenting it was [vi]sited and taken out of its body" (B.6). The context of judgment also implies that there is an opportunity for repentance that this unfortunate soul did not avail. We can confirm this by the Akhmimic text, where there is more evidence of a "time for repentance"[21] in the face of judgment, which becomes the motivation for repentance. Here too, the seer witnesses souls in torment and distress (10.1–8). The angelic guide informs him that these are "catechumens" who have not been faithful to God (10.9). The seer then asks the angel: "'Then do they not have repentance

---

18. In 1QS 1:8–9, there is a striking parallel of this: "May God not have mercy on you when you call on him" and also, "may there be no peace for you by the mouth of those who intercede."

19. O. S. Wintermute, "Apocalypse of Zephaniah" in *OTP* 1:497. A pre-70-CE date might be discerned from the reference to Mount Seir in 3:2, which could attest a pro-Edomite tradition that might have been prevalent until 70 CE.

20. D. S. Russell, *The Old Testament Pseudepigrapha: Patriarchs and Prophets in Early Judaism* (London: SCM, 1987), 114. Wintermute says that the work emphasizes the divine judgment, which faces all men. Wintermute, "Apocalypse of Zephaniah," in *OTP* 1:502.

21. See below. According to Wintermute, this particular text was written "with a strong appeal for repentance." Ibid., 1:502.

here?' He said, 'Yes.' I said, 'How long?' He said to me, 'Until the day when the Lord will judge.'" (10.10–11). Thus for the wicked, the period of torment for theirs souls is also a period of repentance. The provision of such an opportunity also testifies to the mercy of God. As O. S. Wintermute says, "A corollary of God's mercy and patience is his willingness to permit repentance, which could spare man the punishment he justly deserves."[22] Relevant to our purposes, this is evidence from yet another Second Temple text that speaks of current punishment/destruction being a powerful motivator for repentance, which "is capable of changing the ultimate destiny of man."[23] True repentance averts punishment.

This motif occurs in at least three of the *Testaments of the Twelve Patriarchs*. All the testaments follow the framework of Genesis 49, which recounts Jacob's farewell speech to his sons.[24] With the exception of the Christian interpolations, which date to the early second century CE,[25] this is the work of a hellenized Jew, writing after 250 BCE,[26] possibly toward he end of 200 BCE.[27] While this document was not found at Qumran, *sources* for some of the individual testaments have been discovered in Cave 4.[28] Some of the testaments contain an exhortation by the patriarch to an eschatological

22. Ibid.
23. Ibid., 1:503.
24. H. W. Hollander, "The Testaments of the Twelve Patriarchs," in *Outside the Old Testament*, ed. M. De Jonge (Cambridge: Cambridge University Press, 1985), 71.
25. Regarding thee interpolations, apart from being only about twelve in number, H. C. Kee rightly points out that they appear in the latter part of the *Testaments* and are easy to spot since they are "literally incongruous." These would date to around early 200 CE. H. C. Kee, "Testaments of the Twelve Patriarchs," in *OTP* 1:777.
26. This is based on the *Testaments*' use of the LXX. Ibid., 1:777–78.
27. Denis, *Introduction*, 1:285. Lack of any reference o the Maccabees could suggest a date before the nationalist revolt, c. 200 BCE. Some scholars suggest that because of the kinship between the *Testaments* and the DSS, the former literature too might be of Essene origin. Since the Qumran community was in existence from around c. 150 BCE, the *Testaments* too could date to around that period. Kee, "Testaments of the Twelve Patriarchs," 1:778.
28. Sources for *T. Naph.* (4Q215), *T. Jud.* (3Q7; 4Q484; 4Q538), *T. Lev.* (Aramaic Levi Document: 4Q213–14,1Q21), and possibly *T. Jos.* (4Q539). VanderKam, *The Dead Sea Scrolls Today*, 40.

repentance in the lives of his sons' descendents.[29] This exhortation usually follows the Deuternomic pattern of sin → punishment (often exile) → repentance → restoration. In the *Testaments of Judah, Zebulon,* and *Dan*, the eventual destruction of the temple and exile are seen to be the consequence of the unrepentant state of the people. Judah tells of the rise of wickedness (*T. Jud.* 23.1–3), which would lead to destruction of the temple and exile (23.3c). This unfortunate situation would continue "until you return to the Lord in integrity of heart, penitent and living according to all the Lord's commands" (23.5a). Such repentance will lead to restoration (23.5b). Zebulon too speaks to his sons of future wickedness of their descendents (*T. Zeb.* 9.5) and the punishment that will befall them in the form of the exile (9.6). This situation will be reversed by genuine repentance: "And thereafter you will remember the Lord and repent, and he will turn you around because he is merciful and compassionate" (9.7a). Similarly, Dan speaks of future wickedness (*T. Dan* 5.5–6) and the exile (5.8) and return/repentance: "Therefore when you turn back to the Lord, you will receive mercy, and he will lead you into his holy place, proclaiming peace to you" (5.9). For these three patriarchs, it was their hope that future destruction/exile/punishment would motivate the people to repent. Such repentance would carry with it significant blessings.

---

29. This second, general exhortation to a future repentance does not occur in *T. Reu.* and *T. Sim.*

Jubilees[30] is another document that we should note in seeking the repentance-motivated-by-destruction/divine anger motif. Repentance here follows the pattern of wickedness → (punishment) → repentance → restoration, based on repentance texts we encountered in Deuteronomy and Leviticus. God reveals to Moses on Mt. Sinai the blatant wickedness (*Jub.* 1.7, 9, 12) and idolatry (1.9b, 11), which will result in captivity and exile (1.13). This will cause them to repent: "And afterward they will turn to me from among the nations with all their heart and with all their soul and with all their might" (1.15a). This repentance will lead to blessing and restoration: "When they seek me with all their heart and with all their soul, I shall reveal to them an abundance of peace in righteousness" (1.15c). Further on in the document, *Jubilees* reemphasizes that a period of widespread wickedness (23.16–21) will result in captivity (23.22). This is followed by a time of repentance: "And in those days, children will begin to search the law, and to search the commandments and to return to the way of righteousness" (23.26). Thus, while apostasy is responsible for God's punishment, the return of God's favor requires repentance—a return to the "path of righteousness."

In *Pseudo-Philo* (*Liber Antiquitum Biblicarium*),[31] we have a lengthy retelling of biblical history from Adam to the death of Saul.[32] It

---

30. Twelve fragmentary Hebrew manuscripts of *Jubilees* have been found at Qumran. Nickelsburg says that "connections between the *Book of Jubilees* and the Qumran community are especially close." He points out that "the religious ideas, theology, and laws in Jubilees closely parallel and are often identical with those in writings unique to composition at Qumran." Nickelsburg, *Jewish Literature*, 79. While this work can be dated to around the second century BCE (J. Charlesworth, *The Pseudepigrapha and Modern Research* [Missoula, MT: Scholars Press, 1976], 143), Nickelsburg says that "palaeographical evidence from Qumran Manuscripts of *Jubilees* suggest a date closer to 100 B.C.E." Nickelsburg, *Jewish Literature*, 78. More precisely, Denis says, "La date de composition de *Jub.* est en tout cas antérieure au ms. le plus ancien, le fragment 4Q216, que la paléographie date d'environ 150 av. C, et on la situe généralement entre 168 et 105." Denis, *Introduction*, 1:398.

31. For this work, "a date around the time of Jesus would seem most likely" (D. J. Harrington, "Pseudo-Philo," in *OTP* 2:299) or possibly a time before the first Jewish War and the destruction of the temple (Denis, *Introduction*, 1:421).

describes the climate of wickedness that prevailed after the death of Zubul (29.4), the Israelites facing military defeats (30.3) on account of their sins (30.2b, 4b). This motivates them to express their desire to repent in the hope that it will appease God's wrath (30.4c). Hence, they "fasted for seven days and sat in sackcloth" (30.5a). As a result, the Lord sends Deborah to announce deliverance. In other words, repentance averted divine wrath.

Conclusion

Many other examples can be cited from Second Temple Literature, but the above instances are sufficient to show that outside the Hebrew Scriptures, the most common motivation for repentance was divine punishment or even knowledge of imminent punishment. In all of the texts highlighted above, repentance was not just motivated by imminent destruction but could also avert it. The Deuternonomic pattern of sin → punishment (exile) → repentance → deliverance recurs frequently. In some cases, it appears as a stylistic feature; for example, in the *Testaments of the Twelve Patriarchs* oral and ethical exhortations are conveyed to the current generation but are placed in the mouth of the patriarchs. Since these exhortations are often couched in Deuternonomic language, it is not surprising that in such testamentary literature, punishment (described in the language of exile) motivates repentance. Since the order of this pattern is sequential, its employment makes it imperative that repentance has to be motivated by the threat of exile.[33] Thus it plausible to conclude that a prominent theme in both the Hebrew Bible and Second Temple Jewish literature is that of repentance motivated by divine anger.[34]

---

32. Nickelsburg, *Jewish Literature*, 265.
33. This pattern also occurs in narrative-style literature as well (*LAB* 30.2–5; Jud. 5:18–19; *Jub.* 1.7–15).

Intrinsically related to this motif is the eschatological dimension that supports it. History is moving inexorably to its consummation; a return to God ensures blessings; disobedience to the commands of God result in destruction. In order to enjoy the eschatological blessings of God, one is urged to take seriously the consequences of wickedness and disobedience, consider the extent of destruction (or better still, fear imminent destruction), and strive to transform one's life through repentance. Thus the motif of repentance motivated by divine anger/(present or imminent) destruction is inseparably linked with eschatology.

Bearing in mind the frequency of this motif across the literature we looked at, before we move to our next chapter it is worthy noting this observation by B. Nitzan:

> As penitential motifs are found in distinctively sectarian compositions as well as various other types of compositions with no evident sectarian features, including "apocryphal" and "parabiblical" works, examination of atypical penitential motifs in addition to the general content of a composition may give insight to its ideological and historical origin. Moreover, in cases where similar patterns of this kind of data are accumulated from several compositions, these may point to distinct streams of tradition in Second Temple Judaism.[35]

In light of this, hopefully this somewhat lengthy digression will help us ascertain whether the Qumran community's repentance followed this pattern, and to what extent. To understanding something of the religious experience of a separated community in the isolated and

---

34. Closely related to the repentance-motivated-by-wrath motif is the "opportunity-for-repentance" motif that occurs *before* this divine punishment is manifested. This motif appears in the Apocrypha, Pseudepigrapha, and NT (*Wis. Sol.* 11:23:12;10; *Apoc. Zeph*, Sahidic text, B.6; Akhmimic text, 10.10–11; *T. Ab.* 12.12–13; Acts 17:30; 2 Pet. 3:9). There are also texts in which this opportunity is explicitly denied (Wisd. of Sol. 5:3; *1 En.* 13.1–2; 14:7). In 1QS 2:8-9 and 11Q19 59:6-7 also the opportunity for repentance is denied.

35. Nitzan, "Traditional and Atypical Motifs," 187.

barren landscape of the Judean wilderness, it is there that we must begin our investigation. Our journey finally begins.

3

Repentance, Separation, and the Covenant

We begin our analysis of the concept of repentance in the very place where we encounter the community—in the isolated and bleak landscape near wadi Qumran, on the northwestern shores of the Dead Sea in the Judean wilderness. In this chapter, we will discuss how the choice of this location was fundamental to their religious experience, since for the Qumran community, fidelity to the covenant was manifested by separation from the world. We will explore how withdrawal and separation from the world functioned as a powerful metaphor for repentance, reshaping their understanding of covenant in penitential terms. We will also need to evaluate our findings in the light of our working definition, which defines repentance as "the radical turning away from anything which hinders one's whole-hearted devotion to God and the corresponding turning to God in love and obedience."[1] The thrust of this chapter is to show that repentance was the most basic prerequisite for joining

1. Milgrom, "Repentance," 74.

the community and participation in the community's redefined understanding of "covenant."

Repentance as Separation: Penitential Separation

Literal Separation: Formation of the Community

The first members of the community understood the need to turn away from evil and wickedness in terms of an extreme separation. This became the defining factor of their religious experience. We can conclude this because the emphasis on physical separation was primarily for the maintenance of purity. Since the community applied to themselves the biblical rules for ritual purity, when they encountered the incorrect ritual observances of the Jerusalem priesthood (which in their eyes was corrupt), they believed that their own purity could be attained only by separation.[2] M. Newton points out that in the Hebrew Bible, the verb בדל has cultic overtones, so that usually the separation referred to by the verb would result in ritual and cultic purity. This fits in with the community's priestly conception of itself, wherein the priesthood is set apart from the rest of Israel (Lev. 10:10; 11:47; 20:25; Ezek. 22:26; 44:23).[3]

However, at Qumran, further dynamics were at work with regard to their notion of separation: ritual uncleanness was intimately linked to moral uncleanness.[4] Hence, separation from ritual uncleanness involved a separation from moral impurity—in other words, a separation from sin. Thus such separation becomes an analogue for

2. According to 4QMMT, no matter what the reasons were for separation, they ultimately saw their act as a spiritual obligation. Pouilly says: "Même s'il est motivé par l'impiété d'Israël, ce départ dans la solitude est considéré comme un geste prophétique: c'est un nouvel Exode. Dans la piété et l'expiation, les 'élus' de Dieu prépareront la restauration de l'Alliance sainte entre Yahvé et Israël." J. Pouilly, *La Règle de la Communauté de Qumrân. Son Évolution Littéraire* (Paris: Gabala, 1976), 25.

3. M. Newton, *The Concept of Purity at Qumran and in the Letters of Paul* (Cambridge: Cambridge University Press, 1985), 15–19.

4. On this relation between ritual and moral purity, see the discussion in chapter 6.

repentance, since, in the words of our working definition, it implied a "radical turning away from [some]thing which hinders one's whole-hearted devotion to God." Further, this "penitential" separation has direct bearing on the religious experience of the community, as such separation (or failure to separate) ultimately affected their relationship with God.

Since the initial act of separation by a core group resulted in the establishment of a community at Qumran, in the wilderness, it would be helpful to consider the significance of the "wilderness" in the Hebrew Bible. This significance will help us, in turn, understand why the community perceived the wilderness as the locus for the manifestation of repentance.

The Wilderness as a Locus for Spiritual Renewal

S. Talmon observes that in the Hebrew Bible references to מדבר refer roughly to two unequal periods of time: the shorter period (approximately two years) included the Sinai theophany, while the longer period (the remaining thirty-eight years) comprised the actual desert wanderings "imposed on Israel as a divine punishment of their sins and for their doubting God's power to lead them safely into the Promised Land of Canaan."[5] Therefore, the theme of "disobedience and punishment" has a much greater impact on the subsequent formulation of the "desert motif" in biblical literature than does the concept of the desert as the locale of divine revelation and of Yahweh's love for Israel.[6] However, the one text that strikingly stands out in its positive conception of the desert is Isa. 40:3, which

---

5. Talmon, "The 'Desert Motif' in the Bible and in the Qumran Literature," in *Biblical Motifs: Origins and Transformations*, ed. A. Altman (Cambridge, MA: Harvard University Press, 1966), 31–63.
6. Ibid., 48.

emphasizes a new exodus and a new settlement in Canaan and is overshadowed by the "divine benevolence" theme.[7]

Although the desert and the desert period are conceived "originally and basically as a punishment and a necessary transitory stage in the restoration of Israel to its ideal setting,"[8] this motif expresses the idea of "an unavoidable transition period in which Israel recurrently is prepared for the ultimate transfer from social and spiritual chaos to an integrated social and spiritual order."[9] H. Najman too focuses on the spiritual benefits of the desert and sees it as the "locus for healing and moral transformation" and hence "the locus for spiritual purification."[10] She concludes that the concept of wilderness "is used to designate the proper place for purification of holiness. Life in the wilderness is a life that generates spiritual purification."[11] Therefore, for the core group, their departure to the desert could be justified by the use of Isa. 40:3 and an act of separation that not only defined their own religious experience in spatial terms but also in time to come became the determining factor in the religious experience of subsequent members of the community.

Separation and Isa. 40:3

For the community, repentance was manifested by separation and resulted in a withdrawal to the desert. This was not just a random act

7. Ibid., 55.

8. Ibid., 37.

9. Ibid. He points out that for the Qumran community, retreat into the desert is "the hiatus between the "historical" exodus from the Jewish society of their days, and the "eschatological" conquest of Jerusalem and the Land of Israel, which lies ahead of them" (57).

10. H. Najman, "Towards a Study of the Uses of the Concept of Wilderness in Ancient Judaism," *DSD* 13, no. 1 (2006): 99–113. She observes that the wilderness as a locus for withdrawal from corruption and soul-purification is attested in Philo's *De Decalogo* 10–11. In his description of the Therapeutae in *De Vita Contemplative* 2.18–20, Philo attributes their recovery of holiness to the withdrawal, their focus on the law, ritual, and healing the soul, instead of external distractions and so on.

11. Najman, "Concept of Wilderness," 109.

of piety but rather one that stemmed from their reading from their reading of Scripture: according to 1QS 8:12-14, this was a fulfillment of Isa. 40:3. 1QS 8:1-10a refers to a core group of fifteen, "perfect in everything revealed from all the Law." Among other things, they are "to implement truth" and "keep faithfulness." They achieve this with a "firm inclination" (יצר סמוך) and a "broken [repentant] spirit" (רוח נשברה). This last description is significant since the phrase רוח נשברה elsewhere in the scrolls explicitly conveys the idea of an attitude of penitence.[12] The success of this core group[13] is because of their single-minded (יצר סמוך) penitential nature (רוח נשברה). The above context (1QS 8:1-4) is immediately followed by a temporal clause suggesting that the establishment of this core, penitential group leads to the eventual formation of the community:

4 בהיות אלה בישראל
5 נכונה העצת היחד באמת

4. When these things exist in Israel
5. the council of the community council shall be founded in truth.

The temporal clause "when these things exist in Israel" (בהיות אלה בישראל) occurs again in 1QS 8:12b. What exactly "these" (אלה) refers to is quite ambiguous. However, it is plausible to take it as referring to the core group of fifteen *as well as* the virtues they exhibit (1QS 8:1-4).[14] Since this description of a core, penitential group precedes their withdrawal, their actual departure to the desert must

---

12. 4QS[e] has "and in humility and a broken spirit" (ובענוה רוח נשברה). This further conveys the idea of penitence. See also 4Q393 fr. 1-2, 2:7.
13. The righteous atone for the land through sufferings.
14. The group of fifteen and the virtues cannot really be separated. Since the fifteen men exhibit these virtues, these virtues would not exist independently of the core group. See also Brooke's discussion of the pronoun אלה in G. Brooke, "Isaiah 40:3 and the Wilderness Community," in *New Qumran Texts and Studies*, ed. G. Brooke and F. García Martínez (Leiden: Brill, 1994), 117–32.

be seen as the *manifestation* of their penitence. This becomes clear in 8:12-14:[15]

בהית אלה ליחד בישראל [   ] [   ] 12

13 בתכונים האלה יבדל מתוך מושב הנשי העול ללכת למדבר לפנות

שם את דרך הואהא

14 כאשר כתוב פנו דרך**** ישרו בערבה מסלה

לאלהינו

12. And when these exist ^for a community in Israel

13. ^In compliance with these they are to be separated from the midst of the dwelling of the men of sin to walk to the wilderness to prepare there his path.

14. As it is written, "in the wilderness prepare the way of ****, make straight in the desert a highway for our God.

If we understand "these" (אלה) as referring to the core, penitential group as well as the virtues they exhibit, the intralinear addition at the beginning of line 13: ^"in compliance with these" (בתכונים האלה) is significant since it immediately precedes the sentence: "they are to be separated from the midst of the dwelling of the men of sin" (יבדל מתוך מושב הנשי העול, line 13a), indicating that this penitential group is the subject of the verb יבדל. Apart from being a genuine act of physical separation, in the light of our proposal of the analogy between separation and repentance, this verb metaphorically conveys the two-direction "turning language" of repentance. This is clearly expressed in 1QS 8:13, where "they separate" (*turn away from*) the midst of the men of deceit and "walk to" (*turn to*) the desert.[16] Hence,

15. While the text of 1QS 8:12-14 is similar to 4QS^e, the Isa. 40:3 quotation is absent in 4QS^d. Brooke notes that these two 4QS documents are copied on manuscripts that are more or less contemporary to each other. One could argue that an actual move to the wilderness was not universally carried out and some members of the community "preserved an ideology which did not necessitate a wilderness experience." Brooke, "Isaiah 40:3 and the Wilderness Community," 117–32.

16. The italicized words mark the analogous relation between separation and turning: they separated (יבדל מ-) the midst of the men of deceit and walked to (ללכת ל-) the desert. After

there are here two layers in the use of the verb בדל; on the one level, it literally refers to a physical separation,[17] while on a metaphorical level it alludes to repentance. If this is the case, it strengthens my reading of the withdrawal to the desert as the *manifestation* and symbol of the group's repentance. The aim of the separation is expressed by an infinitive of purpose in the next clause: "to walk to the wilderness to prepare there his path" (ללכת למדבר לפנות שם את דרך הואהא). A proof text (Isa. 40:3) is then provided as the biblical justification, and its interpretation emphasizes a study of the law. Talmon observes that the community's literal reading of Isa. 40:3 is for them a summons to disassociate themselves from their sinful contemporaries[18] and to live in the desert as "returners to the Torah" (שבי התורה) (4QpPs 37 1:1–2). This exodus from society makes them into "penitents of the desert" (שבי המדבר) (4QpPs 37 2:1), "with the stress on 'penitents'—who are assured of the future salvation."[19] Once separated, they devoted themselves to the study of the law, which in fact "prepared the way of the Lord." Najman observes that "the members of this community experience this spiritual transformation through meticulous adherence to Mosaic Law, in isolation from those who do not obey the law, or obey it in a twisted form."[20] Thus the community's separation from evil men was "basic to the concept of the community."[21]

the initial group went out to the desert, for the subsequent and prospective members it would have symbolized a "turning to" the *community* in the desert.

17. Some scholars (such as N. Golb) do not accept a literal withdrawal to the desert. Brooke points out that in most cases the use of בדל in 1QS would be understood as "implying some kind of physically spatially oriented act of separation." Based on the cumulative evidence of these other uses he states that the reader of יבדלו in 1QS 8:13 would certainly understand that a physical movement was involved. Brooke, "Isaiah 40:3 and the Wilderness Community," 121. J. J. Collins says that 1QS 8:13b "suggests rather strongly that the retreat to the wilderness be taken literally." J. J. Collins, "Forms of Community in the Dead Sea Scrolls," in *Emanuel*, 105.
18. The wilderness developed a dimension of "retreat." Talmon, "Desert Motif," 63. The "desert" in Isaiah has no negative connotations.
19. Ibid., 60.
20. Najman, "Concept of Wilderness," 106.

In other words, the core group that formed the nucleus of the community was a single-minded, penitential group. Their *physical* separation from deceitful men for cultic purposes also implied a *spiritual* separation from their sinfulness, thus making this separation an analogy for repentance. Their separation was manifested in withdrawal to the wilderness. Thus the withdrawal to the wilderness became both the manifestation of repentance as well as the locus for repentance.

Other Instances of the Repentance-as-Separation Motif

In the Scrolls

A separation from the wickedness of the surrounding nations was at the core of Israel's existence in the Old Testament (Lev. 20:24; Ezra 10:11). However, at Qumran, the call for separation results in the creation of a distinctive, new entity, namely, the community of the renewed covenant. 4QMMT, which reflects an early stage in the community's life, conveys this idea. C 7–8 says to its recipients (who were fellow Israelites):

7 ש[פשרנו מרוב ה]עם . . . [ו] [ו]מכול טמתם
8 ומהתערב בדברים האלה ומלבוא ע[מהם] לגב אלה

7. (that)] we have separated ourselves from the multitude of the pe[ople . . . [and] from all their impurity
8. and from intermingling in these practices and from participating wi[th them] in these practices[22]

Separation (expressed here by פשר) as an allusion to repentance is seen in the quadruple use of the preposition -מ (מן) that describes

21. W. La Sor, *The Dead Sea Scrolls and the New Testament* (Grand Rapids: Eerdmans, 1972), 59.
22. Text: E. Qimron and J. Strugnell, eds., "MMT," *Qumran Cave 4. V. Miqsat Ma'ase Ha-Torah.* DJD 10 (Oxford: Clarendon, 1994), 58.

what the community has turned away from: (מַכוּל, מֵרוב העם
חטאתם, מֵהתערב בדברים האלה, מֵלבוא עמהם לגב אלה).[23] In
short, the reason for the separation is because of the uncleanness
(hence sinfulness) of the rest of Israel and the community's reluctance
to participate in this sinful existence (כול חטאתם). M. Elliott
comments that this text was perhaps written to justify not only the
group's condemnation of the establishment but "perhaps also the
physical separation of the group from Jerusalem."[24] 4QMMT seeks
to convince its recipients to ultimately adopt the senders' point of
view, which can be done only through repentance.[25] E. Qimron and
J. Strugnell suggest that the senders were "'in eirenic' discussion" with
a group that was "not so different from themselves as to be incapable
of being won over to the writers' position and practices."[26] Qimron
and Strugnell therefore conclude that conversion is the intention of
the document.[27] Their conclusion is interesting especially since they
specifically note earlier the *absence* of "conversion" language in the
document.[28] Thus they contradict themselves (and rightly so) when
they now state that conversion was what was intended throughout
the document. Thus, in repenting and accepting the community's
teaching, the recipients would become part of the senders' "separated"
group. That they had already repented of the impurity of the rest
of Israel was manifested in their withdrawal to the desert. Their
separation symbolizes a conscious *turning away* from evil.

In terms of understanding this separation as crucial within the
religious experience of the community, we should note that after the

---

23. I have underlined the preposition for emphasis.
24. M. Elliott, *The Survivors of Israel: A Reconsideration of the Theology of Pre-Christian Judaism* (Grand Rapids: Eerdmans, 2000), 177.
25. In fact, Nitzan comments that the halakic debate between the community and its opponents revolved around correct repentance. Nitzan, "Repentance in the Dead Sea Scrolls," 151.
26. Qimron and Strugnell, "MMT," 114. This "cordial" attitude further endorses the early nature of the document. This cordiality was possible because the split had not yet become irreparable.
27. Ibid., 114.
28. Ibid., 111.

community had been formed at Qumran through an initial act of radical and spatial separation by the core group, for the subsequent members "separation" was less radical and divisive: their "separation" was not going to create in any way a new entity. Thus while such separation became part of the religious experience of subsequent members who joined the community, it was not at the same level of intensity as that of the founders of the community. This is not to say that the spatial dimension of separation was unimportant. In fact, this element was always present whenever a new member joined the now "separated" community.

Other similar texts demonstrate that separation was intimately linked with repentance for the members of the community. The purpose of the *Rule of the Community* is described in 1QS 5:1-2a thus:

1 וזה הסרך לאנושי היחד המתנדבים לשוב מול רע ולהחזיק בכול
אשר צוה לרצונו להבדל מעתד
2 אנשי העול להיות ליחד בתורה ובהון

> 1. And this is the rule for the men of the community who freely volunteer to repent from all evil and to be strengthened in all which he commanded for his will, to separate from the congregation of
> 2. the men of deceit in order to be a community in Law and in possessions.

In all likelihood, "to repent from all evil" (לשוב מול רע) parallels "to separate from the congregation of the men of deceit" (להבדל מעדת אנשי העול) since both verbs convey the need to turn away from wickedness. The object of the verb שוב is impersonal (רע), while the object of בדל refers to persons (עדת אנשי העול). The purpose of this turning/separation ultimately is "to be a community" (להיות ליחד). Assuming that these are parallel statements, "separation language" (בדל) is used synonymously with "repentance language" (שוב). Therefore, this introduction to the *Rule* envisages first of all an act of separation, which in fact is an act of repentance. J. Pouilly asserts: "Devenir membre de la Communauté exige donc une rupture. Il ait se séparer des impies, c'est-à-dire de tous ceux qui n'obéissent pas à Dieu fidèlement et qui sont voués à périr au Jour du Jugement."[29] Thus the verb בדל marks the primary obligation for participation in the community and in the covenant. J. J. Collins describes this need to separate from men of deceit, to turn away from evil as the raison d'être[30] of the community. This is evident not only in the above text but also in the oath taken while joining the community.[31] On entering the covenant, they are to swear to return to the sectarian law of Moses:

8 וקים על נפשו בשבועת אסר לשוב אל תורת מושה

8. He should swear with a binding oath to turn to the law of Moses.

The phrase "to turn to the law of Moses" (לשוב אל תורת מושה) involves a *turning to* that might imply a *turning away from*. A few lines later (1QS 5:10), there is a reiteration of the need to take a similar oath, this time expressed in the language of separation.

10 יקים בברית על נפשו להבדל מכול אנושי העול ההולכים
11 בדרך הרשע

10. He should swear upon his soul by the covenant to be separated from all men of injustice, the ones
11. walking in the path of wickedness.

The injunction in line 10: "He should swear . . . *to be separated from all men of injustice*" (להבדל מכול אנושי העול) is separated from the

---

29. Pouilly, *Le Règle*, 56.
30. Collins "Forms of Community," 101.
31. The only oaths that the sectarians were allowed to take were the covenantal curses (1QS 2:11-18). This type of oath alone was allowed because the only one to be affected (and that too, adversely) was the one who took the oath in the first place. Further, even this oath was taken once a year and in a ritualistic context. See CD15:1 and Josephus's *J.W.* 2.8.6.

earlier one: "to return to the law of Moses" (לשוב אל תורת מושה)
by a description of the Zadokite priests who interpret the law (line
9), but for all practical purposes line 10 reemphasizes the content
of line 8. This is another instance where שוב and בדל are used
interchangeably to refer to aspects of repentance.

There is further justification for understanding separation language
as a metaphor for repentance. 1QS 9 speaks of the perfect behavior
of the men of the community, which enables them to be set apart.
Because of this special status, contact is forbidden with those outside
the community. The latter are described as those who have *not*
separated from their wickedness. Therefore, the community's goods
must not be mixed with the group, which is described thus:

אנושי רמיה אשר 8

9 לוא הזכו דרכם להבדל מעול ללכת בתמים דרך

8. The men of deceit who

9. have not cleansed their path to separate from deceit to walk in the
perfect way.

Obviously "not cleansed their path" (לוא הזכו דרכם) refers to a
lack of repentance. This can be confirmed by the two infinitives
of purpose in line 9 (להבדל and ללכת), which imply that had
these men of deceit cleansed their path (repented), they would have
separated from deceit and walked in perfection. In this context,
separation is the external manifestation of repentance.

In 4Q418 fr. 81, we see another example of repentance as
separation.

[. . .] הבדילכה מכול 1

2 רוח בשר ואתה הבדל מכול אשר שנא והנזר מכול תעבות נפש

1.   [. . .] he has separated you from every

2. spirit of flesh, And you, keep yourself apart from everything he
hates, and be separated from all abominations of the soul.

Commenting on the phrase "every spirit of flesh" (מכול רוח בשר),
J. Frey notes that it is paralleled by "everything he [God] hates" and
therefore refers to "a sphere or entity opposed to God and his will."[32]
In line 1, God "separates" his chosen ones. In line 2, the individual
needs to remain in this "separate" state. This line synonymously uses
two "separation" verbs, בדל and נזר.[33] Further, the sentence "and
you keep yourselves apart from everything he hates" (ואתה הבדל
מכול אשר שמא, line 2) ideologically parallels one of the opening
injunctions from 1QS 1:4c, where one is exhorted to keep apart
from all evil: "to separate from all wickedness" (לרחוק מכול ער).
While the general content is parallel, the 1QS text uses yet another
separation verb: רחק. Since the object from which one "distances
oneself" is "all evil," there is no doubt that it is an exhortation to
repent. Thus 4Q418 fr. 81, 1b–2 and 1QS 1:4c contain various
words used to convey one common idea, namely, separation from
different things ("spirit of flesh, "everything he hates," "abominations
of the soul," and "evil"). This in turn highlights another common
element—separation is a manifestation of repentance.

Thus the texts discussed above further the case that separation
language often metaphorically conveys the idea of removing/
distancing oneself from evil. This repentance-as-separation motif

32. J. Frey, "The Notion of 'Flesh' in 4QInstruction and the Background of Pauline Usage," in
*Sapiential, Liturgical and Poetical Texts from Qumran: Proceedings of the Third Meeting of the
International Organization for Qumran Studies, Published in Memory of Maurice Baillet*, ed. D. Falk,
F. García Martínez, and E. Schuller (Leiden: Brill, 2000), 197–226 (216). He notes that this
phrase goes beyond the common biblical usage and denotes *sinful* humanity (219).

33. Newton observes that the verb נזר is sometimes used in the scrolls to convey a "cultic"
separation (see CD 6:14–15; 7:3). Newton, *The Concept of Purity at Qumran*, 18. Frey comments:
"[Man] is, therefore, called to sanctify himself and to keep away from the abominations that
characterizes the 'spirit of flesh.'" Frey, "Notion of 'Flesh,'" 216.

often employed these following verbs: פרש, בדל, נזר, and רחק. Separation as a manifestation of repentance was the most basic prerequisite for entrance into both the community and the covenant. The locus for this separation/repentance was the wilderness.

In Second Temple Literature

Was this motif unique to Qumran? Does it occur in other Second Temple Jewish literature? Answering this question will help us better understand if the Qumran community was redefining this aspect of their penitential experience in an unprecedented way. G. Brooke points out that there are texts in the Apocrypha and Pseudepigrapha that "provide a ready example of actual physical retreats to the wilderness which the members of the roughly contemporary communities associated with the *Manual of Discipline* may well have known about."[34] We see something of this motif in the first part of the *Martyrdom of Isaiah* (*Mart. Isa.*). While this work was composed not later than 100 CE, the narrative section of chapters 1–5 (1.1–3.12 and 5.1.16) could go back to the period of persecution of the Jews in 167–164 BCE.[35] Our interest lies with a very brief part of chapter 2. Isaiah, seeing the wickedness around him, "withdrew from Jerusalem and dwelt in Bethlehem" (2.7b). Bethlehem too was sinful so again "he withdrew to a mountain in a desert place" (2.8). However, he does not remain on his own; rather, he is joined by several others (2.9); the fact that they are all clothed in sackcloth (2.10) is a clear sign of their penitence. This type of repentance in *Mart. Isa.* is a

---

34. Brooke highlights 1 Macc. 2:29-38, where despite the loss of life, those seeking righteousness/ justice "go into the wilderness so as not to compromise themselves." Brooke, "Isaiah 40:3 and the Wilderness Community," 130.

35. M. Knibb, "Martyrdom and Ascension of Isaiah," in *OTP* 2:149. See also E. Brandenburger, "Himmelfahrt Moses," in *JSHRZ*, vol. 5.2, *Apokalypsen*, ed. E. Brandenburger, U. Müller & A. Klijn (Gütersloh: Gütersloher, 1976), 59–84. Knibb affirms that 1.1–3.12 and 5.1.16 is the "oldest element of this work and is Jewish" (143).

REPENTANCE, SEPARATION, AND THE COVENANT

physical separation motivated by repentance; that is, withdrawing from a polluting and defiling context reminds us of the "penitential separation" motif we are considering. This type of repentance has a spatial dimension to it. It is not merely a separation expressed in a nonassociation from sinful practices; rather, one seeks to distance oneself from evil through a total physical separation. However, because of lack of evidence for this incident, this may well be a textual construct and not an actual, historical act of separation.

The *Testament of Moses* (*T. Mos.*) has an example of this motif. A wide range of dates have been suggested for this document: the period just following the war of 132–135 CE (Zeitlin); during the period of the Maccabean revolt in 168–165 BCE (Licht); first century CE, but before 70 CE (Charles).[36] Despite the various dates, it nevertheless falls within the period of our investigation and therefore is relevant for our purposes. On his deathbed, Moses foretells the sinfulness of the people and the subsequent punishment (8.1) and persecution (8.2–5) that this sinfulness will result in. In this context, Moses commends the faithfulness of a man called Taxo and his seven sons (9.1–2). Because Taxo does not want himself (or his sons) to be tainted by the wickedness around them, he gives to his sons this advice: "We shall fast for a three-day period and on the fourth day we shall go into a cave, which is in the open country" (9.6a).[37] The intention of remaining "separate" from sinfulness is evident. The reason for such a separation is so that they will not "transgress the commandments" of the Lord (9.6b). The penitential nature of this withdrawal can be further confirmed by their act of fasting.[38] Thus

36. J. Priest, "Testament of Moses," in *OTP* 2:921. Scholars generally accept a first-century-ce, date recognizing that at least some of the material reflects an earlier historical period: chs. 8–9 refer to Antiochius IV Epiphanes's persecution, and chs. 5–6 refer to Herod's reign.

37. J. Priest observes that refuge in caves was common in times of persecution (ibid., 2:919–34). See also 1 Macc. 2:29-38; Heb. 11:32-38.

38. "This ritual of penance serves as a preparation for the retreat into the cave in the field." J. Tromp, *The Assumption of Moses: A Critical Edition with Commentary* (Leiden: Brill, 1993), 226.

we have in *T. Mos.* a brief but significant reference to repentance manifested in spatial separation.

What of apparently "separatist" groups such as the Pharisees and rabbinic *Haverim* (חברות) who were governed by their great concern for purity and strict rules of association?[39] This necessarily caused them to see themselves as "separate" from others, so as not to contaminate themselves. However, the separation of the Pharisee or the חבר was not absolute: impurity could be resolved by the performance of appropriate purificatory rituals. "Rabbinic *halacha* would undoubtedly permit an *am ha-aretz* to eat with *haverim*, provided he was willing to undergo a ritual cleansing of his body and his clothing."[40] Thus, even though they maintained a degree of separation from polluting influence, their ultimate concern was avoidance of ritual impurity and not repentance.[41] It must be noted that the separation of the Pharisees (or *Haverim* for that matter) did not involve a physical withdrawal from society and the establishment of a separate, spatially isolated community. In fact, according to J. Maier, the Pharisees, unlike the Qumran community, "tried to find a way to live according to a Torah not restricted to an elitist and extremist group as a way for as many as possible of all the people of Israel."[42]

If we were to read these texts in the light of what we have seen so far with the Qumran community, we notice that although both

39. Collins, "Forms of Community," 102. A. Shemesh refers to *m. Demai* 2:3, which underscores the "separation" aspect between a חבר and the עם הארץ. A. Shemesh, "The Origins of the Laws of Separatism: Qumran Literature and Rabbinic *Halacha*," *RevQ* 70 (1997): 207–39.
40. Shemesh, "Origins of the Laws of Separatism," 232.
41. While they may have "turned away from" ritual impurity, they did not "turn toward" anything. For the Qumran community, genuine repentance had a "turning away from" (sin) dimension as well as a tangible "turning toward" (God/renewed covenant/community) dimension.
42. J. Maier, "The Judaic System of the Dead Sea Scrolls," in *Judaism in Late Antiquity*, part 2, *Historical Synthesis* (Leiden: Brill, 1995), 84–108. He continues, "It may be that the Pharisaic-Rabbinic principle not to impose on the public unbearable burdens had one of its roots in reaction to such extremist tendencies as attested to in the Qumran scrolls" (105).

Mart. Isa. 2.10 and *T. Mos.* 9.6 like the Qumran community express a spatial dimension to their separation (the former portrays the *desert* as the locus for this separation/repentance, while in the latter the *cave* becomes a locus for the maintenance of spiritual purity); however, neither of the texts describes an *organized* separation; For that matter, the separation of the Pharisees and the *Haverim* do not even refer to a *spatial* separation; rather, they allude more to a complete (nonspatial) disassociation from sinful practices; that is, their separation did not involve a separation from society. Particularly helpful is E. P. Sanders's discussion on the "exclusivist" nature of the Pharisees. *Contra* those who liken the separation of the Pharisees to that of the Qumran community, he says, "The [Pharisees] had leaders, but not an alternative priesthood. They had their own interpretations of the law, as well as further traditions, but they did not claim that they had more of the Mosaic law than did the Sadducees or the common people, and their differences of interpretation did not lead to a sociopolitical split. They accepted the temple, they championed the rights of the current priesthood, they brought their sacrifices, and they kept holy days when every one else did."[43] At Qumran, however, the community's separation was primarily an act of repentance since it was not merely ritual impurity from which they turned but also moral impurity. This was manifested in a spatial withdrawal that was absolute—those outside the community (even Jews) could not be purified by ablution. Collins says that "outsiders cannot be rendered fit for association by purificatory baths,"[44] thus pointing to a more extreme degree of separation. Similarly, A. Shemesh too notes that all those outside the sect were "inherently impure" and that "no ablution can purge them of this impurity."[45]

43. E. P. Sanders, *Jewish Law from Jesus to the Mishnah* (London: SCM, 1990), 236–242, esp. 241.
44. Collins, "Forms of Community," 102.
45. Shemesh, "Origins of the Laws of Separatism," 233.

Thus, while we do encounter the repentance-as-separation motif in some Second Temple texts as well as in the religious practices of the Pharisees and *Haverim*, it is alluded to in a completely "nonspatial" way and "nonorganized" way;[46] in the scrolls, it is fundamental to the community's identity as a separate, organized, spatial entity at Qumran. These characteristics clearly rendered the Qumran community different from other "separatist groups" of that era.

There was another feature that rendered the Qumran community's penitential separation radically different: their unique understanding and interpretation of the law, which also, as we shall below, had strong repentance overtones.

Penitential Separation and the Covenant

At Qumran, joining the community involved joining the covenant.[47] This interrelation needs to be borne in mind as we explore repentance, separation, and the covenant. Just as the theme of covenant forms the heart of the Hebrew Scriptures, the Sinai covenant and its renewal constituted the Qumran community's very raison d'être.[48] Even a casual reading of the scrolls confirms the importance of the covenant for the Qumran community. The frequent occurrence of the term ברית attests to this.[49] C. Evans aptly describes the importance of the covenant to the community: "Interest in the covenant, in obeying it as perfectly as possible, provides the *rationale* for the formation of the community, the *guidance* for community development, and the *hermeneutic* for the interpretation

46. Even if the separation of the Pharisees does appear to be organized, it is certainly not absolute separation that is required.
47. 1QS 5:7c–8a states: "All who enter the counsel of the community enters the covenant of God."
48. M. Abegg, "The Covenant of the Qumran Sectarians," in *The Concept of the Covenant in the Second Temple Period*, ed. S. Porter and J. de Roo (Leiden: Brill, 2003), 81–92 (88).
49. The word ברית occurs more that two hundred times in the DSS. C. F. Evans, "Covenant in the Qumran Literature," in Porter and do Roo, *The Concept of the Covenant*, 55–80.

of the scriptures."[50] The Qumran community saw itself as the recipient of a "new" covenant from God. This was not a covenant distinct from and in opposition to the old one; rather, it was a "renewed" one.[51] S. Talmon was the first to describe the Qumran community as "the Community of the Renewed Covenant."[52] He comments that the description "those who entered the renewed covenant" (CD 6:19; 8:29) "underscores their intended self-implantation in the world of biblical Israel."[53] This renewed covenant was occasioned by the apostasy and sinfulness of the rest of Israel, which was in turn a result of the false teaching of the Jerusalem priesthood.[54]

For the purposes of this chapter, this renewed covenant and how the members of the community understood it serve as the basis of understanding repentance as manifested by extreme separation. One's entry into this separated community was identified with entry into the covenant. Pouilly says, "l'infidélité d'Israël provoque la Communauté à retour aux sources, à l'Alliance. S'agréger à la Communauté équivaut à 'entrer dans l'Alliance.'"[55] Therefore, it will help for us to view the repentance-as-separation motif against a covenantal backdrop.

---

50. Ibid., 55–56.
51. Ibid., 79. Kapelrud is alone in arguing that the old covenant had become obsolete and hence a new one was necessary: "Der alte Bund hatte für die Qumranleute seine Bedeutung und seinen Inhalt verloren. Ein Leben ohne Bund war aber undenkbar und unmöglich, deshalb mußte ein neuer Bund anstelle des alten wirksam werden." A. S. Kapelrud, "Der Bund in den Qumran-Schriften," in *Bibel und Qumran*, ed. H. Bardtke (Berlin: Evangelische Haupt, 1966), 137–49.
52. S. Talmon, "The Community of the Renewed Covenant: Between Judaism and Christianity," in *The Community of the Renewed Covenant*, ed. E. Ulrich and J. VanderKam (Notre Dame: Notre Dame University Press, 1994), 3–24.
53. Ibid., 12. The most explicit reference to the renewed covenant in the HB is Jer. 31:31. Scholars see it as being fulfilled by the community. Pouilly says: "Le terme jérémien 'nouvelle Alliance' n'est pas utilisé en 1QS. Il est donc plus exact de voir ici une rénovation de l'Alliance (ancienne)." Pouilly, *La Règle*, 56.
54. Evans, "Covenant in Qumran Literature," 79.
55. Pouilly, *La Règle*, 53.

The following text from 1QS 5:7b-8a confirms this sort of an identification: "Whoever enters the council of the community enters the covenant of God" (כול הבא לעצת היחד יבוא בברית אל). At Qumran, the one act was identical to the other. Hence, whatever was involved in joining the community was equally valid for entering into the covenant. Therefore, since repentance (manifested by separation) was the basic prerequisite for joining the community, then by extension repentance became the basic prerequisite for participating in the covenant as well. As C. Evans points out, "For the community at Qumran, entering the covenant was very much a conversion, from apostasy and damnation, to repentance and salvation."[56] This justifies our overall reading of the repentance-as-separation motif within a covenantal context.

We have in 1QS 1:16—3:12 a clear description of entry into the covenant, which is part of the annual covenant-renewal ceremony. Those who were gathered there were a mixed group with regard to their status in the community/covenant, both new members as well as existing ones. 1QS 5:7b-8 confirms this for us.

7   כולהבא לעצת
8 יבוא בברית אל לעניני כול המתנדבים

7.   whoever enters the council of the community
8. enters the covenant of God in the presence of all who freely volunteer.

Entry into the community/covenant by the new members did not occur in isolation. Rather, it was a public ceremony witnessed by those who had themselves undergone the same entry procedures in the past. It did not matter whether one was joining as a member for the first time or continuing as a member. The *reiteration* of oaths

56. Ibid., 63.

and the subsequent *re*instatement into this covenantal community indicates their annual recommitment to the covenant. This ceremony represented two levels of repentance: First, an initial act of repentance on the part of the *new* members rendered them acceptable to join the community. Second, full participation in this ceremony served as a reaffirmation of repentance for the *existing* members. Therefore, the covenant-renewal ceremony was primarily a penitential occasion by which all members (both new and existing) were reminded annually of their repentance; participation in the rites of the ceremony was an annual recommitment to one's initial repentance. The fact that this ceremony occurred in the Judean desert would have served as a stark reminder that their repentance was very much an act of separation.

In other words, fundamental to the religious experience of the community was an act of repentance manifested through separation that for the founding members established a separate community and for subsequent members enabled them to participate in and identify with this penitential experience. Participation in this community enabled one to participate in the renewed covenant. Penitential separation and annual repentance were the fundamental requirements for both joining and remaining in the community and the covenant.

Covenant and the (Sectarian) Law of Moses

According to 1QS 8:12-14, preparation of the way of the Lord through study of the law was the purpose of being a separated community. Their distinctive understanding of the law served to underscore their separate (and therefore penitential) status. E. Condra says of 1QS that "the overall picture of the community which emerges in this document is a group separated from the evil world with a view to repentance and the 'proper' practice of the Mosaic Law."[57] After separating and "turning away from" evil, they first of all "turned to" (joined) the covenantal community. In doing so, they also turned to the law of Moses in its unique sectarian interpretation.[58] We need to see how their understanding of the law further established them as a separate, penitential community and that the obligation to "return to the law" was in itself an act of repentance.

The centrality of the law of Moses for the members of the community is unambiguous. F. García Martínez describes the life of the men of Qumran as "a life completely dedicated to the observance of the Law."[59] The frequent recurrence of the command to "return to the law of Moses" emphasizes its importance and uniqueness. In fact, it is associated with joining the community. According to 1QS 5:7c-9a, anyone who "enters the council of the community enters the covenant of God in the presence of all who freely volunteer."

8 ויקים על נפשו בשבועת אסר לשוב תורת מושה ככול אשר צוה בכול

9 לב ובכול נפש לכול הנגלה ממנה לבני צדוק הכוהנים שומרי
בריתו ודורשי רצונו

8. He shall swear with a binding oath to return to the law of Moses, according to all that he commanded, with whole

9. heart and whole soul, in compliance with all that has been revealed of it to the sons of Zadok the priests, the keepers of his covenant and seekers of his will.

Since all Israel had gone astray in following the Mosaic law, "it was with regard to the Law of Moses that this repentance was needed, but specifically, a repentance in conformity with the sectarian elaboration of the Law."[60] Hence the return to the law of Moses was primarily an

---

57. Condra, *Salvation for the Righteous Revealed*, 148.

58. S. Fisdel comments that for the community, "only through repentance and return to the observance of the Law was there salvation." Fisdel, *The Dead Sea Scrolls: Understanding the Spiritual Message* (Northvale, NJ: Aronson, 1998), 58.

59. F. García Martínez "The Men of the Dead Sea," in *The People of the Dead Sea Scrolls: Their Writings, Beliefs and Practices*, ed. F. García Martínez and J. T. Barrera (Leiden: Brill, 1995), 35. This frequent exhortation is in accordance with one of descriptions of the members, "men who observe the Law" (1QH 7:10;8:1; 12:4).

act of repentance. This "turning to" the law in fact occurs after they have "turned away" from evil, thereby highlighting the bidirectional aspect of turning. The law of Moses to which the sectarians turned was not the "general" law that was freely available and known to all Israel; rather, it was the distinctively sectarian interpretation.[61]

The exhortation "to return to the law of Moses" also receives emphasis in CD. Allegiance to the covenant is demonstrated through a sincere acceptance of the law with its distinctive sectarian interpretation. Thus, as in 1QS 5:7, wherein the individual is expected to wholeheartedly turn to the law, one encounters a similar command in CD. Not only that, in CD the exhortation occurs four times within a short space of text (15:9, 12; 16:2a, 5a). In CD-A 15:7, there is no doubt that this phrase alludes to repentance. The blank space preceding the beginning of line 7 suggests the beginning of a new paragraph.

וכן [blank]   6
7 המשפט בכל קץ הרשע לכל השב מדרכי הנשחתה

6.   [blank] And thus
7. is the regulation throughout all the age of wickedness, for all the ones who turn[62] from his path of corruption.

The above-mentioned regulation (המשפט) was obviously a consequence of the first and basic act wherein the individual recognizes his corrupt way and repents of it (לכל השב מדרכי הנשחתה). The use of the verb שוב in the overall context of wickedness (קץ הרשע) unambiguously alludes to repentance. Only after this act of repentance can he be enrolled into the community

---

60. Condra, *Salvation for the Righteous revealed*, 127.
61. The community believed that God revealed to them (hence, הנגלות) through the Teacher of Righteousness the true or full meaning that had been hidden (הנסתרות) from Israel (CD 3:12-14; 1QpHab 2:5-10; 7:2).
62. *DSSNT*: "for all who *repent* of their wicked way" (65).

and that after having first sworn to return to the law. To put it differently, repentance is manifested through one's return to the law. Further, the four references of "returning to the law of Moses" occur in two sets. These are expressed in a cause-effect relationship. The first of these sets (a and b) states the need to swear to return to the law and the consequence of breaking it. CD 15:9-10 and 15:12-13 describe the oath a new member takes. He is

a.

9   לש[וב] אל תורת משה בכל לב ובכל

10 נפש אל הנמצא לעשות בכ[ל] קץ ק[ר]בו

9.   to re[turn] to the Law of Moses with the whole heart and

10. so[ul], to whatever is found (therein) to do during the complete period of his appr[oa]ch.

b.

12 וכאשר יקים אותו עליו לשוב אל תורת משה בכל לב ובכל נפש

13 [נק]יאים הם ממנו אם ימעל

12. But when he solemnly undertakes to return to the law of Moses with all his heart and all his soul,

13. they will [exact re]venge from him should he become unfaithful.

The second set (c and d) occurs in CD 16:1-2 and 16:4b-5 and expresses basically the same consequential relationship but differently.

c.

1   על כן יקום האיש על נפשו לשוב אל

2 תורת משה כי בה הכל מדוקדק

1.   Therefore a man must solemnly undertake to return to

2. the law of Moses, for in it all is defined.

d.

וביום אשר יקום האיש על נפשו לשוב 4
אל תורת משה יסור מלאך המשטמה מאחריו אם יקים את דבריו 5

4. And on the day on which he has solemnly undertaken return
5. to the law of Moses, the angel Mastema will turn from following after him if he keeps his words.[63]

It is interesting that these two "sets" are clustered together. In the first set (a and b), the phrase occurs as: "to return to the law of Moses with a whole heart and soul," while the second set (c and d) has an abbreviated form: "to return to the law of Moses." Apart from this minor difference, the language describing the act and its consequence match each other closely.

In the first set, text a states the need to return to the law and text b expresses the consequence of unfaithfulness to the law (the exacting of vengeance). This idea is reflected in the second set, where text c states the need to turn to the law while text d mentions the consequence of this act (the angel Mastema turns away from that individual). Although the overall message of the two sets is the same, text b describes in negative terms (vengeance) the consequence of disobedience to the law while text d describes in positive terms (the removal of vengeance) the benefit of obedience to the law. From these two sets two things become clear.

First, the sectarian interpretation of the law of Moses is central to the community, as seen from attention repeatedly being drawn to this obligation. Its importance lies in the fact that "in it all things are strictly defined" and that it serves to further establish the

63. Nitzan says that "as long as a person fulfils his oath, his repentance is granted the power to overcome the magical power of the curse with which angel Mastemah might have threatened him." Nitzan, "Repentance in the Dead Sea Scrolls," 155.

"separateness" of the community. Second, adherence to the law results in well being (deliverance from destruction).

All that has been mentioned above regarding the benefits of returning to the law of Moses or the consequence of not being faithful to it is the follow-on of the original exhortation in CD 15:7: "[blank] And such is the regulation throughout all the age of wickedness, for all the ones who turn from his path of corruption." This confirms my earlier premise that a return to the law of Moses and all that it involves is a manifestation of repentance.

We can conclude that the sectarian interpretation of law was central to the community. Participation in the covenant and membership in the community meant acceptance of and adherence to this law after one separated from the surrounding wickedness. This "return," then, was an act of repentance since the law of Moses became the object *to* which they turned (after they turned *away* from evil).[64] Acceptance of this sectarian interpretation of the law further accentuated their separation from other Jews. Thus "separation from evil" and a "return to the law" go hand in hand, representing a "turning away" and a "turning toward," both acts being a manifestation of repentance. As D. Lambert notes, Qumran's use of the term *šûb* resembles that of biblical Hebrew in that it focuses on behavioral practice, but is unique in that it refers, not to turn away from generic sin, but specifically to a turn away from nonsectarian practice.[65]

---

64. See 2 Kgs. 23:25, where it is said of Josiah: "Before him there was no king like him, who turned to the Lord with all his heart, with all his soul, and with all his might, according to all the law of Moses; nor did any like him arise after him."

65. Lambert, "Was the Qumran Community a Penitential Movement?," 507.

Covenant of Repentance (ברית תשיבה)

Up to now, I have tried to show that repentance was at the very core of the community's perception of the covenant. This close relation between repentance and the covenant existed primarily because of the *type* of covenant it was; that is, by its very nature the covenant demanded repentance. CD offers some vital information as to how the community understood the covenant. In the context of the sinfulness of the rest of Israel, God chose for himself a faithful remnant to renew his covenant with (CD 1:3-11). C. Hempel notes that in CD the term *covenant* "occurs 44 times in the medieval and ancient MSS not including references that occur in overlapping sections."[66] Of these, a notable description of the covenant and definitely the one much neglected in scholarly discussion is the reference in CD-B 19:16c to the "Covenant of Repentance" (ברית תשיבה).[67] This phrase explicitly indicates the nature of the covenant and enables us to better understand those texts in 1QS and CD that stress the proper attitude required to join this covenant of repentance. For example, in CD-A 8:1b-2, there is a strong criticism of those who enter the covenant insincerely and without repentance.

יכן המשפט כל באי ברית אשר 1

לא יחזיקו באלה לפקודם לכלה ביד בליעל 2

1.   Thus is the judgment of all those entering the covenant, who

2. do not remain steadfast in these [precepts]; to be visited for destruction at the hand of Belial.

The phrase "[those] who do not remain steadfast in these" (לא יחזיקו באלה) refers to the incorrect attitude that is condemned. This

---

66. C. Hempel, *The Damascus Texts* (Sheffield: Sheffield Academic, 2000), 79.

67. This is the only instance in the scrolls where the noun תשיבה occurs.

suggests that a proper attitude is essential to participate in the covenant. Similarly, 1QS 2:11-12b warns:

11 ארור בגלולי לבו לעבור

12 הבא בברית הזות ומכשול עוונו ישים לפניו להסוג בו

> 11. Cursed in the idols of his heart, for the one crossing over
>
> 12. and entering this covenant and setting the stumbling block of his sin before him so that he backslides.

These lines have also been translated thus: "damned be anyone initiated with an unrepentant heart, who enters this Covenant."[68] This confirms that an appropriate attitude is required. CD-B 19:16b-17a throws valuable light on this subject. It makes the following significant addition to CD-A 8:4b-5 on the *type* of covenant that has been entered. CD-A only has:

4 כל מרדים מאשר לא סרו מדרך

5 בוגדים ויתגוללו בדרכי זונות

> 4.   . . . all are rebels because they have not turned from the way of
>
> 5. traitors and have defiled themselves on the paths of fornicators.

Whereas CD-B supplies the first part of the sentence:

16 כי באו ברית התשובה

17 ולא סרו מדרך בוגדים ויתגללו בדרכי זנות

> 16.   They have entered the covenant of repentance but have not turned
>
> 17. from the path of traitors and have defiled themselves on the paths of fornicators.[69]

---

68. *DSSNT* 128.

69. M. Abegg translates: "Truly they had entered the covenant repenting but they did not turn away from traitorous practices; they relished the customs of fornication and filthy lucre." This does not capture the essential nature of the covenant. Further, there is no basis in the above text

Stated differently, they have entered a covenant that *requires* repentance, but have not repented. סרו employs the imagery of turning—they have not "turned" (repented). The phrase "covenant of repentance" (ברית התשובה) unambiguously states that central to the covenant is repentance: without repentance, one has only insincerely accepted the covenant. Furthermore, ברית התשובה is a crucial concept because it is directly related to the need to "return to the law of Moses." For the sectarians, the renewed covenant consisted of the distinctively sectarian interpretation of the law of Moses, and it is this interpretation to which they "turned" in an act repentance. Thus the term ברית התשובה becomes a focal point: knowing that the covenant demanded repentance, only true penitents could participate in it after they had genuinely separated from sin and turned to the law of Moses; the members of the community understood the covenant as one whose very nature demanded repentance. It was not possible truly to join the covenant and *not* turn from evil.

"Repenters of Sin" (שבי פשע)

Following the same line of thought discussed above, the self-designation שבי פשע further emphasizes the penitential nature of the covenant. In the context of God's forgiveness to those in the covenant, it is said of God in CD 2:4b,5a:

4 ארך אפים עמו ורוב סליחות
5 לכפר בעד שבי פשע

4.   patience is his and abundance of pardon,
5. to atone for those who turn away from sin.

---

to take תשובה as a verb. Abegg, "The Covenant of the Qumran Sectaries," in Porter and de Roo, *Concept of the Covenant*, 95.

This text implies that atonement is only for those who repent. Seeing this initial act of repentance (turning from sin), God forgives the penitent and assists him to maintain a state of repentance. The term "those who turn away from sin" (שבי פשע) refers not only to the initial repentance manifested on joining the community but also to repentance even after one joins the community. Similarly, 1QH 6:23b-24a says:

23   ואתה רו[ם] וגדול   [
24 [ורוב הס]דים הסולח לשבי פשע ופוקד אוון רשעים

    23.   [you are lof]ty, great
    24. [abounding in stea]dfastness forgiving those who turn away from offense, and punishing the iniquity of the wicked.

As in 1QH 2:4b,5a, here too God forgives "those who repent from sin" (שבי פשע). Interestingly, this text exhibits parallelism: the forgiveness of the penitent (הסולח לשבי פשע) is juxtaposed with the punishment of the wicked (פוקד אוון רשעים). The penitents are forgiven while the unrepentant are punished. This twofold categorization implies that the criterion for forgiveness is repentance. Those who repent enjoy God's goodness, abundance of steadfastness, and forgiveness, while those who do not repent are deprived of these things. This idea occurs again in the following text from 1QH 8:24-26a:

24   וא[דעה כי אתה אל חנון] ורחום א[ר]וך א[פ]ים ורב חסד ואמת
ונושא פשע
25 ונחם על [רעת אוהביך] ושומרי מצו[תיך ה]שבים אליך באמונה
ולב שלם [...]
26 לעובדך [ולעשות] טוב בעיניך

    24.   and I kn[ow that you are a gracious] and compassionate[God], s[l]ow to a[ng]er, abounding in steadfastness and truth, who forgives offense [...]

25. and has remorse on account of the [evil of those who love you] and keep [your] pre[cepts, those] who turn to you with trust and a perfect heart [...]

26. to serve you [and to do] good in your eyes.

All the above-listed attributes of God and his blessings are relevant for "those who turn" to God (השבים). Although this is a variation of שבי פשע, it retains the entire content of the epithet. They are further described as "those who love you" (אוהביך), implying an ongoing commitment.[70]

Our epithet occurs again in the hymn of the Instructor in 1QS 9:21—11:22, which describes the Instructor's emotions and reactions to various issues. His understanding and attitude to repentance is mentioned in 1QS 10:20b-21a. He says:

20 לוא אטור באף לשבי פשע ולוא ארחם
21 על כול סוררי בדך

20. I shall not sustain angry resentment for those who turn from sin but I shall have no mercy
21. for all those who deviate from the path.

The Instructor will take a tolerant attitude to those who repent. These penitents are described as שבי פשע. Line 21 confirms this when he speaks of not tolerating "those who deviate from the path" (סוררי בדך). In both instances, turning language is used: שוב occurs in 10:20, while סור occurs in 10:21. Further, סוררי בדך is contrasted with שבי פשע. This suggests that while individuals can and do repent, hard-heartedness or an unrepentant attitude is not tolerated. To be noted is that these epithets refer to those *in* the community, thereby emphasizing the penitential nature of the covenant. Thus

---

70. Interestingly, God "has pity on the evil of those who you love" (ונחם על רעת אוהביך). This implies that even the "chosen" who loved God could have evil within them (see 4Q186). The disciplinary sanctions of the community indicates its desire to deal with this evil and remain penitent.

שבי פשע captures the community's deep concern for repentance since it describes those who repent after sinning even while in the covenantal community.

Penitents of Israel (שבי ישראל)

Another epithet that expresses the penitential nature of the covenant is "penitents of Israel" (שבי ישראל).[71] A storm of controversy surrounds its translation and meaning, and has led scholars to exercise caution. If שבי is vocalized as a noun, it means "captivity"; if taken as a participle, it could be given a spiritual meaning ("penitents") or a geographical one ("returnees").[72] S. Iwry prefers "returnees of Israel." He objects to translating the phrase as "repenters of Israel": the word "'repenters' is in construct (שבי) and so could necessarily involve it to be followed by an object from which one repents. For example, in 'repenters of sin' the object from which one repents is 'sin.' By analogy, to say 'repenters of Israel' would be to say Israel is the object from which one repents."[73] J. Murphy-O'Connor argues that the Qumran sect originated in Babylon and emigrated to Jerusalem. Thus שבי alludes to a geographical direction rather than moral transformation.[74] M. Knibb, however, refutes Murphy-O'Connor's theory by pointing out that of the six occurrences of שוב in CD, four have moral connotations, and it is highly possible that the remaining two have a moral meaning.[75] R. Werline accepts Knibb's position and says that the term שוב signifies "moral transformation

71. CD 8:16 // 19:29; CD6:5 // 4Q267 fr. 2:11 // 4Q266 fr. 3, 2:12. See particularly S. Iwry, "Was There a Migration to Damascus? The Problem of שבי ישראל," Eretz-Israel 9 (1969): 80–88.
72. J. Murphy-O'Connor, "An Essene Missionary Document? CD II,14–IV,1," RB 77 (1970): 201–29.
73. Iwry, "Was There a Migration to Damascus?," 86.
74. J. Murphy-O'Connor, "The Essenes and Their History," RB 81 (1974): 215–44 (220).
75. M. Knibb, "Exile in the Damascus Document," JSOT 25 (1983): 99–117 (106–7).

rather than spatial migration." He says, "The Hebrew phrase translates into English as 'the penitents of Israel.'"[76]

As we shall see below, the translation "penitents of Israel" is the most plausible option and is also in keeping with the overall concept of the "covenant of repentance." After mentioning the various people in Israel's history who succumbed to evil ways (CD 2:17—3:12), the author also mentions a remnant who "remained steadfast to God precepts" (CD 3:12-13). However, in spite of being a chosen and faithful group, they too were prone to sin (CD 3:17b-18a). According to the mysteries of God, he pardoned them (CD 3:18b), firmly established them, and blessed them (CD 3:19-20). The author then cites Ezek. 44:15 ("the priests and the Levites and the sons of Zadok who maintained service of my temple when the children of Israel strayed away from me; they shall offer me the fat and the blood")[77] and applies it to the members of this chosen group, who have been forgiven, blessed, and established by God as CD 4:2b-4 states.

2 הכהנים הם שבי ישראל [blank]
3 היוצאים מארץ יהודה והלוים הם והנלוים עמהם [blank] ובני צדוק הם בחירי
4 ישראל קריאי השם העמדים באחרית הימים

2.   [blank] the priests are the penitents of Israel
3. who left the Land of Judah; and the Levites are those who joined them [blank] and the sons of Zadok they are the chosen of
4. Israel, men of renown, who shall stand at the end of days

According to this application of Ezek. 44:15, the group in focus is described as שבי ישראל (CD 4:2). Schechter has "captivity of

76. R. Werline, *Penitential Prayer in Second Temple Judaism: The Development of a Religious Institution* (Atlanta: Scholars Press, 1998).
77. The modification of the MT in the CD citation is ascribed to its author rather than a textual variation.

Israel" in his main text, although he admits in a footnote the possible translation "repentants."[78] C. Rabin suggests another explanation: that it is an abbreviated form of שבי פשע ישראל, although this cannot be verified.[79] In column 4, after a blank space, we have the explanation of the Ezekiel text. The blank space in all probability is a paragraph marker. In this new paragraph, the opening line is significant: "the priests are the penitents of Israel" (הכוהנים הם שבי ישראל). This clearly identifies the priests with the ones described as שבי ישראל. We can then use this positive identification as the starting point for exploring the phrase in more detail. CD 6:2-5 emphasizes again the priestly nature of שבי ישראל:

ויקם מאהרן נבונים ומישראל [blank]   2
3 חכמים וישמיעם ויחפורו את הבאר חפרוה שרים כרוה
הם [blank] נדיבי העם במחוקק הבאר היא התורה וחופרייה 4
5 שבי ישראל

2.   [blank] And he raised from Aaron men of knowledge and from Israel

3. wise men, and made them listen. And they dug the well. "The well that the princes dug,

4. which the nobles of the people delved with a staff." The well is the law and those who dug it [blank] they are

5. the penitents of Israel.

The fact that the men are raised from "Aaron" suggests their priestly background. "Men of knowledge from Aaron" (מאהרן נבונים) parallels "wise men from Israel" (מישראל חכמים), indicating that these two descriptions refer to the same group. Further, in 6:3a, this priestly group "dug a well" (ויחפורו). We know this because the subject of the third person plural imperfect ויחפורו has to be

78. S. Schechter, *Documents of Jewish Sectaries I: Fragments of a Zadokite Work* (Cambridge: Cambridge University Press, 1910), 35n1.

79. C. Rabin, *The Zadokite Documents* (Oxford: Clarendon, 1954), 13n21:2:3.

the "men of knowledge from Aaron" and "wise men from Israel." This action (of digging) was understood in the light of Num. 21:18, where the princes and nobles "dug" (חפרוה) a well (which was interpreted by the community as "the law"). Immediately following this quotation, there is a third reference to the verb חפר in the form of the participle וחופריה. In the new paragraph (marked by the blank space), this participle is further described thus: "they are the penitents of Israel" (הם שבי ישראל). Thus "digging (a well)" imagery uses the verb חפר to tie what precedes the Num. 21:18 citation with what follows it. This device enables us to further identify the "priests" with the "penitents of Israel." This fits into the widely accepted theory that the Qumran community was primarily a priestly community.

Another occurrence of this phrase in CD 8:16 (// CD-B 19:29) throws further light on our argument so far.

16 [blank] וכן המשפט לשבי ישראל סרו מדרך העם

16. so this is the judgment of the penitents of Israel, who have turned away from the path of the people.

The context suggests that they are recipients of God's favor because of God's love for their forefathers and his faithfulness to the covenant made with them (CD 8:16b-18a). Of interest is the sentence "who have turned away from the path of the people" (סרו מדרך העם) since שבי ישראל is now further qualified as those who have turned away from the (wicked) path of the people. Furthermore, סרו מדרך העם is clearly a reference to repentance in terms of "turning away from evil." We noted earlier that the priests are described as שבי ישראל. In further support of this idea, we have here a combination of סרו מדרך העם with שבי ישראל. This reference to a "penitential" group of *priests* who "turn away from the way of the people" bears strong conceptual and linguistic similarity to a 1QSa 1:1-3:[80]

1 וזה הסרך לכול עדת ישראל באחרית הימים בהסף]ם
ליחד להתה[ל]ך

2 על פי משפט <u>בני צדוק הכוהנים</u> ואנושי בריתם <u>אשר</u>
<u>ס]רו מלכת בד]רך</u>

3 <u>העם</u> המה אנושי עצתו אשר שמרו בריתו בתוך רשעה
לכ]פר בעד הארץ

1. And this is the rule for all of the congregation of Israel in the end of days: When they assem[ble as a community to wa]lk

2. according to the regulation of <u>the Sons of Zadok, the priests</u>, and the men of their covenant <u>who have [turned away from living in the w]ay</u>

3. <u>of the people</u>. These are the men of his counsel who have kept their covenant with him amidst the evil to a[tone for the land].

The underlined sentences denote the conceptual and linguistic similarities between this text and CD 8:16. To this we can add CD 2:2: "the priests are the penitents of Israel" (הכהנים הם שבי ישראל). Hence, this priestly group that is described as the penitents of Israel are so described because they are first of all a group of those who have repented. D. Dimant says that they realized their need to repent and sees this as the natural explanation as to why the sectarians called themselves "the repenters of Israel."[81]

When we conflate all that we have seen so far, it further confirms our reading of שבי ישראל as alluding to repentance against those theories that do not accept a spiritual and moral reading of the participle שבי. Murphy O' Connor argues that the religious nuance is not inherent in the שבי but is conveyed to it by the presence of פשע. This leads him to conclude that "identity of construction is absolutely no justification for transferring this religious meaning to שבי ישראל."[82] However, once we accept the spiritual dimensions of

---

80. Since we will discuss this text at some length in a later chapter, it will suffice at this point only to draw out some general observations relating to the immediate context.

81. Dimant, "Qumran Sectarian Literature,", 492.

82. Murphy-O'Connor, "An Essene Missionary Document?," 201–29.

this epithet, it seems plausible to suggest that as a penitent, priestly group, the identification of שבי פשע in CD 2:5 with שבי ישראל of CD 4:2; 6:5; and 8:16 is highly plausible and even likely. Thus, to summarize, שבי ישראל refers to a group of Zadokite priests who repented and joined the covenant and who were the forerunners of the community.

Conclusion

In this chapter, we have explored the "separateness" of the community and argued for its crucial relationship to repentance. This was because repentance was the most basic criterion for entrance into the community, as it involved a conscious decision to "turn away" and separate oneself from evil and to "turn toward" or commit oneself to the community, the covenant, and the law of Moses as defined by the community. This process, as we saw, was considered an act of repentance, one that further perpetuated their separateness. This separated community perceived itself as the sole recipient of the renewed covenant, since the rest of Israel was excluded from because of their wickedness. They understood their covenant as a "covenant of repentance." Thus repentance manifested in separation and adherence to the sectarian law was essential for inclusion into the covenantal community. The locus of this repentance was the wilderness.

We now need consider the findings of this chapter in the light of our working definition, which sees repentance as "the radical turning away from anything which hinders one's whole-hearted devotion to God and the corresponding turning to God in love and obedience." We can break the definition down into individual parts. First, there is *a radical turning away*: Based on our evidence, we are in a position to answer the question, *what* did they turn away from? Joining the covenant meant staying separate from wickedness (1QS 1:2; 5:1). This included those things that God hates (1QS 1:4), the idols of the heart (1QS 2:11), the lot of Belial (1QS 2:4), the sons of darkness (1QS 1:10), men of injustice (1QS 5:1, 2), incorrect halakah (4QMMT), the path of corruption (CD 15:7), and the "spirit of flesh (4Q418 fr. 81). This turning away was characterized by separation. Thus, for the Qumran community, repentance marked a turning away that was so radical it called for a complete, spatial separation (1QS 1:4; 5:1, 10, 14; 9:3, 9, 20; 4Q418 fr. 81; 4QMMT C-7). This was continually reaffirmed in the annual, public covenant-renewal ceremony. This separation itself was an act of repentance whereby one consciously and willingly turned away from defiling and evil influences.

In the second part of the definition, repentance involved a wholehearted *turning to God*. This was seen in the community's acceptance of the covenant of repentance (CD-B 19:16), in their joining of the community (1QS 5:7-10a), and in their wholehearted turning to the special interpretation of the law of Moses (1QS 5:8; CD-A 15:9, 12; 16:2, 5). They turned away from wickedness and turned to the community, its law, and the covenant.

Another factor to be considered is *imagery*. How was this repentance *described*? Repentance was expressed in various ways: while it was generally conveyed by "turning" language (שוב, sometimes סור) and often "separation" language (בדל, נזר, רחק and פרש). It was also spoken of in terms of "joining the covenant" and "returning to the law of Moses." Based on the above, repentance had the following result: It led to the spatial separation of the community, which in turn led to the formation of a new entity. Thus separation had a strong spatial dimension to it. It also symbolized joining a covenant that demanded repentance (CD 19:16). Membership in the community itself expressed a repentance that was manifested through physical separation and withdrawal to the wilderness (1QS 8:13). This separation was coupled by their constant recommitment to the law of Moses (1QS 5:8; CD-A 15:9, 12; 16:2, 5). The wilderness thus became both the manifestation of repentance as well as the locus for it.

When we consider how all this fits into the *religious experience* at Qumran, we see that the spirituality of the core group became the norm and pattern for the spirituality of those who subsequently joined the community. The community itself becomes a controlling agent of the religious experience of its members, which, as we saw, was an experience rooted in repentance. The starting point of religious experience at Qumran was a penitential experience.

We are now in a position to begin to reshape our working definition: for the Qumran community, the turning away was so radical that it involved a *spatial* separation to the extent that an entire, distinctive, separated community was formed; their wholehearted turning to God was manifested in joining the covenantal community with its distinctive understanding of the law. We can call this act *penitential separation*, which as described in this chapter was a key dimension in the religious experience of the community.[83]

---

83. G. Vermes comments that the "sectaries saw in [Isa. 40:3] a divine command to withdraw from the society of the wicked and settle in the solitude conducive to inward spirituality." G. Vermes, "Eschatological World View in the Dead Sea Scrolls and in the New Testament," in Paul, Kraft, Schiffman, and Fields, *Emanuel*, 479–94.

4

—————

Predestined Repentance

In the previous chapter, we explored the function of repentance within a covenantal framework. In joining the separate community, one joined the renewed covenant with its reinterpreted law. Such repentance appears to be the individual's conscious decision. In identifying the Qumran community with the Essenes, we immediately run into a problem. In *Antiquities of the Jews* 18.1, 2, 5 (§11, 18–22), Josephus mentions the three "philosophies" among the Jews, namely, Pharisees, Sadducees, and Essenes. He then says this of the Essenes: "The Essenes like to leave all things to God", which is in fact the very first thing Josephus mentions about the Essenes in this section.[1] He further emphasizes this submission to God in *Ant.* 13.5, 9 (§171–72). Regarding "fate" (εἱμαρμένη),[2] the Pharisees took a midway position, believing in providence while at the same time leaving a certain amount of "freedom" for human

1. T. S. Beall, *Josephus' Description of the Essenes Illustrated by the Dead Sea Scrolls* (Cambridge: Cambridge University Press, 1988), 113.
2. "Fate" (εἱμαρμένη) as used in this text "is probably equivalent to divine providence" and was probably chosen as a term Josephus's gentile readership would understand. Ibid.

beings. The Sadducees rejected the idea of providence altogether, since they believed that the will was completely free. Then he says: "But [the sect] of the Essenes maintains that fate is the ruler of all things [πάντων τὴν εἱμαρμένη κυρίαν ἀποφαίνεται] and that nothing happens to people except it be according to its decree." Josephus thus emphasizes the predestinarian outlook of the Essenes.

Even from a cursory reading of the scrolls, one gets the impression that God is the controller of all things. Based on this idea, P. S. Alexander says that "he [God] is the cosmic puppet-master who pulls everyone's strings."[3] However, other scholars such as A. Marx argue against reducing the members of the community to "controlled puppets"; he therefore comments: "les moines de Qumrân ne sont nullement des marionettes dans la main de Dieu, mais des hommes libres et donc responsables."[4] The appeal in Marx's position lies in his critique of a robot-like system. In the 1970s, E. Merrill made a detailed study on predestination in the scrolls.[5] He concludes: "Predestination is one of the chief doctrines in 1QH, if not *the* most prominent."[6] Nevertheless, he affirms that "the need for repentance is a major theme in 1QH," and that the individual "has the opportunity,

3. P. S. Alexander, "Predestination and Freewill in the Theology of the Dead Sea Scrolls," in *Divine and Human Agency in Paul and His Cultural Environment*, ed. J. M. G. Barclay and S. Gathercole, LNTS 335 (London: T&T Clark, 2006), 27–49 (48).
4. A. Marx, "Y a-t-il une prédestination à Qumrân?," *RevQ* 6 (1967): 161–81 (168). We will consider Marx's anachronistic language at a later stage in this chapter. Interestingly, Marx's position would find more approval than Alexander's. For example, Harris speaks of an inner "impulsion" rather than an "external compulsion." J. G. Harris, "The Covenant Concept among the Qumran Sectaries," *EvQ* 39, no. 2 (1967): 86–92. Dimant in commenting on atonement affirms that members of the community had "their own role to play." Dimant, "Qumran Sectarian Literature, 492. Sutcliffe observes that the many references to God's forgiving nature "show that the theologians of Qumran did not consider men to be fixed independently of their own will in a course of evil conduct." Sutcliffe, *The Monks of Qumran: The People of the Dead Sea Scrolls* (London: Burn & Oates, 1960), 74. Merrill too speaks of the definitive role that the individual plays. E. H. Merrill, *Qumran and Predestination: A Theological Study of the Thanksgiving Psalms* (Leiden: Brill, 1975), 45.
5. .Merrill, *Qumran and Predestination*. As we shall see in this chapter, this could be said of most of the other scrolls as well.
6. Ibid., 13.

even the full responsibility, to repent as a condition for his being admitted among the sons of light."[7] Interestingly, for Merrill, if one repents, it is because he is predestined to do so.[8] He believes that this apparent contradiction between predestination and "voluntarism" was "not considered by the Qumranians." Merrill struggles with his own position throughout his book. Although a strong advocate of predestination, he appears to contradict himself when he says: "The need for repentance is a major theme in 1QH, and, obviously, repentance is an act of the individual on his own."[9] This provides us with an example of the reluctance among scholars to speak (as Alexander does) of an absolute predestination.

While these two positions represent two ends of the spectrum, there is no denying that both polarities are present in the scrolls; despite the fact that God comes across most often as the one who predestines all things, there are also texts that confirm individuals as having a key role to play, especially in the area of repentance. Our task, then, is to look at textual evidence on both sides and see how this issue squares up on balance. We must reconsider how God's sovereign control of one's actions fits in with the apparent individual *voluntary* decision to repent. To put it differently, we need to explore whether the repentance of the Qumran community was in fact a voluntary act.

In the previous chapter, we looked at repentance as an act of separation wherein one consciously withdraws from surrounding wickedness in order to join the community. Let us continue with this line of thought, placing the focus on repentance as a voluntary act.

---

7. Ibid., 42.
8. Ibid., 49. Although Merrill acknowledges the importance of repentance, he does not dwell on it with as much detail as one might expect. Although to be fair to Merrill, we cannot expect much detail in a work that is fifty-eight pages long and confined only to 1QH and written before the entire collection of scrolls became available.
9. Ibid., 45.

What follows is well expressed in a question Merrill raises regarding salvation at Qumran: "Does God absolutely and arbitrarily determine such matters? Is there no room for human freedom and responsibility in Qumran Soteriology?"[10]

Before we proceed, let us turn to a very early source and consider another of Josephus's view of the Essenes. In *Jewish War* 2.8, 2–13 §119-61 he says of the Essenes in §120: "They turn aside [ἀποστρέφονται] from pleasure as an evil, and regard self-control [ἐγκράτειαν] and not succumbing to the passions as a virtue." This suggests the general idea of repenting from all evil. Hence "turning aside" (ἀποστρέφονται) coupled with the exercise of "self-control" (ἐγκράτειαν) seems to suggest an emphasis on individual responsibility. Josephus's observation suggests that the Essenes were well aware of the role that they had to play to remain holy, even though they believed that God was in control of all things.[11]

Repentance by the Individual

"Volunteers" (המתנדבים)

Emphasis on the role of the individual in the area of repentance is best seen in the voluntary aspect of membership as defined by the epithet "those who freely volunteer" (המתנדבים). M. Hengel says that "entrance into the *yahad* was a personal decision based on an act of individual conversion."[12] Essential to admittance into the

10. Ibid., 37. M. Bockmuehl observes that the scrolls reflect a more individualized understanding of religious affiliation and experience, in keeping with late Second Temple Judaism. M. Bockmuehl, "1QS and Salvation at Qumran," in *Justification and Variegated Nomism*, vol. 1, *The Complexities of Second Temple Judaism*, ed. D. A. Carson, P. O'Brien, and M. Seifrid (Tübingen: Mohr-Siebeck, 2001), 381–414 (394).
11. We will return to this apparent paradox later in a chapter when assessing our finding in the light of religious experience at Qumran.
12. M. Hengel, "Qumran and Hellenism," in *Religion in the Dead Sea Scrolls*, ed. J. Collins and R. Kugler (Grand Rapids: Eerdmans, 2000), 46–56 (48). He observes that the form of a strictly organized, hierarchically established free community, where entrance was an individual

community was a conscious, voluntary decision on the part of the one entering the community, as 1QS 5:1 implies.

והזה הסרך לאנשי המתנדבים לשוב מכול רע ולהתחזק בכול אשר
צוה לרצונו

> This is the rule for the men of the community who freely volunteer to repent of all evil and to keep themselves strong in all that he commands for his will.

This text clearly states that the following rule is applicable to those who join the community. These men are further described as "volunteers" (המתנדבים). This description is qualified by stating that they freely volunteer "to repent from all evil" (לשוב מכול רע) and "to remain strong in God's will" (ולהתחזק בכול אשר צוה לרצונו). These two infinitives of purpose (לשוב and ולהתחזק) confirm that "repenting" and "remaining steadfast" to God's will are the very reasons why they considered themselves as המתנדבים in the first place. Further, 1QS 5:7b-8 states that they make this voluntary commitment in the presence of those who have voluntarily done the same in the past.

7 כול הבא לעצת היחד
8 יבוא בברית אל לעיני כול המתנדבים

> 7. whoever enters the council of the community
> 8. enters the covenant of God in the presence of all who freely volunteer.

---

decision and a sign of personal conversion is without analogy in ancient Israel (ibid., 50). This emphasis on the individual entering the community/covenant represents a shift from the Old Testament regarding the covenant. In the Old Testament, the whole nation entered into the covenant with God; it was the election of a nation. G. Forkmann comments: "The individual is central here, the individual is the partner in the covenant, not the nation." G. Forkmann, *The Limits of the Religious Community* (Lund: Gleerup, 1972), 72.

Those witnessing the entry of the new members into the community are themselves described as המתנדבים, men who have themselves made a voluntary commitment to the community. Central to the above two texts is the *hitpaʿel* participle המתנדבים.[13] Thus it might be helpful to examine this term in more detail. In the Old Testament, the term נדב had become something of a technical term[14] that was used in a Holy War context (Judg. 5:2, 9; Isa. 13:2-3) to denote the generous dedication without reservation of those who came to participate. It was also used in a cultic context, referring to the "free contributions" of the people in the building of the temple (Exod. 25:2, 21; 1 Chron. 29:5-6, 9, 14, 17; Ezra 1:6; 2:68; 3:5; Neh. 11:2). Thus the term נדב fits with the community's military and cultic outlook.[15] In the context of repentance, מתנדבים denotes a *voluntary turning away* from evil men and a *voluntary turning to* the community. J. G. Harris comments: "The impulsion of inner response to the obligations that the covenant implied was the motive of entry and not external compulsion."[16] Harris's view is representative of scholars who reject a complete predestination. For example, Marx says:

> C'est volontairement qu'ils se plient aux précepts de Dieu, qu'ils se convertissent du mal, qu'ils s'attachent aux commandements du Seigneur, qu'ils se séparent des hommes pervers, qu'ils marchent dans les voies de Dieu et obéissent à sa volonté.[17]

---

13. Légasse says: "dans la littérature qumranienne, les participes nifʿal et hitpaʿel de *ndb* deviennent une manière de terme technique servant à désigner la Secte." S. Légasse, "Les pauvres en espirit et les 'voluntaries' de Qumrân," *NTS* 8 (1961/1962), 336-345 (338).

14. A. Fitzgerald "*MTNDBYM* in 1QS", *CBQ* 36 (1974): 495–502 (496).

15. In the community's reading of 1 Chron. 29:1-22, they saw a parallel between David and the Israelites willingly contributing their personal wealth for the building of the first temple and their own (the community) dedicating their efforts and resources to the renewal of the Jerusalem temple. The cultic dimension is further emphasized since the community set itself the task of establishing itself as the temple where true worship was offered.

16. Harris, "Covenant Concept," 89.

17. Marx "Predestination à Qumrân?," 164.

For Harris, S. Légasse, and Marx, individual voluntary participation in the covenant through an act of repentance is paramount.

If מתנדבים describes the requirements of those joining the community, then the command in 1QS 1:3b–5a at the time of joining is significant.

ולאהוב כול   3

4 אשר בחר לשנוא את כול אשר מאס לרחוק מכול רע

5 ולדבוק בכול מעשי טוב

3.   to love all
4. which he has chosen and to hate all what he rejects, to keep oneself from all evil
5. and to become attached to all good works.

The very purpose of joining as expressed by the two infinitives "to detach oneself" (לרחוק) and "to attach oneself" (ולדבוק) describe an initial act that is voluntary, implying that one's membership in the covenant depended on one's own decision, a conscious and deliberate commitment of oneself, a voluntary act of repentance. But not all scholars see it like this. Regarding the term מתנדבים, D. Lambert challenges that it implies some notion of free will operated at Qumran. Rather, he talks of an "inner compulsion" and says that any suggestion that the initiates have made a rational *choice* to adopt sectarian ways over their own is absent.[18]

Repentance by the Individual Reflected in *Hodayot*

E. Sutcliffe attributes absolute freedom to the individual when he says: "That man is responsible for his actions and is free to do good or to do evil the men of Qumran were well aware. For students of the Bible such as they were this could not be in doubt."[19] This conclusion, however, is not viable especially since as students of the

18. Lambert, "Was the Qumran Community a Penitential Movement?," 504.

Bible, they would have certainly encountered texts that emphasize God's control over all things. Thus, rather than taking human freedom in the area of repentance as a foregone conclusion (as Sutcliffe implies), we will examine select texts that highlight the individual's effort in staying penitent by his own resolve. This is often seen in humanity's frequent affirmation of new conduct. In 1QH 6:17-18a the author says:

17 [וא]ני ידעתי ברוב טובך ובשבועה הקימותי על נפשי לבלתי
חטוא לך
18 [ול]בלתי עשות מכול הרע בעיניך

17. [ ] [But] I, I know, thanks to the abundance of your goodness, and I have enjoined my soul with an oath not to sin against you
18. [and no]t to do anything which is evil in your eyes.

While the motivating factor for one's right conduct might be God's goodness (ברוב טובך), there is also a conscious (וא]ני ידעתי) and binding decision (בשבועה הקימותי על נפשי) to remain in a right relationship with God. This is characterized by the desire to stay turned away from sin (לבלתי חטוא לך) and not do any evil (ולבלתי עשות מכול הרע). This suggests an ongoing need for penitence. Such affirmations of the conscious effort one makes to stay in a proper relationship with God recur regularly. Consider 1QH 7:13-14:

13 [...] . . . ואהבכה בנדבה ובכול לב ובכול נפש בררתי . . . [...]
14 חק[ימותי לבלתי] סור מכול אשר צויתה

13. [. . .] . . . I love you freely, with (my) whole heart and with (my) whole soul I have purified [. . .]
14. [I have] imp[osed on myself] not to turn aside from all that you have commanded

19. Sutcliffe, *Monks*, 72. On the other hand, D. Winston talks of a "relative freedom" and says that within the framework of relative freedom, the concepts of determinism and predestination may freely coexist with that of voluntarism. D. Winston, *The Wisdom of Solomon* (Garden City, NY: Doubleday, 1979), 57.

The three verbs in first person: "I love you freely" (ואהבכה), "I have purified" (בררתי), and "[I have] imp[osed on myself]" (הקימותי) imply that the writer was well aware of his own responsibility to stay penitent. Particularly significant is the phrase "and I love you *freely*" (בנדבה). The use of נדב suggests that one's love to God may be likened to a freewill offering and also echoes the "voluntary" overtones of the epithet מתנדבים.

The phrase "who walk on the path of your [God's] heart" (הולכי ללכת בדרך) also conveys the individual's decision to remain penitent. This "path of his heart" is loved by God, so walking on such a path implies living in a manner acceptable to God. A brief description of "God's path" would enable us to see better the relation between this epithet and repentance. This can be constructed from 1QH 14:20-21a, which speaks of the privileged status of the community.

20 ואתה אל צויתם להועיל מדרכיהם בדרך קו[דשכה אשר ילכו]בה
ועול וטמא ופריץ
21 אל יעוברנה ויתמוטטו מדרך לבכה

20. You God commanded them to seek fortunes far from their paths, on your holy path, on which the uncircumcised, the unclean the vicious
21. do not walk. They have staggered off the path of your heart.

Here God's path, which is described as "your holy path" (דרך קו[דשכה), is contrasted with "their [the wicked one's] path" (דרכיהם). Access onto this path is restricted since the uncircumcised, unclean, and vicious are not allowed on it. Therefore, only those who consciously repent of sin alone can walk on it. That they walk on it *after* they repent[20] provides another example of "staying penitent."

20. "They left their own paths" is a metaphor for repentance that implies a turning away from one's (evil) ways and turning to God's way.

Further, 1QH 12:21-22a indicates that for such persons, the reward is great.

21 ואשר כנפשכה יעמודו לפניכה לעד והולכי
בדרך לבכה
22 יכונו לנצח

21.   those who are in accordance with your soul, will stand in your presence always; those who walk in the path of you heart
22. will be established permanently.

The first part of the sentence, "those in accordance with your soul" (אשר כנפשכה), parallels the third part, "those who walk in the path of your heart" (הולכי בדרך לבכה). Similarly, the second part: "[they] will stand in your presence" (יעמודו לפניכה) parallels the fourth part: "[they] will be established permanently" (יכונו לנצח). This parallelism emphasizes not just repentance (being "in accordance" with God, that is, after having turned to him) but also the reward for such repentance (standing permanently in God's presence). We could strengthen our case for taking this phrase as alluding to repentance and the life thereafter from one further text in which this epithet appears, namely 1QH 12:24-25.

24 וישמעוני ההולכים בדרך לבכה ויערוכה לבה
25 בספר קודשים

24.   those who walk on the path of your heart have listened to me, they have aligned[21] themselves before you
25. in the council of the holy ones.

The phrase "they have aligned themselves to you" (ויערוכה לבה) is significant because the verb ערך ("to arrange," "to set in order") implies that they have consciously turned their direction toward God.

---

21. *DSSNT* 96: "they are *drawing themselves* up."

This is in keeping with the phrase "those in accordance with your soul" (1QH 12:21). Thus to translate it as "align" forcefully brings out the "remaining turned to God" aspect of repentance. The participle ההולכים also confirms the ongoing nature of the commitment. 1QH 14:6-7 further supports this interpretation and helps pull everything that we have seen about this epithet together.

6 ואדעת כי יש מקוה לשבי פשע ועזבי חטאה בה] . . .[ולהתהלך

7 בדרך לבכה לאין עול

   6. And I know that there is hope for whoever turn from offence and relinquish sin [. . .] to walk

   7. on the path of your heart, without injustice.

The "repenters of sin" are described also as "relinquishers of sin" (ועזבי חטאה). The infinitive להתהלך shows that the reason for which they repented of sin was in order to walk in the path of God's heart. Thus the above text unambiguously locates the epithet "those who walk on the way of you heart" (להתהלך בדרך לבכה) in a context of repentance. It can also be taken as an allusion to the penitential life since only the "repenters of sin" (שבי פשע) and the "relinquishers of iniquity" (עזבי חטאה) can walk on this path. Thus the epithet "whose walk [themselves] on the way of your heart" (להתהלך בדרך לבכה) is a reference to an ongoing penitential life.

Repentance as Part of God's "Fixed" Design

Despite this emphasis on the role of the individual in the area of repentance, our struggle lies in reconciling this fact with the unambiguous emphasis in the scrolls on predestination and God's sovereign control over all things. 1QH 9:7-8 says of God,

Before you created them, you knew all their workings . . . and without you nothing can be accomplished, or be known except by your will.[22]

An abundance of similar texts has led several scholars to believe that the Qumran worldview is largely a "closed" one, with predestination dominating all things, including one's spirituality.[23] Likewise, M. Mansoor says that "God's foreknowledge and providence encompass everything that happens in the world."[24] A. Lange notes that the idea of a preexistent order of creation regulating all things may be derived from sapiential circles. This theology was adopted and used by the Qumran community to understand their own worldview.[25] In order for us to look at this strong predestinarian attitude and the extent to which it affected the community's religious experience relating to repentance, a good place to start is a text from the two-spirit theory.[26]

The Two-Spirit Theory

One of the clearest theological formulations in the scrolls is the treatise on the two spirits (1QS 3:13—4:26). When confronted by the clarity and logic of this work, H. G. May comments rather unreasonably: "The Qumranians were not theologians seeking a system of beliefs neatly and consistently set forth in theological terms. They did not permit their 'system' to deny the responsibility of man."[27] However, the members of the community certainly *knew* what they believed. The systematic exposition of the two-spirit treatise is a clear example of their systematic theologizing.

---

22. Mansoor describes this as "one of the most significant and clear passages on predestination and foreknowledge." M. Mansoor, *The Thanksgiving Psalms* (Leiden: Brill, 1961), 55.
23. Alexander speaks of "a profoundly dualistic and deterministic worldview which was all-pervasive in Qumran theology." Alexander, "Predestination and Freewill," 47. Limitations of space and words force us to confine ourselves to only a few sample texts in this section.
24. Mansoor, *Thanksgiving Psalms*, 53.
25. A. Lange, "Wisdom and Predestination in the Dead Sea Scrolls," *DSD* 2 (1995): 340–54.
26. Our discussion of 1QS 3:13—4:26 is limited to its specific contribution to our understanding of repentance within a predestinarian framework.
27. G. H. May, "Cosmological References in the Doctrine of the Two Spirits and OT Imagery," *JBL* 82 (1963): 1–14 (50).

According to the treatise on the two spirits, God's control over the universe is unquestionable. 1QS 3:15–16 says,

15 מאל הדעת כול הויה ונהייה ולפני היותם הכין כול מחשבתם
16 ובהיותם לתעדותם כמחשבת כבודו ימלאו פעולתם ואין להשנות

15. From the God of all knowledge stems all there is and all there shall be. Before they existed he established all their designs.

16. And when they have come into being, at their appointed time, they will execute all their works according to his glorious design, without altering anything.

Right at the outset, God is established as the source of all existence, as the preposition מ- conveys in "from God" (מאל). All things are preordained (הכין כול מחשבתם) and preprogrammed (כמחשבת כבודו ימלאו פעולתם), and irrevocably so (אין להשנות). According to 1QS 3:17-19, humanity has been accordingly equipped for this situation.

17 והואה ברא אנוש לממשלת
18 תבל וישם לו שתי רוחות להתהלך בם עד מועד פקודתו הנה רוחות
19 האמת והעול במעון אור תולדות האמת וממקור חושך תולדות העול

17. And he created man for the dominion of
18. the world and placed within him two spirits so that he would walk with them until the appointed time of his visitation: they are the spirits
19. of truth and of deceit. From the spring of light stem the generations of truth, and from the source of darkness the generations of deceit.

The infinitive להתהלך in 3:18 suggests this is the very purpose for the bestowal of the two spirits. As a result, the inherent goodness or evil of an individual is determined by the amount of either "the spirit of truth or deceit" (רוחות האמת והעול) one possesses, which according to 1QS 4:24-26 determines humanity's action in the world.

24 וכפי נחלת איש באמת יצדק וכן ישנא עולה וכירשתו בגורל עול ירשע בו וכן

25 יתעב אמת כיא בד בבד שמן אל עד קץ נחרצה ועשות חדשה והואה ידע פעולת מעשיהן לכול קצי

26] עולמיד[ם וינחילן לבני איש לדעת טוב[ורע... ו][ל[ה]פיל גורלות לכול חי לפי רוח ב[...עד מועד] הפקודה

24. In agreement with a man's inheritance in the truth he shall be righteous and so abhor injustice; and according to his share in the lot of injustice, he shall act wickedly in it, and so

25. abhor the truth. For God has sorted them into equal parts[28] until the appointed end and the new creation. He knows the result of their deeds for all the end of

26. [appointed ti]mes and has given them as a legacy to the sons of man for knowledge of good [. . . and] to cast the lots of every living being according to his spirit in [. . . until the time of] visitation.

The twofold categorization of humankind is clear. Further in 4:24 "inheritance in the truth" (נחלת באמת) is contrasted with "lot of deceit" (גורל עול), which in turn contrasts the resultant actions "he will be righteous" (יצדק) with "he will be wicked" (ירשע). Further, one's behavior is predetermined and fixed by God: "[God] knows the result of their deeds" (ידע פעולת מעשיהן), suggesting a worldview wherein all is fixed. Thus 1QS 3:12—4:26 confirms that if repentance is possible at all, it is because this is one's predestined lot. But this rigid outlook is not confined to the scrolls alone. *Jubilees* too expresses a rigid determinism[29] on the whole. Relevant to our

---

28. In the phrase כיא בד בבד, the division is qualitative and not quantitative. Wernberg-Møller translates "separately" rather than "equally," thereby alluding to the "irreconcilability of the two spirits." P. Wernberg-Møller, *Manual of Discipline*, Studies and Texts of the Desert of Judah (Leiden: Brill, 1957), 84.

29. The reference to this text from *Jubilees* is not about predestination per se, but is limited to its specific contribution to our understanding of repentance within a predestinarian framework.

purposes, *Jubilees* asserts that Israel's anticipated repentance has been "written and ordained" (5:17):

> And he made for all his works a new and righteous nature, so that they should not sin in all their nature for ever, so that they might be all righteous each in his kind, always.
>
> And the judgment of all of them has been ordained and written in the heavenly tablets without injustice. And if any of them transgress from their way with respect to what has been ordained for them to walk in, or if they do not walk in it, the judgment of every sort of nature and every kind has been written.
>
> And there is nothing excluded which is in heaven or on earth, or in the light or in the darkness or in Sheol or in the depths or in the place of darkness.
>
> And all their judgments are ordained, and written, and engraved. He will judge concerning everyone: the great one according to his greatness, and the small according to his smallness, and each one according to his way.
>
> And He is not one who accepts persons, and he is not one who will accept gifts when he says that he will execute judgment upon each one. If one gave everything which is in the earth, he would not accept anything from his hand, because he is a righteous judge.
>
> And for the children of Israel it has been written and ordained: "If they return to him in righteousness, he will forgive all of their transgressions and he will pardon all their transgressions."
>
> It is written and it is ordained, "He will have mercy to all who return from all their error once each year.] (*Jub.* 5:12–18)[30]

This heavily predestinarian view, which describes a foreordained repentance, is akin to the scrolls' idea of predestined repentance as expressed in the treatise of the two spirits. It is therefore no surprise that *Jubilees*, with its strong predestinarian outlook, was of much importance at Qumran.

---

30. Wintermute, "Jubilees", in *OTP*, 2:65.

Physiognomy

Quite unusual from other texts we have been looking at that express God's sovereign control over an individual, 4Q186 describes how one's physical characteristics testify to the ratio of light or darkness within that individual. P. S. Alexander says that this text attempts to determine the nature of a person's spirit by observing the form of certain parts of their body.[31] M. Delcor mentions that astrological horoscopes were a common contemporary phenomenon, especially in the Greco-Roman world. He also notes: "Il est probable que ces pratiques astrologiques assez répondues dans les milieu esséniens de Qumrân ont contribué pour une grande part à forger la doctrine deterministe de la secte."[32] As part of the elaborate and lengthy entry procedure, the final test is based on a discreet[33] examination of the candidate's physical characteristics, and if a person "in the mystery of divine choice has received as his lot more parts of light than of darkness, [he] is finally considered suitable to be a member with full rights of the community. He can enter to become part of the new covenant."[34] Alexander mentions that the parts listed are those that can be observed discreetly without the subject being aware of this scrutiny.[35] According to this text, the light-darkness ratio is

31. Alexander, "Predestination and Freewill," 40.
32. M. Delcor, "Recherches sur un horoscope en langue hébraïque provenant de Qumrân," *RevQ* 5 (1964–1966): 521–42 (533).
33. 4Q186 is an encoded document. Alexander says that this is to conceal the content from *insiders*. Thus no one (other than those carrying out the examination) who came across the text by chance would have understood it. This, he says, is "probably the major reason why certain Qumran texts were put into code." Alexander, "Predestination and Freewill," 41. According to M. Popovic, coded writing was to control the accessibility of the learning contained in the text. It was a "scribal means to prevent easy access to the information in the text." M. Popovic, "Physiognomic Knowledge in Qumran and Babylonia: Form, Interdisciplinarity, and Secrecy," *DSD* 13, no. 2 (2006): 150–76 (176).
34. García Martínez, "The Men of the Dead Sea,", 38.
35. P. S. Alexander, "'Wrestling against Wickedness in High Places': Magic in the Worldview of the Qumran Community" in *The Scrolls and the Scriptures: Qumran after Fifty Years*, ed. S. Porter and C. Evans, JSPSup 26 (Sheffield: Sheffield Academic, 1997), 318–37 (331).

numerically described: the first individual has six part of light and three parts darkness (fr. 1, 2:7-8a); the second has eight parts of darkness and one part light (fr. 1, 3:6b-7); the third has eight parts of light and one part of darkness (fr. 2, 1:6c-8a).[36] This physiognomic text states that one's outward behavior is determined by one's internal makeup. Because of this, no individual is totally good or totally evil since there can be no balance between the two forces, with the uneven number of spirits (nine) making a tie impossible.[37] Thus "what ultimately determines that one can succeed in being a perfect member of the community of 'the sons of light' is the fact that from the beginning he has received more parts of light than of darkness."[38] In other words, 4Q186 shows that one's behavior (and by implication, repentance itself) was predestined by God based on the amount of "light" he had placed within him.

The "Predestined Repentance" Motif
in Other Second Temple Texts

However, it should also be recognized (in the light of such highly deterministic texts as the ones examined above) that the motif of predestined repentance in itself is not distinctive to the scrolls; both Qumran and non-Qumran material are united in affirming God's sovereign control and reign over the created order.

The *Sibylline Oracles*, for example, highly emphasize God's sovereign control. *Sibylline Oracles* 4.153–169 contains a description of the impiety in the last times (4.153–159) and of God's wrath

36. More recently, M. Popovic has challenged the reconstruction of 4Q186 fr. 2, 1:7 (ואחת הנומש) because "the reading of a *nun* in this line is practically impossible." Although he concedes that the present reconstruction is reasonable, "it unfortunately lacks the textual basis in 4Q186 that it once seems to have had." M. Popovic, "A Note on the Reading of הנומש and דומא ינשה in 4Q186 2 I 7," *RevQ* (2004): 635–41 (638).
37. G. Boccaccini, *Beyond the Essene Hypothesis: The Parting of Ways between Qumran and Enochic Judaism* (Grand Rapids: Eerdmans, 1998), 63.
38. García Martínez, "The Men of the Dead Sea," 37.

manifested in a "great conflagration" (4.161). In light of this, the people are urged to change their ways (4.163–165) and demonstrate repentance through ritual washings[39] and supplications. Attached to this process of repentance is the injunction: "Stretch out your hand to heaven and ask forgiveness for your previous deeds and make propitiation" (4.166). Then "God will grant repentance [φεος δώσει μετάνοιαν] and not destroy" (4.168b–169a). This indicates that despite human involvement (manifested in the performance of correct acts), repentance was ultimately granted by God.

Sirach's[40] reference to repentance, though brief, is significant to the task at hand, since it explicitly states that repentance only comes from God.

> Yet to those who repent he grants a return [μετανοοῦσιν ἔδωκεν ἐπάνοδον] and he encourages those who are losing hope. Turn back to the Lord and forsake your sins; pray in your presence and lessen your offence. Return to the Most High and turn away from iniquity, and hate intensely what he abhors. (Sir. 17:24-26)

Regarding this text, P. Skehan and A. Di Lella comment: "Repentance is possible only because the sinner can freely choose to abandon sin and return to the Lord's way."[41] These verses describe

---

39. John the Baptist's call to a baptism of repentance in the face of imminent eschatological destruction is the "most obvious parallel" to this text. Collins dismisses any relation of this text with the ritual washings of the Essenes. He says, "All that we know of the baths of the Essenes from Josephus or from the Qumran scrolls points to daily purification, not to a baptism of repentance." J. Collins, "Sibylline Oracles," in *OTP* 1:388n. e.2.

40. Sirach was composed between 198 and 175 bce in Hebrew and was translated into Greek about 117 bce. D. Harrington, *Invitation to the Apocrypha* (Grand Rapids: Eerdmans 1999), 79. Its relevance to our investigation lies in that fact that fragments of two manuscripts of the Hebrew text have been found at Qumran (2Q18 and 11Q5 21:11-17. G. Sauer says, "Die funde von Qumran und auf Masada konnten für diese Frühzeit die hebräische Textform nachwiesen." G. Sauer, *JSHRZ*, vol. 3.5, *Jesus Sirach* (Gütersloh: Gütersloher Verlaghaus; Gerd Mohn, 1981), 484; and at the fortress in Masada (G. W. E. Nickelsburg, *Jewish Literature between the Bible and the Mishnah* [London: SCM, 1981], 64), confirming that Sirach was read at Qumran (J. van der Ploeg describes Sirach as "part of the devotional reading of Qumran, as the remains of it testify." J. van der Ploeg, *The Excavations at Qumran*, 115.

the various acts sinners must do and attitudes they must cultivate if conversion is to be sincere.[42] However, by thus emphasizing only the voluntary nature of repentance, the authors do not do justice to the verb ἔδωκεν in verse 24. If a return is possible, it is only because God *grants* it. As in the case of what we saw in the *Sibylline Oracles*, here too individuals have a role in repentance, but it is "granted" by God, albeit in a slightly nuanced form. So too *Wisdom of Solomon* describes how in some instances God gives a *time* for repentance: "But you are merciful to all, for you can do all things, and you can overlook peoples' sins, so that they may repent" (11:23). Similarly, of God's gradual judgment of the sins of the Canaanites, it is said: "but judging them little by little you gave them an opportunity to repent"[43] (12:10). If the above texts speak of God giving a *time* for repentance, 12:19 speaks of God giving repentance itself: "You have filled your children with hope, because you give repentance for sins [ὅτι διδοῖς ἐπὶ ἁμαρτήμασιν μετάνοιαν]." The hope of God's children is in fact the hope of repentance. Thus, in the Wisdom of Solomon, we see that God not only desires repentance but also gives the *opportunity* to repent,[44] while sometimes God grants repentance itself.

---

41. P. Skehan and A. Di Lella, *The Wisdom of Ben Sira*, AB 39 (New York: Doubleday, 1987), 283. They conclude that because of human freedom repentance is possible.

42. Ibid., 284.

43. Winston believes that this idea might be based on a contemporary Greek idea that God is quick to bless but slow to chastise. Winston, *Wisdom of Solomon*, 235.

44. See also *Apoc. Zeph.* 10.10–12; *Let. Aris.* 187–188; *LAB* 52.3. O. S. Wintermute describes this motif as the "corollary of God's mercy and patience, which could spare man the punishment he justly deserves." Wintermute, "Apocalypse of Zephaniah," in *OTP* 1:502. It is worth mentioning that there are instances when this opportunity to repent is denied (Wisd. of Sol. 5:3; *1 Enoch* 13.2; 1QS 2:8-9; 11Q19 59:6-7). Nevertheless, the bringing about (or denial) even of this opportunity to repent is still in the hands of God.

Predestined Repentance at Qumran

H. Ringgren has noted, however, that when compared to other Jewish literature, emphasis on a "deterministic" worldview does not occur so consistently as it does in Qumran literature.[45] Lambert too says: "*shuv* does not constitute a desideratum incumbent upon the individual or even the nation, but a foreordained component of God's eschatological plan."[46] He further notes while talking about human transformation: "It is clear that only through God's intervention that the worshipper is purified, forever susceptible to falling back on his true nature."[47]

The theme of God's assistance in the context of repentance is dominant in the scrolls. However, what stands out is the fact that God not only predestined a select group for repentance but also assisted them in this task. This recognition is most often expressed in relation to humanity's helplessness. This motif can be detected even in the earliest stages of joining the community, as seen in the exhortation to those who are entering the covenant. CD-A 2:2-3a reads,

2 [blank] ועתה שמעו אלי כל באי ברית ואגלה אזנכם בדרכי
3 רשעים [blank]

    2. [blank] and now, listen to me, all who enter the covenant, and I will open your ear to the paths of the
    3. wicked. [blank]

While the end of line in CD has a blank space, 4Q266 fr. 2, 2:2-3a provides an amplified reading since the above lacuna at the end of the line can be read thus:

45. Ringgren, *The Faith of Qumran*, 55.
46. Lambert "Was the Qumran Community," 508.
47. Ibid., 510.

2 [blank] ועתה שמ]עו אלי כל באי ברית ואגלה אזנכם בדרכי רשעים[
3 ומכול שבילי חט]אים אזיר אתכם

2. [blank] and now, lis[ten to me, all who enter the covenant, and I will open your ear to the paths of the wicked]
3. And from all the tracks of the sin[ners I shall divert you.

Taken together, in the first part God makes them aware of the ways of the wicked (CD) and sets before them the paths of good and evil, reassuring them of his assistance by diverting (אזיר)[48] them from evil (4Q266). Further, reading the CD text alongside the 4Q266 fragment suggests that these two acts of God occur *after* one has entered the covenant: "all who come into the covenant" (כל באי ברית). Thus once the individual repents and turns away from evil, God enables them to stay penitent by keeping them turned away from evil while in the covenant. E. P. Sanders says: "God's ruling providence can be depicted not only as the decisive factor in entering the covenant, but also as preventing those within from straying."[49]

Similarly, in the 4QDibHam, the idea of God's sovereign control in the area of repentance continues. The vital role that God plays in directing an individual's life is seen in the description of God "planting his law in the person's heart" to "free them from sinning against him [God]," as 4Q504 fr. 1–2, 5:11–14 says:

11 ותחון את עמכה ישראל בכול
12 [ה]ארצות אשר הדחתם שמה להשיב
13 אל לבבם לשוב עודך לשמוע בקולכה
14 [כ]כול אשר צויתה ביד מושה עבדכה

11. you were gracious to your people Israel among all
12. [the] countries into which you drove them there, to cause to turn

48. The use of the *hip'il* of נזר is significant, considering the strong penitential overtones of this verb.
49. Sanders, *Paul and Palestinian Judaism*, 261. This is the main thrust of Sanders's twofold categorization of "getting in" and "staying in" the covenant.

13. their heart to turn to you and to listen to your voice,
14. [according to] all that you commanded through the hand of Moses your servant.

In all the verbs used in this text, *God* is the subject. *He* was "gracious" (תחון) to his people in the countries where *he* himself had driven them (הדחתם). Further, *his* graciousness motivated the people to "return" (to him) as seen in the phrase: "to cause them to turn their heart to turn to you" (להשיב אל לבבם לשוב עודך). This reference to repentance implies that the heart has been turned away from evil and has now been turned toward God. In this combination of לשוב and להשיב, the *qal* infinitive (לשוב) is subsumed into the *hip'il* infinitive (להשיב): if they have turned to God, it is because God caused them to turn. E. Merrill, in his study on predestination in the scrolls, affirms that the need for repentance is a major theme.[50] He says that the individual "has the opportunity, even the full responsibility, to repent as a condition for his being admitted among the sons of light."[51] Nevertheless, according to Merrill, if one repents it is because he is predestined to do so.[52] Similarly, in P. Garnet's study of salvation in the scrolls,[53] he describes repentance as "choosing God's will and displaying his attitude in resisting contamination for Israel."[54] However, like Merrill, he too sees repentance as the "work of God in the human heart."[55]

Apart from explicitly describing God's role in bringing about repentance, the 4Q504 fr. 1–2, 5:11-14 text shows that להשיב also conveys that the purpose of this action was that they obey him: "to listen to your voice" (לשמוע בקולכה); in other words, they

50. He highlights that this "need for repentance" is especially noticeable in 1QH.
51. . Merrill, *Qumran and Predestination*, 42.
52. Ibid., 49. He believes that this apparent contradiction between predestination and "voluntarism" was "not considered by the Qumranians."
53. P. Garnet, *Salvation and Atonement in the Qumran Scrolls* (Tübingen: Mohr-Siebeck, 1977).
54. Ibid., 60.
55. Ibid., 117.

need to stay penitent. Further, if "you were gracious" (תחון) refers to those blessings that have been realized in the past, then "Israel," the recipients of God's graciousness, repented (in the past) purely by God's action. Although repentance spoken of here has occurred in the past, 4QDibHam consists of prayers used on a weekly basis, thereby serving as a continuous reminder to its users of God's role in bringing about repentance even in the present.[56] This constant emphasis on God's control over all things leads one to naturally conclude that the members of the community are predestined for salvation and therefore predestined for repentance, since on its own, sinful humanity can achieve nothing. Thus D. Flusser states:

> The elect Essene was a person whose election was predetermined. He lived within the world, and it was predetermined that at a certain date he would leave the vanities of the world, enter the sect and accept its discipline and rules, and live as one of the Sons of Light, of the true Israel. The Essenes called this turning point repentance and the covenant of the sect was called the "Covenant of Repentance"[57]

The ability to repent is a gift given to those already predestined for it. L. Schiffman says that "it is possible for one to repent if one is predestined to be among those who turn away from iniquity and join the community."[58]

---

56. The members of the community who would have recited this prayer are elsewhere described as שבי ישראל and thereby could easily have understood their own repentance and their need to stay penitent (CD 6:5; 8:16; 4Q267 fr. 2, 11//4Q266 fr. 3, 2:12. According to Garnet, one of the functions of the community is to "provide a concrete opportunity for repentance." Ibid., 111.

57. D. Flusser, *The Spiritual History of the Dead Sea Sect* (Tel Aviv: MOD, 1989), 129. Sutcliffe, however, says that although there is a continual struggle for mastery over a man's soul, neither side imposes a decision. Each one decides to which part he will belong. The individual membership of the parties is *not* fixed once and for all. Sutcliffe, *Monks of Qumran*, 75.

58. Schiffman, *Reclaiming the Dead Sea Scrolls*, 152. He also draws attention to the converse when he says, "If it has been predetermined that a person belongs to the lot of Belial, then one will not repent of one's transgressions."

Repentance through a Divinely Appointed Agent

A variation on the view is effected by God is that repentance is effected by a divinely appointed being, normally an angelic being. The emphasis of *Joseph and Aseneth*[59] is on repentance. Aseneth's idolatry is introduced early in the narrative (2.3). Thereafter, her "conversion and its implications are the main subjects of chaps. 2–23."[60] M. Philonenko says that "la Μετάνοια n'est plus le repentir qui ramène dans la voie droite les fils d'Israël égarés, c'est la conversion au judaïsme."[61] In response to Joseph's prayer for Aseneth's conversion, "she wept with great and bitter weeping and repented of her (infatuation with the) gods whom she used to worship and spurned all the idols" (ch. 9). This "internal" turning is accompanied by conventional (external) penitential acts such as the use of sackcloth, ashes (10.2, 14), and lament (10.3, 15; 11.1), thus combining the internal and external aspects of repentance. Nickelsburg mentions that "she points to her acts of penitence and repudiation as signs of her true repentance and asks forgiveness for her idolatry."[62] Relevant to our purposes, Aseneth's conversion is assisted by a spiritual being called "Repentance" who assists all who repent. *Joseph and Aseneth* 15.7 describes this being as a personification of repentance: Her name is "Repentance" (ἡ Μετάνοια).[63] Her task is to intercede (15.7c) "for all those who

---

59. *Jos. Asen.* originated in the Jewish Diaspora of Egypt, "no later than c. ad 100 and perhaps as early as the first century bc." C. Burchard, "Joseph and Aseneth," in *Outside the Old Testament*, ed. M. de Jonge (Cambridge: Cambridge University Press, 1985), 94. It has been suggested that *Jos. Asen.* is a Christian work of the fifth century ce originating in Asia Minor. C. Burchard, "Joseph and Aseneth," in *OTP* 2:187. However, Collins observes: "The fact that the conversion does not involve baptism weighs heavily against Christian composition and against a late date for the story. Unlike so many pseudepigraphic writings about biblical figures, this story has no unequivocally Christian elements." J. J. Collins, "Joseph and Aseneth: Jewish or Christian?," *JSP* 14, no. 2 (2005): 97–112 (112).

60. Nickelsburg, *Jewish Literature*, 260.

61. M. Philonenko, *Joseph and Aséneth* (Leiden: Brill, 1968), 54.

62. Nickelsburg, *Jewish Literature*, 259.

repent" (τῶν μετανοούντων) in the name of the Most High (15.7c).
Further, she renews and waits on those who repent (15.7d). Thus,
while individuals repent, there is an angel of repentance (sent from
God) who assists them in the process.

In the *Testament of Dan*, Dan speaks of future wickedness (5.5–6)
and the exile (5.8) and return/repentance: "Therefore when you turn
back to the Lord, you will receive mercy, and he will lead you
into his holy place, proclaiming peace to you" (5.9). However, this
anticipated repentance does not come about unassisted. Dan assures
his sons that there shall arise from Judah and Levi the "Lord's
salvation" (5.10). Although the specific identity of this individual is
unclear, one of his salvific acts will be to facilitate repentance: "And
he shall turn the hearts of the disobedient ones to the Lord" (5.11b).
One cannot but notice the lexical and conceptual similarity in the
angelic prophecy to Zechariah regarding the ministry of the yet
unborn John the Baptist, one of his tasks is this: "He will turn many
of the people of Israel to the Lord their God" (Luke 1:16); another
facet of his ministry is "to *turn the hearts* of parents to their children,
and *the disobedient* to the wisdom of the righteous, to make ready a
people prepared for *the Lord*" (Luke 1:17). The italicized words show
the identical words in the description of "the Lord's salvation" in *T.
Dan.*[64] This repentance through a divinely appointed facilitator is a
new dimension of repentance that *T. Dan* introduces, absent in the
other *Testaments*.

63. Philonenko describes the angel Repentance as "la personification d'une vertu." Philonenko,
Joseph and Aséneth, 57. See also *1 Enoch* 40:9, where the angel of repentance is called Phanuel. *T.
Dan* 5.11 speaks of repentance mediated through an angelic being called the "Lord's Salvation."
See below.
64. John the Baptist may be seen as an intermediary who facilitates repentance. However, a primary
difference between John the Baptist and the "Lord's Salvation" of *T. Dan* 5.10 is that the former
is a human being while the latter is an angelic being. Jesus too facilitates repentance through
his preaching (according to the Gospels), but his divinity greatly supersedes the divine status of
the other angelic intermediaries that we have encountered.

This motif also appears in *1 Enoch*. Enoch sees in a vision the dwelling place of the righteous elect (39.4–5), whose dwelling was in the presence of God, continually praising him (39.6–7). He then see four figures around the presence of God, each with their own task cut out (40.1–7). On inquiring about their identity, Enoch is told that they are the angels Michael, Raphael, Gabriel, and Phanuel (40.8–9); significantly, the last angel is described in this manner: "and the fourth, who presides over repentance, and the hope of those who will inherit eternal life, is Phanuel" (40.9). Clearly, repentance was mediated by this angelic figure, appointed by God.

This, along with the other texts I have highlighted above, shows a variation of the "repentance-granted-by-God" motif; rather, although repentance is from God, it is mediated through a divinely appointed figure, in this case the angel Phanuel.

In the *Life of Adam and Eve* (*VAE*), the couple's acts of penitence involve fasting and standing in neck-deep water (6.1—8.3) in order to gain God's pity (6.3). Satan, in attempting to deceive Eve (9.1–2), appeals to the sufficiency of her repentance. He says to her in 9.3a, "the Lord God has heard your sighs and accepted your repentance." In the *Apocalypse of Moses*, we find a section on Eve's account of the fall that is not present in the Greek and Latin *VAE*. It describes the consequences of the fall (15–31) and her repentance through the confession of sin (*Apoc. Mos.* 32.1–2). After a period of punishment, she is visited by an angelic messenger who informs her of Adam's death and who says: "Rise, Eve from your repentance" (32.4a). Her confession is perceived as her repentance. But more relevant to our exploration is the fact that her penitential acts are mediated to her—in one instance by a "false" agent and in another by a genuine one. Nevertheless, we see the repentance-mediated-by-an-agent motif at work.

Given the strong predestinarian approach emphasizing repentance as preordained by God, it is not surprising that in the scrolls there is normally no place for an angelic intermediary in granting repentance.[65] Hence, it is highly significant when such an idea does occur in 11Q13.[66] Column 2 describes the festival of Jubilee and make use of the word "return" in Lev. 25:13 and Deut. 15:2. Although both these texts in their original contexts allude to a "return to" material and financial situations,[67] in 11Q13 the "returning" imagery is transferred into a spiritual turning. The righteous captives of Melchizedek imprisoned by Belial (lines 4–5) would be eventually "brought back"—literally "turned back" (ישיבמה).

5   והמה נחל[ת מלכי צ]דק אשר
6 ישיבמה אליהמה וקרא להמה דרור לעזוב להמה] משא [כול
עוונותיהמה

5.   But they are the chil[dren of the lot of Melchiz]edek who

6. will bring them back, and proclaim liberty to them, relieving them [of the burden] of all their iniquities.

"Relieving them [of the burden] of their sins" in this context indicates that Melchizedek's role of saving the captives who were captured by Belial is clearly an allusion to repentance. Melchizedek then becomes the agent who facilitates repentance since he causes them to repent (ישימה).[68] The fact that this group is his, "these are the sons of

65. The disciplinary system of the community served to regulate and control repentance since it explicitly stated in which offenses repentance was possible and which offenses precluded the possibility of repentance. Hence in an indirect way the community itself "mediated" repentance. See below.

66. M. de Jonge and A. S. van der Woude, "11QMelchizedek and the New Testament," *NTS* 12 (1965): 301–26 (304).

67. In the Leviticus text, the "return" is to one's property and in the Deuteronomy text, the "remission" pertains to monetary issues.

68. In 2:24, there is a reference to "those who turn aside [הסרים] from walking [in the w]ay of the people," which parallels those referred to in 2:6.

the lot of Melchizedek" (line 8) (והמה בני גורל מלכי צדק), serves as a motivational factor for Melchizedek's actions. The mediatory role of Melchizedek stems from his priestly role: this text therefore introduces an eschatological agent who is instrumental in bringing about a spiritual return (repentance) and enabling those of his lot to turn from the way of the people. Put differently, those who repent do so because they have been aided by Melchizedek. On the whole, this motif remains distinctive from the regular teaching of the scrolls regarding repentance as the result of predestination. However, since it is the only instance of an angelic agent of repentance, it possibly represents a minority (or temporarily held) position in the community.

The Community as an Agent of Repentance

That said, another aspect needs to be borne in mind. While repentance was granted by God and there was no place for an agent as such (which is why the above Melchizedek text stands out), the community itself becomes an agent of repentance. This is a distinctive feature with regard to repentance at Qumran. We saw in the previous chapter that the community provides the locus for repentance—adherents become part of the separate community; the law is defined by the community for the community; one's predestined, penitential state finds expression in the rituals of the community—and again, the insulation provided by the community's detachment from all polluting influences creates a temple-like purity in which these rituals can be performed. The community itself had mechanisms in place to regulate and control the repentance of its members. For example, 1QS 5:5b-6 states that when those entering the community have repented by "circumcising the foreskins of their inclination and of their stiff necks" (1QS 5:5a), they are able to do two essential things:

5   ליסד מוסד אמת לישראל ליחד ברית

6 עולם לכפר לכול המתנדבים לקדוש באהרון ולבית האמת

בישראל הנלוים עליהם ליחד

> 5.   to lay a foundation of truth for Israel, for the community of the
>
> 6. eternal covenant, to make atonement for all who freely volunteer for holiness in Aaron and for the house of truth in Israel and for those who join them for a community.

Genuine repentance resulted in "laying a foundation of truth" and also enabled them "to make atonement." The two infinitives (ליסד and לכפר) confirm that this is the purpose for repentance in the first place. The recipients of these two acts are the other members of the community: "for the community of the eternal covenant" (ליחד ברית עולם). 5:6b suggests that atonement is possible even for "those who join them for a community" (הנלוים עליהם ליחד). Thus, as members continued to willingly and sincerely repent and join the community, they were able to atone for one another. A. R. C. Leaney describes the community as a "cleansing community which purifies those who join it by absorbing them into its life."[69] The penitent members of the community made atonement for their fellow members. In short, the entire community itself was both the facilitator of repentance and the locus for it. At Qumran, the attainment of atonement and salvation was a corporate effort.

Evidence of the community itself facilitating and controlling repentance can be seen in its elaborate disciplinary system. Physiognomic texts such as 4Q186 speak of the unchangeable light-darkness ratio in all men. One could repent and join the community because it had been predestined thus. Nevertheless, even these

---

69. A. R. C. Leaney, *The Rule of Qumran and Its Meaning* (London: SCM, 1966), 168. Pouilly describes the community's main function thus: "exercer les uns par rapport aux autres une médiation sacerdotale, une libération du péché." Pouilly, *La Règle de la Communauté de Qumrân.*, 52.

"predestined" individuals had an amount of "darkness" in their makeup. This indicates that no one was completely sin-free or incapable of error even *within* the community. Therefore, because of this possibility of sin on the part of the members of the community, there existed within their daily life a system designed to deal with such situations. The offender could not get off lightly. He had to be punished according to the seriousness of his offense. M. Weinfeld observes that ostracism for either a limited or permanent banishment was "the most customary punishment of the Qumran sect."[70] To speak of a "limited" banishment, however, conveys that for most offenses, after a period of punishment, eventual reinstatement into community life was possible. It is plausible to believe that genuine repentance for one's error led to his reinstatement.

1QS 6:24—7:25 contains a list of offenses and the subsequent disciplinary acts involved, thereby shedding further light on the community's understanding of repentance. For example, for offenses such as lying, stubbornness, and impatience, the punishment involved reduced rations (6:25) or even temporary expulsion from the community for two years (7:18-19), one year (6:25, 27), six months (7:3-4, 12, 18), three months (7:6, 9), sixty days (7:8), thirty days (7:10,12), and ten days (7:10-11, 15). The fact that punishment was restricted to a limited and therefore temporary period is significant. It suggests that during this time of expulsion and banishment, the offender would realize his error and repent of it. When an offender exhibited genuine repentance, he would then be reinstated after the required period came to an end. In the case of disobedience to the community's laws, an offender was first banished from the pure food and from knowing the community's councils. However, this

70. This form of penalty was also practiced in Egyptian and Hellenistic associations. M. Weinfeld, *The Organizational Pattern and the Penal Code of the Qumran Sect* (Fribourg: Éditions Universitaires, 1986).

banishment was also temporary and provided for repentance, as 1QS 8:16b-19 states.

16 וכול איש מאנושי היחד ברית [blank]
17 היחד אשר יסור מכול המצוה דבר ביד רמה אל יגע בטהרת אנושי הקודש
18 ואל ידע בכול עצתם עד אשר יזכו מעשיו מכול עול

16. [blank] and anyone of the men of the community, the covenant of

17. the community who turns away in a high-handed manner from anything commanded, cannot approach the pure food of the men of holiness

18. and cannot know anything of their counsels until he cleanses his deeds from all deceit.

We have here in 8:17 the phrase: "who turns away . . . in a high handed manner" (יסור . . . ביד רמה). We can take the turning (יסור) here as metaphorical since the object of the verb is "all the commands" (מכול המצוה), thus implying a straying from the command. This needs to be read alongside 8:18: "until he cleanses his deeds from all deceit" (עד אשר יזכו מעשיו מכול עול). Regarding the verb וזכו, in the Hebrew Bible, זכה often carries with it connotations of repentance since it is always used in a moral and ethical sense (Ps. 73:13; 119:9; Prov. 21:8b). If we take it as a *pi'el* ("keep clean"), then we can translate it as "until he keeps clean from all deceit," or to paraphrase, "until he repents from all deceit." Thus the short-term expulsions that we saw above hint at what is explicitly expressed in 1QS 8:18, namely, the possibility of repentance during the period of banishment. We can draw support for this from CD 10:3, which shares verbal and linguistic similarities in the text just discussed. CD 10:2-3 contains the following caution:

אל יאמן איש על רעדהו [blank] 2
3 לעד עובר דבר מן המצוה ביד רמה עד זכו לשוב

    2.   [blank] Not to be believed as a witness against his fellow

    3. someone who had deliberately transgressed any precept until he has been cleansed to return.

Evidently "until he has been cleansed to return" (עד זכר לשוב) in line 3 is used metaphorically of repentance. As in 1QS 8:18, here too עד introduces a temporal dimension that is in keeping with the earlier idea of a "limited" banishment, implying the possibility of repentance. The presence of the verb שוב confirms this. Further, the combination of זכה, symbolizing an external purification, and שוב, implying an internal attitude, is totally consistent with what we have seen of the relation between rituals and repentance.[71]

It is clear that a temporary period of punishment presupposes the possibility of repentance. This idea becomes more plausible when juxtaposed with three specific offenses, namely, a deliberate transgression of the law (1QS 8:22- 23), slandering the many (1QS 7:16a-17b), and finally, senior members backsliding and acting treacherously to the community (1QS 7:22-24). In each of these references, the punishment is expressed in the same way: such a person "will not return again to the counsel of the community" (ולוא ישוב עוד על עצת היחד). The use of שוב (ישוב) operates on two levels, one literal and the other metaphorical. On the literal level, it refers to the nullification of a physical return to the community.[72]

---

71. 1QS 7:18b-21 concerns a person who turns away from the authority of the community and "walks in the stubbornness of his own heart" (וללכת בשרירות לבו). For such a person, "if he returns" (אם ישוב), he may be reinstated. There is in the first instance a turning away from the community; and in the second, a turning back to the community, making it clear that repentance is being spoken of.

72. B. Nitzan observes that most of the occurrences of the verb in the penal code "are in the meaning of returning to the congregation." Although she points out that there are very few references of שוב occurring in the penal code with the meaning of repentance, she does

On the metaphorical level, it refers to the nullification of a spiritual turning (repentance). Such an offender who is denied repentance can no longer be part of the penitential community. Since there is no qualifying time span for the expulsion as in the case of the "lesser" offenses, it is evident that the punishment is absolute and that for such offenses, repentance is not possible.

The disciplinary framework at Qumran served as a check for erring members within the community. Discipline meted out varied according to the offense. However, whether the member could repent of their error or not became the determining factor as to whether he could continue in the community. Thus the penal section shows that the community actually controlled and regulated the repentance of its members, thereby serving as an agent of repentance.[73]

If were reflect on the textual evidence gathered thus far, we are faced with something of a paradox: both the Qumran and non-Qumran material accept God's sovereign control (hence the possibility of a predestined repentance)—and yet there are texts that equally talk of repentance as a voluntary response, initiated by the individual itself and free from external input; in some instances, we saw that both aspects (divine and human agency) in the area of repentance are held together in tension in the same texts. A variation on this (that still maintains God's control) involves God providing an opportunity for repentance (and that humans repent of their own accord when they realize this God-given opportunity). Sometimes repentance is the

call attention to CD 10:3. B. Nitzan, "Benediction and Instructions for the Eschatological Community (11QBer; 4Q285)," *RevQ* 16 (1993): 77–90 (86n40).

73. There is concrete evidence that such disciplinary actions were implemented. 4Q477 contains a list of names of offenders and a note regarding their offenses. See E. Eshel, "4Q477: The Rebukes by the Overseer," *JJS* 45 (1994): 111–22.

result of an angelic intermediary who facilitates/effects repentance or urges an individual to repent.

Despite these polarities, scholars usually opt for conscious, voluntary action, as in the case of Marx, Merrill, Harris, Légasse, and Sutcliffe, to name a few. However, there has never been any consensus even among those espousing a particular view. For example, Holm-Nielsen says that the concept of predestination "has always been a matter of "theoretical speculation" and that practical experience demonstrates man's own responsibility."[74] This is indicative of the difficulty this apparent paradox has caused scholars. Winston accurately observes, "What baffles the reader of this ancient literature . . . is the easy coexistence in it of two apparently contradictory strands of thought."[75] He says: "Much of the perplexity of modern critics at the seeming contradictions . . . has been occasioned by their attempt to view the ancient documents through the lenses of later theological conceptions and needs."[76]

E. P. Sanders argues that this apparent contradiction was not a problem in the ancient world, since Jews who combined God's providence and human free will "did not work them out philosophically . . . they did not see the need to solve the problem of the incompatibility between God's providence and human free will, and they simply asserted both."[77] A. Deasley too observes that "the Qumran sectaries were apparently able to tolerate a high degree of unresolved tension in their thought. This does not mean that they threw consistency to the winds, but it does mean that they were ready

---

74. S. Holm-Nielsen, *Hodayot: Psalms from Qumran* (Aarhus: Universitetsforlaget, 1960), 16.

75. Winston, *Wisdom of Solomon*, 48.

76. Ibid., 58.

77. Sanders, *Judaism*, 251. For an amplified treatment of the predestination–free will debate with regard to the scrolls, see Marx "Prédestination à Qumrân?"; Merrill, *Qumran and Predestination*; Sanders, *Paul and Palestinian Judaism*, 257–70; Alexander, "Predestination and Freewill."

to affirm positions which commended them as real and true, whether or not they were able to reconcile them."[78]

While there is certainly accuracy in Sanders's and Deasley's position, it also means that for these scholars, both predestination and free will, although two opposite ends of the spectrum, *coexisted* in Qumran thought. But it is important to realize that we are not merely talking about a *coexistence*, a paradox that was nevertheless *accepted* by the Qumran community. Rather, textual evidence clearly favors predestination, however else one attempts to understand the role of the individual. For the Qumran community, God predestined repentance. Once in the community, one had to manifest this repentance by the performance of various rituals—this *appears* to be by one's own efforts,[79] but in reality, whatever ritual they performed, whatever prayer they uttered, was because they had been predestined to do so. Repentance, then, and the manifestation of it,[80] is best demonstrated in an interesting statement in 1QpMic fr. 8-10, 7. This is what is said of the Teacher of Righteousness:

6 פשרו ע[ל] מורה הצדק אשר הואה
7 [יורה התורה לעצת]ו ולכ[ו]ל המתנדבים לסוף בחירי
8 [אל עושי התורה] בעצת

---

78. Deasley, *The Shape of Qumran Theology*, 139.

79. In attempting to fit individuals' role into this predestinarian scenario, Sanders suggests that in documents that were used primarily for instruction the emphasis understandably is on the role and requirements of the individual, whereas in liturgical documents used for worship it is quite natural to focus the attention on God and on all that he does for his creation. E. P. Sanders, "The Dead Sea Sect and other Jews," in *The Dead Sea Scrolls in Their Historical Context*, ed. T. Lim (Edinburgh: T&T Clark, 2000), 7–43 (30). D. Carson says, "There is no doubt that [the various DSS] slightly reflect different positions on the sovereignty-responsibility tension." D. A. Carson, *Divine Sovereignty: Biblical Perspectives in Tension* (Atlanta: John Knox, 1981), 82.

80. See chapter 6, in which I discuss the external acts and rituals associated with repentance that needed to be performed by members of the community, albeit in the sure and certain knowledge that this is what had been ordained by God.

6.   Its interpretation con]cerns the Teacher of Righteousness who

7. [teaches the law to] his [council] and to a[l]l those volunteering to join the chosen of

8. [God, observing the law] in the council of the community.

He teaches the law to a group described as those "who volunteer to join the chosen of God." The tension lies in the fact that the members of the community on the one hand are "those who freely volunteer to join" (המתנדבים לסוף) and on the other hand join the "chosen of God" (בחירי אל). D. Dombkowski comments: "The Qumranians believed that they were 'volunteers' and that even though the volunteer service of the rest had been preordained, it was nonetheless truly voluntary because it was sincere, given with a whole heart and a willing soul." He further indicates that although their place is "chosen" by God, they have to accept it voluntarily.[81] Boccacinni succinctly explains this paradox.

> Human beings are saved because they are righteous, but they are righteous because they have been chosen. What they are does not depend on what they have done or will do. On the contrary, what they have done and will do depends on what they are and what they are is totally out of human control, because it has been predestined by God.[82]

The manifestation of repentance in their daily life through various rituals and cultic acts served to almost consciously maintain an ongoing penitential state, which in turn emphasized to themselves (and to those outside the community) their special status as the (penitential) community of the renewed covenant in the wilderness according to the fixed design of God.

81. D. Dombkowski, "The Qumran Community and 1Q Hodayot: A Reassessment," *RevQ* 39 (1981): 323–64 (346).
82. G. Boccaccini, *Beyond the Essene Hypothesis: The Parting of Ways between Qumran and Enochic Judaism* (Grand Rapids: Eerdmans, 1998), 64.

Conclusion

We return once again to our working definition to see how the findings of this chapter advance or modify it. According to our definition, repentance is "the radical turning away from anything which hinders one's whole-hearted devotion to God and the corresponding turning to God in love and obedience." As in the previous chapter, we can break the definition down. It talks of *a radical turning away*: If we ask the question "from *what* did they turn?" in the texts we examined above, we see that repentance involved a radical turning away from sin and offense (1QS 5:1; 1QH 4:11-15; 5:20-21), incorrect behavior (1QH 26:14-15), the paths of the wicked or sinners (CD 2:2; 4Q266 fr. 2, 2:2-3; 1QSa 1:1-3), deeds of injustice (1QH 10:3), the lot of wickedness (1QH 10:8), those things God hates, a guilty inclination (CD 2:15,16), and all those who deviate from the path (1QS 10:21). The second part of the definition talks of a wholehearted *turning to God*. Our evidence in this chapter suggests that this turning included a turning in obedience to God (4Q504, fr. 1–2, 5:11-14), to obedience to God's will (1QS 5:1), to the covenant (1QS 5:7), to good works (1QS 1:5), to the path of God's heart (CD 1:11; 1QH 12:21, 24; 14:20), to whatever pleases God (CD 2:15), and to what God commands (1QH 7:14; 1QH 8:25).

How was this repentance *described*? What *images, language*, or *metaphors* were used? Repentance was spoken in terms of divine control over one's destiny (in some genres, this appears to be of human agency). Further, physiognomic imagery (in which humans have a fixed amount of light and darkness) was used (4Q186). Repentance seen in terms of divine assistance (4Q501; 4Q266 fr. 2, 2:2-3; 1QH 4:11, 14-15) was sometimes described as a "straightening of the heart" (1QH 10:3), "turning the heart" (4Q504 fr. 1–2, 5:11-14), and "strengthening of the steps" (1QH 10:8). We encountered epithets such as מתנדבים (1QS 5:1, 8), and "walkers on the way of God's heart" (CD 1:11; 1QH 12:21, 24).

When we collated the above findings, we saw that there was a strong emphasis on the need to "stay turned" to God (1QH 6:17-18a; 7:13-14; 4Q266 fr. 2, 2:2-3; 4Q504 fr. 1–2, 5:11-14). Thus repentance was always accompanied by the need to stay penitent—God had given them the privileged status of being part of the community and enabled them to manifest this privileged status though a continuous life of repentance.

How then does this chapter fit in with the conclusion of our previous chapter, where repentance involved a spatial and geographical separation? The members of the community knew themselves to be a faithful remnant in the midst of the wicked. This required a spatial separation that could only be achieved by God's help since he had already predestined them for this special status. Once in this community, they needed to continuously remain "turned" from sin. They did this wholehearted and joyfully because God had predestined them to do so. This ongoing penitential life that characterized their daily existence within the community was central to their religious experience. Their repentance was real because God had foreordained it. Their response was to live each day in total submission to his will in performing cultic acts that ensured that their privileged status was maintained.

In the light of our working definition, repentance now involved a turning from evil, turning to God, and *staying turned* toward God. If we incorporate this into our evolving understanding of the religious experience of the community, then at Qumran, repentance was a predestined spatial separation from those factors that hindered one's devotion to God; it was accompanied by the continuous and necessary manifestation of this penitent, separate state. Remaining penitent was an ongoing task; we have already alluded to a system of checks and balances and cultic acts within the community by which the members of the community achieved this. We will explore these checks and balances and cultic acts in chapter 6.

5

The Extent of Repentance

Before we move on, we must pause here and consider the implications of the conclusions of the previous chapter, which showcases the strong predestinarian worldview of the community, one that affected all aspects of their religious experience, including their understanding of repentance. Members of the community were predestined to repent; the community itself served as an agent that facilitated repentance. In the following chapter, we will see that there were clearly defined cultic expressions that were connected to the community's understanding that they had been predestined to be part of this community and that this predestined, penitential community alone had the responsibility of enabling the arrival of the eschatological age in its totality (ch. 7).

If, as I argue, this penitential separation, first undertaken by the founders of the community, then became the pattern of those who subsequently joined the community for the ultimate purpose of bringing about the long-promised eschatological age, then what was the extent of repentance? That is, who could repent in such a manner? Was it available to all or just a chosen few? How did Jews contemporaneous to the Qumran community see their own repentance? How did the community's understanding that they were the "chosen of God" fit in with the prophetic annunciations, made long before the community came into existence, that the eschatological age will ultimately dawn on all people? Was predestined repentance a distinctive feature of religious experience at Qumran? In order to explore these questions further, we need to investigate broadly the "extent of repentance." The safest place to start is to look at select texts from the Hebrew Scriptures that address these issues; my assumption is that the Hebrew Scriptures provide us with a common text base for both the community and their contemporaries.[1]

In the Hebrew Bible, repentance is a call to return to God and live in obedience to him and may be "subsumed and summarized by one verb—שוב. This root combines in itself both requisites of repentance: to turn from evil and to turn to the good." Regarding terms used to describe repentance in the Hebrew Bible, W. A. Quanbeck says,

> The commonest term for "repentance" in the OT is שוב, "turn back" (Jer 8:4; Ezek 33:19), which occurs frequently in the prophets. Less common is נחם, "to be sorry, repent" (Ex 13:17; Ps 106:45). The LXX translates שוב by *epistrefo*, "turn about," and *apostrefo*, "turn back." נחם is translated by *metamelomai*, "to change one's mind," and by *metanoeō*, "repent."[2]

It should also be noted that this turning is almost always spoken of as an exhortation to Israel to maintain covenant faithfulness—that is, to

---

1. For example, G. Brooke notes that Genesis, Deuteronomy, Isaiah, and Psalms were particularly significant (and "authoritative") for the Qumran community. G. Brooke, "'The Canon within the Canon' at Qumran and in the New Testament," in *The Scrolls and the Scriptures*, 242–66 (266).

2. "Repentance," by W.A. Quanbeck in G.A. Buttric (ed.), *The Interpreter's Dictionary of the Bible*. Vol.4 (New York: Abingdon, 1963), 33.

turn back to the covenant in faithfulness and obedience. For example, consider this text:

> But if they confess their iniquity and the iniquity of their ancestors, in that they committed treachery against me and, moreover, that they continued hostile to me—so that I, in turn, continued hostile to them and brought them into the land of their enemies; if then their uncircumcised heart is humbled and they make amends for their iniquity, then will I remember my covenant with Jacob; I will remember also my covenant with Isaac and also my covenant with Abraham, and I will remember the land. (Lev. 26:40-42)

Confession of their iniquity is equated with admission of their hostility to God and is the starting point for repentance. It is only *after* their repentance that God will remember his covenant with their ancestors (26:49). In Deuteronomy, Moses, in recapitulating the Lord's goodness to the people (4:20), warns them of the perils that will befall them because of unfaithfulness (4:23-28). Even then, if they sincerely repent, God would be merciful to them and keep the covenant (4:31):

> From there you will seek the Lord your God, and you will find him if you search after him with all your heart and soul. In your distress, when all these things have happened to you in time to come, you will return to the Lord your God and heed him. (Deut. 4:29-30)

Moses also reminds the people of God's faithfulness in providing for them during the forty years in the desert (29:5) and of their own unfaithfulness to God (29:4). Moses underscores the need to swear allegiance afresh to God before entering into the promised land (29:10, 12-13). However, he cautions them that there is only destruction and devastation for those who enter insincerely (29:19-28). Then he says in 30:1-2:

When all these things have happened to you, the blessings and the curses that I have set before you, if you call them to mind among all the nations where the Lord your God has driven you, and return to the Lord your God, and you and your children obey him with all your heart and with all your soul, just as I am commanding you today.

Repentance here is the outcome of knowledge of punishments (30:1) and is coupled with complete obedience to God's commandments. Such repentance results in great blessings by the Lord (30:3-5, 7-10). Turning *to* God is the necessary criterion to avail the covenantal blessings of God.

> For the Lord will again take delight in prospering you, just as he delighted in prospering your ancestors, when you obey the Lord your God by observing his commandments and decrees that are written in this book of the law, because you turn to the Lord your God with all your heart and with all your soul. (Deut. 30:9-10)

These select Deuteronomic texts clearly talk of Israel's repentance, which ultimately leads to their restoration and blessings; the "extent of repentance" in these texts is directed toward Israel. When we come to the biblical prophetic books, we see a more nuanced version of this—God desired the repentance of Israel, and Israel's repentance would then lead to the repentance of all nations. For example:

> In days to come
> the mountain of the Lord's house
> shall be established as the highest of the mountains,
> and shall be raised above the hills;
> all the nations shall stream to it.
> Many peoples shall come and say,
> "Come, let us go up to the mountain of the Lord,
> to the house of the God of Jacob;
> that he may teach us his ways
> and that we may walk in his paths."
> For out of Zion shall go forth instruction,
> and the word of the Lord from Jerusalem.

He shall judge between the nations,
and shall arbitrate for many peoples;
they shall beat their swords into plowshares,
and their spears into pruning hooks;
nation shall not lift up sword against nation,
neither shall they learn war any more.

O house of Jacob,
come, let us walk
in the light of the Lord! (Isa. 2:1-5)

Or

And the foreigners who join themselves to the Lord,
to minister to him, to love the name of the Lord,
and to be his servants,
all who keep the sabbath, and do not profane it,
and hold fast my covenant—
these I will bring to my holy mountain,
and make them joyful in my house of prayer;
their burnt offerings and their sacrifices
will be accepted on my altar;
for my house shall be called a house of prayer
for all peoples.
Thus says the Lord god,
who gathers the outcasts of Israel,
I will gather others to them
besides those already gathered. (Isa. 56:6–7)

Or

Many peoples and strong nations shall come to seek the Lord of hosts
in Jerusalem, and to entreat the favor of the Lord. Thus says the Lord of
hosts: In those days ten men from nations of every language shall take
hold of a Jew, grasping his garment and saying, "Let us go with you, for
we have heard that God is with you." (Zech. 8:22-23)

Thus the "extent of repentance" according to the prophets was
ultimately universal. The prophetic call for repentance therefore

represents a two-stage universalism, where *all* Israel first returns to God, and then *all* gentiles do likewise (Israel being the reason for the gentiles to return to God).

It is fair to say that this two-stage universalism was more or less reflected in Second Temple Jewish literature, albeit with modifications and variations. The book of Tobit portrays a faithful reflection of this two-stage universalism of the prophets. After the exile, Jerusalem once again becomes the center of religious devotion (Tob. 13:8) of penitent Israel (13:6). The result is that Israel becomes a "bright light," attracting "many nations" to Jerusalem. Tobit therefore describes the repentance not only of Israel but also of the gentiles: in his deathbed exhortation to his sons (14:3), Tobit foresees the destruction and eventual restoration of the temple and also the "return" of the nations.

> Then the nations in the whole world will all turn and worship God in truth. They will all abandon their idols, which deceitfully have led them into their error and they will bless the eternal God in righteousness. (Tob. 14:6)

In this universal repentance, a "returning to God" is accompanied by a "turning" from idols. Israel's repentance and return to God will result in the repentance of the nations.

Another modification to the prophetic two-stage universalism is found in Wisdom of Solomon: 11:23 says of God:

> But your are merciful to all, for you can do all things,
> and you overlook people's sins, so that they may repent.

The goodness and mercy of God are motivations for repentance; in thus withholding immediate destruction, God grants them the chance to repent.[3] The *Testament of Zebulun* too tells of how God will "turn all nations to be zealous for him" (*T. Zeb.* 9:8). No clear distinction is made between Jewish or gentile repentance. Rather, the inclusion of the gentiles is deemed to be of great importance. A subtle difference in understanding of the two-stage universalism of the prophets is seen in Judith. The conversion of Achior the Ammonite might be alluded to in his deep understanding of Jewish spirituality when he gives Holofernes a brief overview of the people of Israel, starting with their origins right up to heir conquest of Canaan (5:5-16). Achior says that Israel's God is one "who hates iniquity" (5:17) and who remains with them as long as they are faithful to him. In the past, the Israelites experienced defeat "when they departed from the way he had prescribed for them" (5:18). However, in 5:19, they have become faithful once more: "But now they have returned to their God, and have come back from the places where they were scattered, and have occupied Jerusalem, where their sanctuary is, and have settled in the hill country, because it was uninhabited" (Jth. 6:17).

The third Sibylline oracle records the repentance of the Greeks: "Greece, also by offering the holocausts of oxen and loud-bellowing bulls, which she has sacrificed, at the Temple of the great God, will escape the din of war and the panic and pestilence and will again escape the yoke of slavery" (3.564–657). The extent of repentance is "open" enough to accommodate even Greeks (*Sib. Or.* 3.546–67).[4] *Joseph and Aseneth* emphasizes the repentance of a non-Jew. Early in the narrative, the Egyptian Aseneth's idolatry is introduced (2.3). Thereafter, her "conversion and its implications are the main subjects of chaps. 2–23."[5] M. Philonenko says that "la metanoia n'est plus le

---

3. Furthermore, this mention of God's mercy "to all," which could lead to repentance, is reminiscent of similar, possibly contemporary ideas in the NT (Rom. 2:4; 2 Pet. 3:9).
4. The *Letter of Aristeas* mentions that "all mankind" is converted by God (*Let. Aris.* 17).
5. Nickelsburg, *Jewish Literature between*, 260.

repentir qui ramène dans la voie droite les fils d'Israël égarés, c'est la conversion au judaïsme."[6]

It is noteworthy that in the conversions of Achior, Aseneth, and even of the Greeks is that all of the above *first become Jews*. Achior apparently defected to the Israelites (Jth. 6:17). In fact, D. DeSilva describes Achior's latter status as being a "converted Jew";[7] Aseneth's conversion is often seen as a "conversion to Judaism" from paganism;[8] The Greeks' penitential acts at "the Temple of the Great God" strongly suggest their conversion to Judaism.[9] Thus we see in these three examples that gentiles repent, but they also need to become Jews. Since gentiles do not *become* Jews in the prophetic literature, we see here a modification of the prophetic anticipation of the nations. Thus, according to this variation, the extent of repentance is qualified because in reality, although the ones who repent are of gentile origin, since they have become proselytes, they are now Jews. Thus it is not Israel *and the nations* who repent, but rather an *expanded* Israel. This modification of the prophetic conception of universal repentance played an important role in the formative struggles of the earliest church (Acts 15:1-2, 7). Earliest Christianity still maintained a distinctively Jewish character. Thus for gentiles to turn to Christ, they had to first become like Jews. As a result, when repentance is given "even to the Gentiles" (Acts 11:18), there were sections of the church that were unhappy; this lack of consensus regarding the

6. Philonenko, *Joseph and Aséneth*, 54.
7. D. DeSilva, *Introducing the Apocrypha* (Grand Rapids: Baker Academic, 2002), 89. He further says, "God stands ready to receive the Gentile who turns from false gods to acknowledge and serve the Living God, as Achior does." However, we must be aware that the text does not actually refer to Achior's conversion (102).
8. C. Burchard, "Joseph and Aseneth," in *OTP* 2:189.
9. Admittedly, there is not explicit evidence that the Greeks actually became Jews; however, it seems the most plausible explanation for their Jerusalem-based penitential activities and devotion.

"extent of repentance" eventually lead to the Jerusalem Council (Acts 15).

It is worth highlighting a couple of relevant examples from the New Testament. John the Baptist's call to repentance was responded to even by Roman (hence gentile) soldiers (Luke 3:14). Nevertheless, for John, the extent of repentance was not completely universal since it was primarily, although not exclusively, directed to Israel. While John the Baptist offers the possibility of repentance to non-Jews, this is not the case with the author of *Psalms of Solomon*. He states that because of their desecration of the temple, the gentiles will be "purged from Jerusalem" (*Pss. Sol.* 17.22, 28, 30). There is no chance of their conversion.[10] Similarly, *Jubilees* offers no place for those outside the covenant (15.26). This in itself is interesting especially since *Jubilees* records the promise and blessings to Abraham (15.7-8). Hence we see here a perception of Abraham that is radically different from that of Paul's: although Abraham is to be the father of many nations, this work implies that there is no place for the ultimate repentance of the nations—Israel alone has the opportunity to repent (5.17). In *1 Enoch*, there is a clear dichotomy between the "righteous" and the "sinners." At the final judgment on all (1.7), mention is made of the preservation of the righteous elect, presumably of Israel (1.8).[11]

In the Dead Sea Scrolls, there is certainly no place for the gentiles. P. S. Alexander rightly comments: "There is a lack of a theology of the Gentiles in Qumran thought."[12] The extent of repentance for Israel itself is further qualified—it could be appropriated only by

---

10. R. B. Wright, "Psalms of Solomon," in *OTP* 2:645.

11. However, in the allegorical recapitulation of the history of Israel, the author alludes to the *universal* repentance anticipated by the prophets (90:30-34).

12. He further asserts that "Qumran basically writes the Gentiles off: they were never in any sense within the covenant; they were damned to outer darkness, possibly because they rejected the Torah whereas Israel accepted it, though not all Israelites obeyed the Torah, and so most of Israel will also be damned." Alexander, "Predestination and Freewill in the Theology of the Dead Sea Scrolls," 44.

those who had been predestined for repentance. It is interesting to note that the documents that limit the extent of repentance to Israel alone were found at Qumran (except of *Pss. Sol.*). Like *Jubilees*, the scrolls attest the piety of Abraham but do not see him as a prototype for those outside the covenant to be included with Israel as Paul does. While *1 Enoch*'s idea of the salvation of the righteous elect is in conformity with Qumran thought, the presence of a text that describes the repentance of the nations (*1 Enoch* 90.30-34) could be problematic. The same applies to Tobit, which ends on a note of anticipation of the conversion of the gentiles (13:11; 14:6).

These passages are merely echoes of the biblical prophetic works. The biblical texts themselves were found in the caves at Qumran. Presence of such texts in the prophetic works did not alter their overall importance for the community. Although Isaiah's hope for the conversion of the gentiles was not taken on board, the influence the rest of the book had on the thought of the community cannot be overstated. In the pesharim, the gentiles (*Kittim*) are seen as instruments of destruction (1QpHab 3:10-11) and essentially unrighteous and wicked (1QpHab 2:12—3:2). Further, they are able to lead other Jews astray (1QpHab 2:14-15). In the light of the strong negative attitudes toward the gentiles based on the community's perception of reality coupled with their reading of especially the prophetic books, there could be no place for gentiles in their understanding of who could repent. *Jubilees* anticipates the repentance of all Israel (5:17). This again was incompatible with Qumran thought since repentance was possibly only for the members of the community. Nevertheless, the importance of *Jubilees* itself was never undermined at Qumran. Interestingly, 1QSa 1:1-2 describes itself as the rule for "all Israel." Commenting on this passage, C. Hempel observes that on the one hand this "all Israel" perspective could indicate the self-understanding of the community behind 1QSa as the "true Israel." On the other hand, "it seems equally possible that the author of this text addressed 'all Israel.'"[13] However, the very paucity of this "all Israel" motif in the scrolls denotes that it might well represent a minority trend or even a temporarily held one in the Qumran conception of repentance.[14] Thus the scrolls go one step further than those works that limit the extent of repentance to Israel; at Qumran, it was further limited to the chosen within the chosen.

Thus, to summarize these observations regarding the extent of possible repentance, we see various perceptions emerging:

1. some documents are in conformity with the prophetic anticipation of a two-stage universal repentance—Israel first and then the nations.
2. Some works qualify this by stating that first a conversion to Judaism is necessary.
3. Some narrow down the extent of repentance, limiting it to Israel alone.
4. In the scrolls, this is further narrowed down to a chosen remnant within Israel, those who have been predestined to repent and consequently join the community.

Now that this minor but nevertheless necessary detour has been accounted for, we are ready to proceed to the next chapter, in which we look at how this predestined repentance, available only to the community, was expressed in their daily life.

---

13. C. Hempel, "The Earthly Essene Nucleus of 1QSa," *DSD* 3 (1994): 253–69 (261). "All Israel" terminology occurs in CD 15:5 and 16:1 (see 262).
14. 4QMMT C 26-30 too requires the repentance of those outside this community, but this too reflects a very early stage of the community's thought. 11Q19 59:9-10 anticipated the repentance of all Israel, but then this work is an echo of the prophetic understanding of repentance.

6

Repentance in Daily Life: Cult and Rituals

In chapter 4, we saw that the Qumran community could separate from wickedness because they believed that God had predestined them for it.[1] Not only was this predestined state taken to be an act of repentance, but it was also one that required them to *remain penitent.* Paradoxically, although members of the community were well aware that they were predestined thus, this did not prevent them from "responding" to this predestination by striving to remain truly penitent, thereby seeing themselves as a penitential community in the wilderness. In other words, their penitential actions within the community, although predestined, were nevertheless real since there was a constant awareness that their daily existence was a loving and devotional response to the God who had made them do so. As we saw in chapter 4, there was no incompatibility in this. They saw their worship and devotion (and in this context, penitential acts) as a true offering on their part to God.

---

1. They were "a chosen people drawn out from among the people of Israel," thus "a chosen from the chosen." Evans, "Covenant in the Qumran Literature," 80.

The main expression of community members' genuine devotion and worship involved the performance of daily cultic rites. These cultic rites were a manifestation of the ongoing penitential state to which the members of the community had been preordained. We saw in our introductory chapter that scholarly attention to repentance in the context of *rituals* at Qumran has predominately highlighted what I referred to as the "lustration text" (1QS 3:1-12).[2] Most scholars, especially in the early days of scrolls research, used this text to emphasize that at Qumran the internal dimension of rituals was important (and rightly so). However, in doing so, the rituals themselves as penitential acts are almost neglected. O. Betz's comment is representative of such a view. He says: "soviel wichtiger als das aussere Zeremoniell ist die innere Reinheit."[3] Throughout this chapter, I will highlight that while repentance certainly served to validate "outward" religiosity, these external rituals provided a necessary vehicle for genuine repentance on a daily basis, ensuring that one *remained* penitent. From the point of view of religious experience at Qumran, we will explore how wholehearted devotion to God, though preordained, was inseparable from cultic acts.

In order to do what I intend to do, I first need to highlight the place of rituals in the wider world contemporaneous with the Qumran community. As T. Hägerland says: "Repentance, as commonly

2. I acknowledge that there has been much extremely valuable work on rituals, prayers, and other cultic acts at Qumran. My focus is purely on the relationship of these rituals and repentance. It is this interconnectedness of rituals and repentance that I believe has not been given enough attention, or rather, constitutes a relationship that has been taken for granted; hence the implications have not been sufficiently explored.

3. O. Betz, "Die Proselytentaufe der Qumransekte und die Taufe im Neuen Testament," *RevQ* 1 (1958): 213–34 (217). Similarly, G. R. Driver says that what was important for the community was "not lustration but penitence." G. R. Driver, *The Judean Scrolls: The Problem and a Solution* (New York: Schocken, 1965), 500. C. Toews too overemphasizes the internal element to the neglect of the external one. C. Toews, "Moral Purification in 1QS," *BBR* 13, no. 1 (2003): 71–96 (see below). Cross speaks of repentance, denying the "*ex opere operato* nature of the water rites," thereby focusing on inner purity. Cross, *The Ancient Library of Qumrân*, 70 n96. For a similar view, see also Dupont-Sommer, *The Essene Writings from Qumran*, 76n3.

understood in first-century Judaism, entailed not only moral reform but also ritual elements."[4] He speaks of the "set of symbolic actions" that first-century Jews would normally perform as an integral part of repenting. These rituals are in general conformity with the penitential rites prescribed in the Hebrew Bible. These include weeping, sacrifices, washings, fasting, and the use of sackcloth and ashes, to name but a few penitential rites. Furthermore, according to Hägerland, all these ritual acts and external expressions constituted repentance.[5] Normally, these were associated with temple worship.[6] In such a context, it is plausible to assume that one's perception of the temple largely determined and shaped one's conception of rituals of repentance. In the Hebrew Bible, there are texts that advocate the Jerusalem temple as exerting a centripetal force on Israel and the nations.

> In days to come
> the mountain of the Lord's house
> shall be established as the highest of the mountains,
> and shall be raised above the hills;
> all the nations shall stream to it.
> Many peoples shall come and say,
> "Come, let us go up to the mountain of the Lord,
> to the house of the God of Jacob;
> that he may teach us his ways
> and that we may walk in his paths."
> For out of Zion shall go forth instruction,
> and the word of the Lord from Jerusalem. (Isa. 2:1-3)

Or

> Thus says the Lord of hosts: Peoples shall yet come, the inhabitants of many cities; the inhabitants of one city shall go to another, saying,

4. Hägerland, "Jesus and the Rites of Repentance," 171.
5. Ibid., 174.
6. Provision was made where a visit to the temple was not possible (e.g., 1 Kgs. 8:46-50; 2 Chron. 6:36-39). However, this was the exception and not the rule.

"Come, let us go to entreat the favor of the Lord, and to seek the Lord of hosts; I myself am going." Many peoples and strong nations shall come to seek the Lord of hosts in Jerusalem, and to entreat the favor of the Lord. Thus says the Lord of hosts: In those days ten men from nations of every language shall take hold of a Jew, grasping his garment and saying, "Let us go with you, for we have heard that God is with you." (Zech. 8:20-23)

Others, however, explicitly condemn temple-based religious acts:

I hate, I despise your festivals,
and I take no delight in your solemn assemblies.
Even though you offer me your burnt offerings and grain offerings,
I will not accept them;
and the offerings of well-being of your fatted animals
I will not look upon.
Take away from me the noise of your songs;
I will not listen to the melody of your harps.
But let justice roll down like waters,
and righteousness like an ever-flowing stream. (Amos 5:21-24)

What to me is the multitude of your sacrifices?
says the Lord;
I have had enough of burnt offerings of rams
and the fat of fed beasts;
I do not delight in the blood of bulls,
or of lambs, or of goats.
When you come to appear before me,
who asked this from your hand?
Trample my courts no more;
bringing offerings is futile;
incense is an abomination to me.
New moon and sabbath and calling of convocation—
I cannot endure solemn assemblies with iniquity.
Your new moons and your appointed festivals
my soul hates;
they have become a burden to me,
I am weary of bearing them.
When you stretch out your hands,
I will hide my eyes from you;

even though you make many prayers,
I will not listen;
your hands are full of blood.
Wash yourselves; make yourselves clean;
remove the evil of your doings
from before my eyes;
cease to do evil. (Isa. 1:11-16)

Whoever slaughters an ox is like one who kills a human being;
whoever sacrifices a lamb, like one who breaks a dog's neck;
whoever presents a grain offering, like one who offers swine's blood;
whoever makes a memorial offering of frankincense, like one who blesses an idol.
These have chosen their own ways,
and in their abominations they take delight. (Isa. 66:3)

These sample texts suggest two very different attitudes to the temple. In the first two texts, we have a description of an eschatological and ideal situation; while in the latter three texts, the condemnations do not *reject* the temple but seek rather to correct an attitude and expose and address the superficiality of worship at the time. Thus, in the light of these two opposing views, we get an insight into the religious experience of worshipers when confronted by an indifferent or perhaps apathetic leadership at the temple: those who accept the temple as it is, and those who find alternative ways of worship so as not to participate in the corrupt system. Thus repentance is manifested through external, penitential acts normally expressed by temple-based rituals. However, one's interaction with the corrupt temple and ritual system became the determining factor regarding how one understood rituals.

For example, the author of *Psalms of Solomon* is conscious of the corruption of the temple[7]—he talks of the time "when the sons of Jerusalem defiled the sanctuary of the Lord" (*Pss. Sol.* 2.2). As a

7. See R. B. Wright, "Psalms of Solomon," in *OTP* 2:645.

result, God rejects their offerings (2.4). However, we do not know whether he advocates temple-less rituals. Similarly, *Sib. Or.* 3.564–567 describes how the Greeks perform penitential acts in the temple of the Great God. It could be that the (Greek) proselytes described in this text wanted to affirm their commitment to Judaism. On the other hand, John the Baptist's offer of baptism occurred independent of the temple. The locus of the only "rite" of repentance John demanded was the Judean wilderness. However, we have no evidence of whether or not John was hostile to the current setup in Jerusalem.

This was not the case, however, with the Qumran community since there was no ambiguity regarding their attitude to the temple. Rather, because of their hostility to the Jerusalem establishment, their "rites" of repentance (washings, communal confession, penitential prayers) all occurred quite independently of the temple. It could be that the frequency of water rituals made up for their separation from the temple—they strove hard to maintain a temple-like purity at all times. D. Falk comments that the Qumran community "developed an extensive and comprehensive liturgical cycle without parallel in the Second Temple period among the average population of Jews."[8] J. Baumgarten suggests the reason for this: "The sectarian abandonment of the Temple Cult was facilitated by (or gave impetus to) the development of sacred institutions within the covenant community."[9] Thus the community's withdrawal to Qumran was for an interim period. As a result, the cultic life of the community evolved to tide them through over through this period of transition[10]

---

8. D. Falk, *Daily, Sabbath, and Festival Prayers in the Dead Sea Scrolls* (Leiden: Brill, 1998), 253.

9. J. Baumgarten, *Studies in Qumran Law* (Leiden: Brill, 1977), 51. Similarly, E. Chazon says that the members of the community, "in the wake of their split from the Jerusalem Temple, cultivated prayer as a substitute for sacrificial worship." E. Chazon, "Prayers from Qumran and Their Historical Implications," *DSD* 1 (1994): 265–84 (265).

10. For the idea of "community as temple," see the "Qumran" section in B. Ego, A. Lange, and P. Pilhofer, eds., *Gemeinde ohne Tempel* (Tübingen: Mohr Siebeck, 1999).

until they could return to the temple.[11] We now turn to this cultic life.[12]

When considering the cultic rites performed at Qumran, one is confronted by a wide spectrum. On the one hand, there are the *Hodayot* that capture a nonliturgical expression of spirituality.[13] On the other hand, there are other elements of worship that reflect a more "formal" and fixed climate, testifying to a clearly defined liturgical and ritualistic tradition at Qumran. Prayers for particular occasions (*Festival Prayers*) or times of the day (*Daily Prayers, Dibrei ha-'merot*) also exhibit this formal dimension to worship. There are still other texts that describe elaborate rituals (*Rituals of Purification, Tohorot, Ordinances, Communal Confession*). Some texts describe cultic obligations such as the Day of Atonement ceremony or other immersion practices. Our task is to look at these expressions of worship specifically in order to understand how these rituals provided a penitential framework for the religious experience of the community.

Prayers of Confession

During the Second Temple period, it became increasingly popular to express repentance through confession and prayers. In fact, repentance was characteristic of an entire genre of supplication in the

11. R. Kugler points out that "the community's prayer, praise, study, and priestly cultic self-definition did not replace the act of sacrifice, at best they mimicked or mirrored it." R. Kugler, "Rewriting Rubrics: Sacrifice and the Religion of Qumran," in *Religion in the Dead Sea Scrolls*, 90–112 (92). Some believe that at Qumran rituals replaced the temple cult: "c'est donc tout le rituel du temple de Jérusalem actuellement profané qui se trouve remplacé et dépassé par la simple existence de la communauté priante et sainte." D. Barthélemy, "La sainteté selon la communauté de Qumrân et selon l'évangile," in *La secte de Qumrân et les origines du Christianisme*, ed. J. van der Ploeg et al. (Leuvan: Desclée De Brouwer, 1959), 203–16.
12. Understanding such liturgical elements "provide[s] a key to understanding the life and thought of that community." Chazon "Prayers from Qumran," 265.
13. No doubt 1QH (or the hymn at the end of 1QS) was well thought out and carefully composed. However, such texts are less *liturgical* than a document such as the *Songs of the Sabbath Sacrifice*.

late Second Temple period.[14] Such prayers, initially used in specific contexts, came to be used in ordinary occasions as well. Hence confession (and through it, repentance) came to be a liturgical element. D. Lambert, however, is cautious in too readily identifying rites of confession at Qumran with repentance: "In confession, we do not have an inner experience of consciousness, but a performance designed to highlight God's magnanimity and the sect's status as its recipient."[15] Thus, for Lambert, it is more mechanical and not necessarily indicative of an inward state that accompanies with it a desire to change.

In Qumran literature, the confession genre is most evident in the psalms and prayers. These can be divided into "explicit" confessions, which employ distinctive formulas, and "implicit" confessions, which vary in vocabulary but are nevertheless confessions.

Explicit Confessions

We will begin with the confession recorded in the covenant-renewal ceremony in 1QS. The recitation of blessing and curses by the priests and Levites respectively (1QS 2:1-4a; 2:4b-9) is accompanied by a confession of sin (1QS 1:24-25). After the Levites enumerate the sins of Israel, the sectarians (both new and old) identify themselves with those sins and repent of them. They acknowledge their sinful state. This acknowledgment of sin may be seen as a "confession" of sin. Sincere confession involving genuine repentance resulted in blessings, while an insincere confession devoid of repentance resulted in curses. Thus confession of sin was a means to repentance (Neh. 9:5-37; Psalm 106; Acts 7:2-53).

Such a confession was necessary new entrants into the community. Thus D. A. Carson says: "Those who enter the Qumran community

---

14. Nitzan, "Repentance in the Dead Sea Scrolls," 160.
15. Lambert, "Was the Qumran Community a Penitential Movement?," 502.

begin by confessing their sins."[16] This is the confession as stated in
1QS 1:24-25:

24 [וכו]ל העוברים בברית מודים אחריהם לאמור נעווינו

25 [פ]שענו [חט]אנו הרשענו אנו [וא]בותינו מלפנינו

24. [and al]l those who enter the covenant shall confess after them and
will say we have acted [s]infully,

25. we have [tran]sgressed, we have [si]nned, we have committed
evil, we and our [f]athers before us.[17]

The use of these four verbs (נעווינו, פשענו, חטאנו, הרשענו) is
interesting since it presents us with "a four-verb instead of the usual
three-verb formula" (see 1 Kgs. 8:47; 2 Chron. 6:37; Ps. 106:6; Neh.
9:33; Ezek. 2:3; Dan. 9:5).[18] CD-B 20:28c-29 has an almost identical
confession. Here, those who remain faithful and obedient to the
Teacher's voice and the commandments of God will "confess" before
God:

28 חטאנו

29 רשענו גם אנחנו גם אבותינו בלכתנו קרי בחקי הברית

28.   We have sinned,

29. we have acted wickedly, even us, even our fathers, when we
walked contrary to the ordinances of the covenant.

The most obvious difference between this and the 1QS confession is
the use of only two confessional verbs (חטאנו and רשענו). In CD,
confession is made even on behalf of the sinfulness of past generations

---

16. Carson says this with particular reference to 1QS 1:24–2:1a. Carson, *Divine Sovereignty*, 77.

17. This confession results in their acceptance of God's judgments: "[ ] truth and just [. . .] his
judgment upon us and our fathers" (1QS 1:26). This is almost identical to what is expressed after
the confession in CD-B: "justice and truth are your judgments against us." CD 20:30.

18. Leaney, *The Rule of Qumran and Its Meaning* (, 129. Similarly, 4Q508 fr. 3, 1 acknowledges "we
have acted wickedly" (הרשענו). However, the text is too fragmentary for us to know whether
הרשענו was accompanied by the other confession words and if so, how many. See also T.
Muraoka, "Notae Qumranicae Philologicae," *RevQ* 17 (1996): 573–83.

(so also 1QS). The specific sin being confessed involves covenantal unfaithfulness: "when we walked contrary to the ordinances of the covenant" (בלכתנו קרי בחקי הברית). Taken together, the confessions in 1QS and CD formally acknowledge the need to be detached from evil and to have a renewed relationship with God. Nitzan says of both these texts that "confession is considered as a formal expression of repentance."[19]

For a similar "explicit" confession, we turn to 4Q504 fr. 4, 5b-7 (// 4Q506 fr. 131-32, 12-14):

```
5                                    . . . [רחמנו . . .]
6 [ואל תז]כור לנו עוונות רשונים בכול גמולם הר[ע ואשר]
7 קשו בעורפם אתה פדינו וסלח [נא] לעוונינו ולח[טאתנו]
```

5.   . . . [. . . Have pity on us]

6. [and do not rem]ember to us the iniquities of the forefathers in all their wicked actions and who

7. were stiff-necked. You redeem us and forgive, please, our iniquity and our sin.

The reciters of the prayers take responsibility for the "sins of the ancestors" (עוונות רשונים).[20] Similarly, the confessions of 1QS and CD both have reference to the sins of the fathers (1QS: גם אנחנו גם אבותינו, and CD: "even us, even our fathers" [גם אנחנו גם אבותינו]). This consciousness of sin brings this confession in line with other explicit confession in the scrolls. The various verbs used to beseech God (סלח נא and פדינו, ואל תזכור, רחמנו) affirm the intensity of their desire to repent. We must remember that the prayers of

---

19. Nitzan, "Repentance in the Dead Sea Scrolls," 157. J. Krašovec says, "Confession must be seen against the background of two results of sin: separation from God and evil effects in the world. Forgiveness can re-establish union with God, but evil effects remain until they are confessed and atoned for in some way." J. Krašovec, "Sources of Confession of Sin in 1QS 1:24-26 and CD 20: 28- 30," in *The Dead Sea Scrolls: Fifty Years After the Discovery*, ed. L. Schiffman, E. Tov, and J. VanderKam (Jerusalem: Israel Exploration Society, 2000), 306–21 (321).

20. Line 6a is in fact an exact citation of the first part of Ps. 79:8 (אל תזכר־לנו עונת ראשנים).

4Q*DibHam* were "explicitly intended for daily recital" and were not just used on special occasions.[21] Thus, from this daily usage, we can conclude that confession and repentance were matters of daily concern.

A further example of an explicit confession is be found in 4Q393 fr. 1–2, 2:4c-7.[22] Although the text is rather fragmentary,[23] it preserves communal confession.

אלוהינו הסתר   4

5 פניך מחט[אינו וכו]ל עונותינו מחה ורוח חדשה

6 ברא בנו וכונן בקרבנו יצר אמונות ולפשעים...ך.

7 וחטאים השב אליך וא[ל] רו[ח נשברה מלפניך ת]ה[דף

4.   Our God, hide
5. your face from o[ur] si[ns, and] wipe out [a]ll our iniquities. And a new spirit
6. create in us, and establish in us a faithful inclination, and to the transgressors (teach)
7. and bring back sinners to you. And do n[ot] thrust the broken [sp]irit nfrom you.

This confession represents a turning to God motivated by dissatisfaction with their sinful condition. Particularly significant to our discussion is line 7: "and bring back sinners to you. And do n[ot] thrust the broken [sp]irit from you" (וחטאים השב אליך וא[ל] רו[ח נשברה מלפניך ת]ה[דף). The first part of the line is a cry to God to "return" (redirect and reorient) sinners to himself.[24] This calls to mind the penitential force of שוב, which we know by now is a

---

21. D. Falk, "Qumran Prayers Texts and the Temple," in *Sapiential, Liturgical and Poetical Texts from Qumran*, 106–26 (109).

22. Text: D. Falk, "Works of God and Communal Confession," in *Qumran Cave 4. XX. Poetical and Liturgical Texts, Part 2*, ed. E. Chazon et al., DJD 29 (Oxford: Clarendon, 1999).

23. From what remains of the opening lines, it evidently speak of an acknowledgement of sin: ". . . [ ] . . . in order that you are just in [your] verdict . . . [ ] . . . in our iniquities . . ." 4Q393 fr. 1–2, 2:2-3.

24. In the MT, the psalmist says that *he* will teach transgressors God's ways and as a result, "sinner will return to you [God]" (Ps. 51:13[15]). Falk notes that in 4Q393 fr. 1–2, 2:6-7, the MT

well-established metaphor for repentance at Qumran. The reference to repentance (השב) is further substantiated by the use of "broken spirit" (רוח נשברה) in 2:7. Those turned to God (by God) are the ones with broken spirits who are not thrust away (by him). Further, the conceptual and sometimes verbal similarities of Psalm 51 with 4Q393 are uncontested. Thus, if this penitential psalm from the MT provided the basic thought content for the latter, then the penitential dimension of our confession in 4Q393 can never be overemphasized.

In the psalms scroll from Cave 11, we see a similar phenomenon. The psalmist cries out in 11Q5 19:13c-15a (// 11Q6, fr. 4-5):

13   סלחה **** לחטאתי

14 וטהרני מעווני רוח אמונה ודעת חונני אל אתקלה

15 בעויה

13.   Forgive, **** my sin
14. and cleanse me from my iniquity. Bestow upon me a spirit of faithfulness and knowledge. Let me not stumble
15. in transgression.

The psalmist's state is marked by sin (חטא), iniquity (עוון), and transgression (עויה). He is aware of this sinful state and acknowledges that God alone can forgive and redeem his situation. Again, this confession expresses the psalmist's desire to break out of and rectify his present state, thereby remaining penitent.

In all the explicit confessions above, there is an unambiguous penitential dimension. Those confessing are not happy with their present (sinful) state; they desire to "turn away from" their sin and "turn to" God. Further, the ones confessing see themselves as helpless and totally dependent on God. Underlying these liturgical confessions is the desire to remain penitent.

has been transformed from a vow into a petition, with God as the subject. However, "such a tendency is characteristic of this prayer."

Implicit Confessions

Explicit and often liturgical confessions as important means of repentance are not the only type of penitential confessions one encounters in the scrolls. Confessions often occur in a nonformulaic way. We could describe these as *implicit* confessions. These are most frequently seen in the *Hodayot*. This scroll's emphasis on human helplessness and inherent sinfulness is striking.[25] In describing the human situation as portrayed by 1QH, M. Mansoor says: "Man as a moral creature is frail, sunk in sin, and utterly dependent upon God."[26] Awareness of sinfulness and of dependence on God create an atmosphere for confession. This confession is sometimes expressed through the acknowledgment of one's helplessness. When the author constantly confesses his sinfulness and the wickedness of human nature in general, he does so with the intention of repenting of it, as 1QH 19:19-21a states:[27]

19 ואני נפתח לי מקור לאבל מרורים [. . .] לא נסתר עמל מעיני
20 בדעתי יצרי גבר ותשובת אנוש [אחבונן ואכירה] לחטאה ויגון
21 אשמה

19. As for me a source of bitter sorrow has opened for me, [...] grief had not been hidden from my eyes

20. when I knew man's inclinations. I considered the response of mankind [and paid attention] to sin and the anguish of

21. guilt.

1QH 19:20 begins with: "when I knew" (בדעתי). The temporal use of the prefix -ב alludes to the immediate context of confession: *when*

---

25. The sometimes pessimistic approach to life in 1QH is unique to Jewish literature. Merrill, *Qumran and Predestination*, 37.

26. Mansoor, *The Thanksgiving Psalms*, 53.

27. Expression of dissatisfaction at his situation reveals his desire to turn away from it. Consider this text: ". . . But my heart is disturbed . . . [. . .] [. . .] and my heart melts like wax on account of offense and sin" (1QH 22:13-14).

confronted by man's evil inclination (יצרי גבר), sorrow is the result, which is obviously the reason for confession. The confessional nature of this text is further expressed by "I considered" (אחבונן) and "I paid attention" (אכירה). The objects of these two verbs are "the response of mankind" (תשובת אנוש), "sin" (חטאה), and "the anguish of guilt" (יגון אשמה). Such an acute consciousness of sin conveys to us that the author is in fact *confessing* his sin (with the view to repentance).

A similar "implicit" confession occurs in 1QH 4:17-19. It is a recapitulation of pardon for earlier offenses have already occurred.

17 אמצאה מענה לשון לספר צדקותיך וארוך אפים
18 [במשפטי]ך ומעשי ימין עוזך [סליח]ות על פשעי ראשונים
ולה[תנפ]ל ולהתחנן על
19 [...] ... מעשי ונעוית לבי כי בנדה התגוללתי ומסוד [אמת
הלכ]תי ולא נלאיתי

17.　　　　May I find a reply on (my tongue) to recount your just acts and patience

18. Of your judgments and works of your mighty right hand, forgiveness of my former transgressions, to prostrate and to ask favor concerning

19. [. . .] . . . my works and the depravity of my heart for I defiled myself with impurity, I walked (away) from the foundation of truth and I was not allied with.

1 QH 4:17 contains a jussive, which effectively states his intention: "may I find . . ." (אמצאה) This is to be read in the context of the infinitive in line 17: "to recount" (לספר) and the two *hitpaʿel* infinitives of purpose in 4:18: "to prostrate" (להתנפל) and "to ask favor" (להתחנן). The author recounts God's goodness, which encourages him react thus. These two verbs convey the idea of self-humiliation, which is in fact repentance. Recalling God's forgiveness in the past stimulates confession and repentance in the present. We find support of such a reading of the text (i.e., as a penitential

confession) from 1QH 8:14 based on close verbal and conceptual echoes:

אמצאה מענה לשון להתנפל ולה[תחנן...ע]ל פשעי ולבקש [...]
14 רוח

14. Let me find a reply for my tongue to prostrate myself and to seek fav[or . . . con]cerning my sin, and to seek a spirit of [. . .]

In these examples of implicit confessions, we notice that, over and over again, the reason and motivation for confession is dissatisfaction with one's present (sinful) state. To put it differently, this is a confession with a view to repentance.

Hence we may conclude that penitential confessions at Qumran occurred in different forms, primarily explicit confession (as in the case of 1QS 1:24-45; CD 20:28-30; 4Q504 fr. 4, 5b-7; 4Q393 fr. 1–2, 2:4c-7; 11Q5, 19:13c-15a) or implicit confession (as in three examples from 1QH: 4:17-19; 8:13; 19:19-21). The common element in both these types of confessions is the basic dissatisfaction with one's sinful nature and consequent separation from God. Confessing this underlines one's intention to repent of this sinfulness in order to live a meaningful life and thus "return to God." Confession thereby becomes the means for repentance, and repentance the goal of confession.

Hymnic and Liturgical Texts with Repentance Language

Many liturgical texts from Qumran speak of repentance through various images and metaphors. I will highlight repentance texts in two liturgical documents. As I have said, the general criteria for identification of such repentance texts is their conformity to the "turning toward/turning away" idea and also to repentance language, images, and motifs in the Hebrew Bible.

Barkhi Nafshi Hymns

The *Barkhi Nafshi* hymns describe "praise to God for the salvation of the pious and for giving them a pure heart that will keep them away from temptation."[28] These devotional hymns provide a clear example of repentance in worship at Qumran. We will explore the phrase "circumcision of the heart" as an established metaphor for repentance in these hymns. To do this, I will begin with a text from the *Barkhi Nafshi* hymns and then examine its occurrence in other scrolls. Next I will show how this image of a "circumcised heart" was accompanied by the idea of a "penitent heart" in the 4Q*Barkhi Nafshi*.

Circumcision Language: A Circumcised Heart

The most common leitmotif in the *Barkhi Nafshi* texts is the term "heart," which occurs fifteen times in 4Q434, 4Q436, and 4Q437.[29] There is a recurrent idea of God changing the heart of those whom he has delivered, which is a description of God bringing about repentance. To talk of repentance in terms of "circumcision of the heart" was common in biblical literature (see Deut. 10:16; 30:6; 2 Kgs. 22:19; Ps. 51:10; Jer. 4:4; Rom. 2:29). This connection between repentance and circumcision of the heart is described by R. Le Déaut: "le coeur circoncis est un coeur ouvert à son influence, obéissant à sa voix, malleable à son action."[30] More in line with our immediate task, Le Déaut says that "à Qumrân, le theme de la circoncision du coeur est donc employé pour illustrer les conditions morales d'une vie de perfection."[31] For instance, 4Q434 fr. 1, 1:1-3 elaborates the many

---

28. M. Weinfeld "Grace after Meals in Qumran," *JBL* 111 (1992): 427–40 (427).

29. M. Weinfeld and D. Seely, "Barkhi Nafshi," in Chazon et al., *Qumran Cave 4*, 275.

30. R. Le Déaut, "Le Thème De la Circoncision de Coeur (Dt. XXX, 6; Jer. IV, 4) dans les versions anciennes (LXX et Targum) et à Qumrân," in *Congress Volume: Vienna 1980*, ed. J. Emerton, VTSup 32 (Leiden: Brill, 1982), 178–205 (183).

31. Ibid., 193.

things God has mercifully done. Then in 4Q434 fr. 1, 1:4, it is said of God:

4 ימול עורלות לבם ויצילם למען חסדו ויכן לדרך רגלם

4. he has circumcised the foreskins of their heart and delivered them because of his steadfastness and has established their feet to [on] the path.

The phrase "he has circumcised the foreskins of their heart" (ימול עורלות לבם) is a direct echo of the Hebrew Bible's call to repentance, where the verb מול is used metaphorically of repentance. Further, "he has circumcised" (ימול) is coupled with "[he] has established" (ויצילם), thereby tying circumcision (repentance) to deliverance (salvation), making the soteriological implications of this circumcision all the more clear.[32] The purpose of these two verbs (ימול and ויצילם) is expressed by "in order that" (למען) and thus refers to a change that has been brought about by the action of God. This change results in "the establishment of their feet on the path" (ויכן לדרך רגלם). In the light of what we saw in the previous chapter regarding the repentance epithet "walkers on the path of your heart" (הולכי בדרך לבכה), we may assume that the דרך of 4Q434 fr. 1, 1:4 could refer to this same "path." Further, it conforms to the imagery of turning. Since "the establishment of their feet on the path" (ויכן לדרך רגלם) sequentially follows *after* the heart is circumcised, we may conclude that prior to this circumcision-repentance, one was not "turned" in the right direction.

The importance of a "circumcised heart" as a metaphor for repentance can be confirmed by looking at its usage in other scrolls.[33] In 1QS, there is an admonition to curb one's evil inclination. This is

---

32. We will discuss this in more detail below.
33. The phrase occurs also in 4Q177 2:16 and 4Q509 fr. 287, but these texts are very fragmentary.

conveyed through the imagery of circumcision.[34] 1QS 5:4-5 says of those joining the community:

לוא ילך איש בשרירות לבו לתעות אחד לבבו 4

5 ועינוהי ומחשבת יצר יאאם[35] למול ביחד עורלת יצר ועורף קשה

4. No one should walk in the stubbornness of his
heart to go astray after his heart
5. and eyes and plans of his inclination. Rather [he is] to circumcise in
the community the foreskin of the inclination and a stiff neck.

In 1QS 5:4, the "heart" imagery is introduced in negative terms: "stubbornness of his heart" (שרירות לבו) and "to go astray after his heart" (לתעות אחד לבב), stating first of all what *should not* be done with the heart, before actually stating (in line 5) what *should* be done "circumcise . . . the foreskin" (מול . . . עורלת). Although the "foreskin of the inclination" (עורלת יצר) is circumcised rather than the "foreskin of the heart" (עורלת לב), it is used as a parallel for "heart."[36] Pouilly comments: "il est bien question de la circonsision, main celle-ci ne sera plus seulement un acte extérieur opéré dans la chair. Elle consistera dans l'ascèse: retrancher toutes les passions."[37] This confirms what we earlier saw regarding joining the community through an act of separation from all wickedness, thereby making it a manifestation of repentance.

Another example of circumcision language outside the *Barkhi Nafshi* cycle is found in the *Habakkuk Pesher*. In the section that

---

34. Seely describes 1QS 5:5 as the "most notable parallel" to 4Q434 fr. 1, 1:4. D. R. Seely, "The 'Circumcised Heart' in 4Q434 *Barkhi Nafshi*," *RevQ* 17 (1992): 527–35 (529).

35. This is probably an error for כיא אם. (4QS [b] and [d] have כי אם).

36. R. E. Murphy, "*Yeser* in the Qumran Literature," *Biblica* 39 (1958): 334–44 (343). Seely too affirms that the two words are synonymous. He sees the heart as the seat of all moral behavior, thereby justifying the synonymous nature of יצר and לב. Weinfeld and Seely, "Barkhi Nafshi," 275. Leaney observes that in 1QH 10:23, the evil inclination is described as "an inclination of flesh" (בשר יצר). He believes this to be the "most interesting parallel" of 1QS 5:5 since it alludes to the יצר as "a physical organ surrounded by fleshy skin." Leaney, *Rule of Qumran*, 167.

37. J. Pouilly, *La Règle*, 56.

describes the wicked priest's ultimate punishment at God's hand, it is said that his disgrace exceeded his glory (1QpHab 11:9-11). The continuing interpretation provides the reason for this punishment:

12 פשרו על הכוהן אשר גבר קלונו מכבודו
13 כיא לוא מל את עורלת לבו וילך בדרכי
14 הרויה

12. Its interpretation concerns the priest whose disgrace was greater than his glory.
13. For he did not circumcise the foreskin of his heart and walked in paths of
14. excessiveness.

"For" (כיא) in 11:13 introduces the explanation, that his "disgrace was greater than his glory" (גבר קלונו מכבודו). It also tells us the very reason for his downfall: "he did not circumcise the foreskin of his heart" (לוא מל את עורלת לבו). The "circumcision of the heart" is referred to here negatively: "he *did not* circumcise" (לוא מל). This is to be seen in the larger context of 1QpHab 8:8-11. The priest's initial integrity is pointed out (8:9). Then his gradual degradation is described in terms of "arrogance of heart" (8:10a, רם לבו), which led him to "desert God" (8:10b) and "betray his laws" (8:10c). In this context, if the starting point of the priest's downfall is seen as רם לבו, then it is logical to read "he did not circumcise the foreskin of his heart" of 1QpHab 11:13 against this background. Another reason for the priest's disgrace is described by 1QpHab 11:13-14a thus: "[he] walked in the paths of excessiveness" (ילך בדרכי הרויה). This implies that he did not change his evil way. In other words, because he did not circumcise his heart (repent), he continued to walk in excessive ways. On the whole, 1QpHab 11:12-14, with its reference to the failure to "circumcise" the heart and not change one's excessive way, is a negative parallel of 4Q434 fr. 1, 1:4, where the heart *is* circumcised, resulting in the establishment of the feet on the *right* way.

This relation to "circumcision" and walking on the "right way" occurs also in 4Q504, fr. 4, 11-13, where we have the following plea to God to circumcise the heart:

11   מולה עורלת [לבנו . . .]
12 [. . .] . . . עוד חזק לבנו לעשות [. . .]
13 [. . .] . ל[ל]כת בדרכיכה [blank] [. . .]

11.   Circumcise the foreskin of [our heart . . .]
12. [. . .] . . . again strengthen our hearts to do [. . .]
13. [. . . to] walk in your ways [blank] [. . .]

Because this text is very fragmentary, the object of circumcision in line 11 is lost and therefore has to be supplied: "our heart" (לבנו). The definite reference in line 12 to "strengthen our heart" (חזק לבנו) makes it plausible to read לבנו in line 11. Further, line 13 too could strengthen this argument, since circumcision is followed by the desire "to walk on [God's] ways." Thus, although fragmentary, there is a conceptual and terminological similarity evoked by מול, עורלה, לב, and בדרך that definitely echoes the other circumcision-repentance texts discussed above.[38]

The occurrence of circumcision language in 4Q434 fr. 1, 1:4 is not an isolated occurrence. There are enough parallels in other scrolls to show that it was a well-established metaphor for repentance at Qumran. However, it does not end here. In the *Barkhi Nafshi* hymns, the circumcised heart becomes a "penitent heart." The image of a

---

38. Despite its poor condition, I mention it here because what exists is interesting: 4Q177 2:16 says: "[. . . who have turned the foreskin of the he[art] of their flesh in the l[ast] generation [. . .]" (...חס[יר]רו ערלות ל[ב ב]שרם בדור חא[חרון...). To be noted in this text is the reference to לב בשרם and, more importantly, the occurrence of circumcision imagery without the use of the verb מול. סור is used instead, thereby conveying the spiritual turning that a metaphorical circumcision would involve.

"penitent heart" abounds in these hymns and through them, in the worship of the community.

Transformation Language: A Penitent Heart

Heart imagery is not confined to the "circumcised heart." It is also used to denote a complete transformation of the heart, the "penitent heart." Circumcision is frequently accompanied by a complete change of behavior. D. R. Seely speaks about a "series of reversals" in the *Barkhi Nafshi* hymns—an uncircumcised heart has been circumcised; a heart of stone is driven away and a pure heart is put in its place; the evil inclination is driven away and replaced by a spirit of holiness; the haughtiness of heart has been replaced with a broken spirit.[39] All these reversals add up to a transformation of character that has been brought about by repentance. The *Barkhi Nafshi* hymns therefore "eloquently teach God's total conversion of his people and his ability to transform them by implanting in them pious qualities."[40]

Let us now consider the motif of a "penitent" heart as expressed in transformation language. Our first text (4Q434 fr. 1, 1:4) is one that we have looked at before since it brings together the ideas of a circumcised heart and a penitent one.

4 ימול עורלת לבם ויצילם למען חסדו ויכן לדרך רגלם

4. he has circumcised the foreskins of their heart and delivered them because of his steadfastness and has established their feet to [on] the path.

This text answers several questions: What did God do? He "circumcised the foreskins of their heart" (ימול עורלת לבם). How did he do it? Through his "loving kindness" (למען חסדו); Why or

39. Weinfeld and Seely, "Barkhi Nafshi," 331.
40. Ibid.

for what did he do it? To "establish their feet on the way" (ויכן לדרך רגלם). The purpose of the circumcision was to establish them on the right way—there is a transformation of life. Throughout the *Barkhi Nafshi* hymns, these two ideas go together—the circumcised heart becomes the penitent heart. The one is the consequence of the other—the heart is circumcised *so that* the right way might be chosen. The "way" represents the path to salvation followed by the sons of light, as opposed to the way to destruction followed by the sons of darkness.[41]

Similarly, 4Q436, fr. 1, 1: 4b–7a says:

4   ותחזק על לב

5 [נדכה] ללכת בדרכיכה לבי פקדתה וכליותי שננתה בל ישכחו חוקיכה

6 [על לבי פקד]תה תורתכה וכליותי פתחתה ותחזק עלי לרדוף אחרי דרכי[כה

7 [לעשות כול רצו]נכה

4.   And you have *prevailed over* the heart

5. [of the contrite], so that he should walk in your ways. You have *commanded* my heart, and my inmost parts you have *taught* well, lest your statutes be forgotten.

6. [On my heart] you have *enjoined* your law, on my inmost parts you have *engraved* it; and you have *prevailed upon* me: so that I pursue after you[r] ways,

7. [and perform all] your [good plea]sure.

This text appears to be a carefully constructed chiastic structure with an overlap of conceptual, terminological, and verbal similarities.

---

41. D. R. Seely, "Implanting Pious Qualities as a Theme in the *Barkhi Nafshi* Hymns," in L. Schiffman, E. Tov, and J. VanderKam, *Dead Sea Scrolls*, 322–31 (326).

B		A
ללכת <u>בדרכיכה</u>		<u>ותחזק על</u> לב נדכה

D		C
בל ישכחו חוקיכה	<u>וכליותי</u> שננתה	<u>לבי פקדתה</u>

D'		C'
<u>וכליותי</u> פתחתה		על <u>לבי פקדתה</u> תורתכה

B'		A'
לעשות כול רצונכה	לרדוף אחרי <u>דרכיכה</u>	<u>ותחזק עלי</u>

The above structure emphasizes and provides further evidence that circumcision of the heart results in transformation of life. The use of six forceful action verbs (see the underlined words) with God as the subject shows that God effects this transformation in the first place. In A and A', the verb חזק על recurs (1:4b and 1:6a). In both cases, as B and B' show, the result of "prevailing upon the heart" is the "setting out on the right way" (1:5 and 1:6b). The use of פקד (C and C') refers to the thorough investigation of the heart by God. D and D' show that the effect reaches the very depths of one's being (כליותי).[42] This clearly denotes a transformation. In this text, although circumcision language is absent, the reference to God "prevailing over" the heart could be synonymous with his "circumcising the heart" since the end result is one and the same: a penitent and transformed heart. Another example of a penitent heart is found in 4Q434 fr. 1, 1:10-11:

---

42. The image of the heart and inmost parts being commanded and instructed is a metaphor for the "internalization of religious belief." Ibid., 327.

10 ולב א[ח]ר נתן לדם וילו בד[רך]

11 בדרך לבו גם הוא הגישם כיא ערבו את רוחם

10. And he gave them an[ot]her heart and they walked in his w[ay].

11. In the way of his heart he also brought them near because they pledged with their spirit.

As in the case of the earlier text where we took the phrase "you have prevailed over" (חזק על) as a reflection of circumcision language, we may assume here as well that the phrase "and he gave them an[ot]her heart" (ולב אחר נתן לדם) is synonymous with the idea of circumcision. The language of "another heart" (לב אחר)[43] suggests a transformation. Here, the "new [another] heart" is the penitent heart, filled with the resolve to remain penitent. This is seen by the fact that they "walked in his way."[44] The reason for this is because they repented, expressed thus: "he also brought them near" (כיא ערבו את רוחם). This idea is affirmed also in 4Q436 fr. 1, 1:10 (// 4Q435 fr. 1, 1):

10 [לב האבן ג]ערתה ממני ותשם לב טהור תחתיו יצר רע גער[תה]

מן [כליותי]

10. [the heart of stone] you have [dri]ven with rebukes far from me, and you have set a pure heart in its place. The evil inclination [you] have driven with rebukes [from my inmost parts].

In this text, "heart of stone" (לב האבן) stands in parallel relation to "evil inclination" (יצר רע). Similar parallelism is used to describe the removal of these unwanted elements. Furthermore, the heart of stone and the evil inclination are both "driven with rebukes" (גערתה מן כליותי and גערתה מן), where the "heart of stone" (לב

---

43. Either לב אחד or לב אחר are possible. However, אחר is preferred based on Jer. 32:39. See Weinfeld and Seely, "Barkhi Nafshi," 271.

44. See also 4Q436 fr. 1, 1:4-7.

האבן) is exchanged for a "a pure heart" (לב טהור). It is interesting that the "heart of stone" is not replaced by a "heart of flesh," which would have been its natural opposite.[45] The *pure* heart of this text possibly carries with it connotations of cultic purity as well. It also confirms the Qumran position that ritual purity and moral purity were identical. Thus the sinful heart of stone (moral) could be replaced by a *pure* heart (moral *and ritual*). The end result is a transformed life and a penitent heart. This transformation is even more vividly described with further help of the "heart" metaphor in the next column (4Q436 fr. 1, 2:2-4) of the same hymn:

ע[רוף קשה שלחתה ממני ותשמו ענוה זעף אף הסירותה [ממני ותשם] 2

[לי רוח אר]וך אפים גבה לב ורום עינים התנ**תה ממני 3
[רוח שקר]

אבדת] ולב [נד]כה לי 4

2. S]tiffness of neck you have sent away from me, and you have made it into humility. Wrathful anger you have removed [from me and have set]

3. [in me a spirit of lo]ngsuffering. Haughtiness of heart and arrogance of eyes you have forg[ott]en to reckon to me [A spirit of deceit]

4. you have destroyed] and a br[ok]en heart you have given to me.

The transformation that God effects is expressed in the language of removal. For the sake of clarity of argument, the negative qualities removed are italicized: "*S]tiffness of neck* you have sent away from me" (ערוף קשה שלחתה ממני); "*Wrathful anger* you have removed [from me" (זעף אף הסירותה ממני); and "*arrogance of eyes* you have forg[ott]en to reckon to me" (ורום עינים התנ**תה ממני).[46] Furthermore, the process of transformation involves a substitution

---

45. Ezek. 11:19; 36:26. In fact, the imagery goes beyond the idea of circumcision—it is not just the removal of the "foreskin" but of the whole heart!

46. Regarding the restoration of התנ]ה[, Weinfeld and Seely suggest התנשיה with the meaning "forget so as no longer to reckon it to my account." Weinfeld and Seely, "Barkhi Nafshi," 304.

that has taken place, the replacement of that which is tainted by that which is pleasing to God (again, the new attributes are italicized for clarity): stiffness of heart by *humility* (ענוה); wrathful anger by a *spirit of longsuffering* (ארוך רוח); a spirit of deceit by a *broken heart* (לב נדכה). This last instance is particularly significant since it alludes to a penitent heart.[47]

It is worth noting that repentance and its consequence —transformation of life—provides adequate reason for one to bless God. 4Q437 fr. 4, 3b-6 // 4Q438 fr. 4, 2:3-6 in fact expresses the core of the *Barkhi Nafshi* hymns.

3 [   ]ב [רע ל]העב]יר ממני ורו
4 [רחמים] [אנוש או רוח] אורח חיים ו]ללכת בא[
הבת חסד
5 [ובמשפת צדק ולהצניע ללכת בכו]ל דרכי אל ותעב
ת[א ממני יר]
6 [רוח מחיתה ורוח ישועת הלבשתני על כול אלה אברך

3. remov]ing evil from me, and with the abun[dance
4. [of mercy a man or spirit] the way of life and [to walk in the l]ove for mercy
5. [and in righteous judgment, walking humbly in al]l the ways of God. And you have remov[ed from me t]he
6. [spirit of destruction and with the spirit of salvation you have clothed me.] Because of all these things I will [bless.

Although the text is fragmentary, the lacunae can be filled in from 4Q438. Enough of it remains to establish the general picture of what is being said. It is clear that here too a transformation has taken place: "evil" and a "spirit of destruction" have been removed. The *hip'il* infinitive at the opening of line 3, "remov]ing" (ל]העב]יר), speaks of a separation from evil, initiated by divine agency, which is

---

47. Both 4Q435 and 4Q436 are fragmentary at this point. However, the reconstruction of "broken heart," which is based on Ps. 51:19 (לב נשבר ונדכה). Ibid., 299. In 4Q393 fr. 1–2, 2:7, there is a mention of a "broken spirit" (רוח נשברה).

followed by an emphasis on the need to stay penitent. This can be seen in the phrase: "to walk humbly in all the ways of God" (ולהצניע ללכת בכו]ל דרכי אל).[48] The final emphatic acclamation of praise: "Because of all these things I will [bless" (על כול אלה אברך) at the end of the text is significant, where על implies that for all the reasons just listed God is worthy of praise—and the reasons listed above all speak of a transformation of life. From these examples, we see that a transformed life is synonymous with a penitential life and is the result of repentance. Hence, a circumcised heart results in a penitent heart. Thus, in the *Barkhi Nafshi* hymns, there is a constant gratitude to God for repentance and the subsequent penitential life that he has brought about—which is consistent with the predestined-repentance motif while at the same time emphasizing the devotion of the worshiper, the only appropriate "response."

Songs of the Sabbath Sacrifice

While identifying motivations for repentance, we saw in chapter 3 that the repentance-motivated-by-divine-judgment motif was by far the most common motivation in the Hebrew Bible, and was common as well to the Second Temple texts that we considered, texts contemporaneous with the scrolls. We also observed that this was not a major motif in the scrolls. We have come to discover in chapter 4 that the possible reason for this is because at Qumran, the heavy-handed predestinarian approach almost completely eliminates an external motivation for repentance. That said, we do have a liturgical text that tells us that repentance occurs when confronted by divine anger. This motif is uncommon in the scrolls. We may

---

48. According to TWOT, the only use of the *hip'il* of כנע in the HB occurs in Mic. 6:8, where it appears in the *hip'il* infinitive absolute. Apart from this striking similarity, there are other verbal and conceptual exact parallels with Mic. 6:8.

assume that this was possibly a less developed idea in the community's conception of repentance. This motif occurs in 4Q405 fr. 23, 1:12:[49]

12 ל[ו]א ירחם בממשלת עברת כל[ת חרו]נו לוא ישפט במושבי
אף כבודו

> 12. He will n[o]t[50] show compassion in the dominion of the fury of his annihilat[ing wrath] (but) he will not judge those who are made repentant by his glorious anger.

The first part of the line (1:12a) alludes to the righteous and impartial wrath of God. The identity of those who are the objects of God's wrath is not mentioned. However, the identity of another group (1:12b) who are spared *because they repent* is less difficult. They are described as "those who are made repentant" (מושבי). I have adopted Newsom's translation "those made repentant by his glorious anger" (במושבי אף כבודו).[51] Some scholars, however, translate it as: "he will not judge while his glorious wrath *resides.*" This arises because the *hop'al* construct מושבי (from שוב) is reduced to מושב from ישב "dwell," "reside." Let us assume, based on the overall context, that Newsom's reconstruction is correct and that מושבי refers to a group of penitents; I will try to confirm this by first attempting to identify those who do not repent and thereby become the objects of divine wrath. Although such an identification will be limited by the hypothetical nature of the task, I hope that this tentative identification would aid our understanding of the repentance-motivated-by-wrath motif.

49. Text and translation: C. A. Newsom, "Songs of the Sabbath Sacrifice," in *Qumran Cave 4. VI. Poetical and Liturgical Texts, Part 1*, ed. E. Eshel et al., DJD 11 (Oxford: Clarendon, 1998), 182.
50. Some translations have "*For* (כיא) he will have compassion during the rule of the severity of his obliterating wrath" reconstructing כיא rather than לוא. See *DSSSE* 2:835. For a detailed reconstruction/translation of this line, see Newsom's discussion in "Songs," 357–58.
51. She alternatively suggests, "'those turned back by his glorious anger' i.e. those who repent before God's anger." Newsom, "Songs," 360.

For this task we turn to the first song (4Q400). It extols the holiness of the angelic beings and their priestly functions in the heavenly sanctuary (4Q400 fr. 1, 1:14–16). In 4Q400 fr. 1, 1:14, God purifies them. Thus one of the angelic duties is described thus:

14 [להבל]⁵² כול נעוי דרך ויכפרו רצונו בעד כול שבי פשע

14. [to destroy] all who pervert the way. And they shall atone his will for all who repent from sin.

In the above text, two contrasting groups are described: one receives punishment while the other receives God's good pleasure. The imagery of turning is used; in the case of the first group, a negative turning is implied in the phrase "all who pervert the way" (כול נעוי דרך), suggesting that they have *turned away* from what is acceptable. For the second group, it is a positive turning and denotes a *turning back* to God in repentance (כול שבי פשע). It is possible that there is a conceptual connection between the שבי פשע of 4Q400 fr. 1, 1:16 and the מושבי אף כבודו in 4Q405 fr. 23, 1:12, as both apparently refer to the members of the community. While this kind of identification is hypothetical, it could be supported by another text outside the *Songs*. In the concluding song of the Instructor in 1QS 10:20b–21a, he says:

20   לוא אטור באף לשבי פשע ולוא ארחם
21 על כול סוררי דרך

20.   I will not hold my anger against the repenters of sin but I will not have mercy
21. for all those who turn from the path.

52. Newsom suggests להבל in her reconstruction since it serves as a plausible contrast to יכפרו, thereby maintaining the negative parallel present in the contrast of נעוי דרך with שבי פשע. Ibid., 182.

185

We see here a contrast between "withheld judgment" (לוא אטור) for the penitent (שבי פשע) and "withheld mercy" (לוא ארחם) for sinners (סוררי דרך).[53] The primary difference, however, between 4Q405 fr. 23, 1:12 and 1QS 10:20b-21a is that in the former text, the subject of the wrath is God, while in the latter it is the Instructor. Also, the 1QS text first speaks of mercy and only then does it speak of punishment, while in the 4Q405 text the order is reversed: first punishment is spoken of and then mercy/good pleasure. Barring these differences, there is a strong conceptual similarity between the three texts discussed above, allowing us to postulate that the ones most likely to be destroyed in the dominion of God's annihilating wrath in 4Q405 fr. 23, 1:12 is a group similar to the ones described as נעוי דרך (4Q400 fr. 1, 1:16) and סוררי דרך (1QS 10:20b-21a). This becomes clear from the contrast in the two distinct ideas present in line 12: we encounter again the contrast of לוא ירחם ב-, ("mercy withheld," which is the lot of one group) and לוא ישפט ב- ("judgment withheld," which is enjoyed by the second group). If we continue to assume that the identity of the first group in 4Q405 fr. 23, 1:12 is akin to the נעוי דרך, then they are the ones who are in fact contrasted with מושבי אף כבודו. Thus we have two groups standing in the face of this same divine anger, one that is destroyed and another that repents. Thus, in 4Q405 fr. 23, 1:12, divine anger serves as a motivation for repentance. By introducing such an idea into liturgical texts such as the *Songs*, it would have served as a reminder of the importance of repentance and the consequences due to lack of it. While this might have been especially appropriate in the context of worship, repentance motivated by divine anger is not a predominant theme in the scrolls.

---

53. This reference to סוררי דרך supports our earlier reading of נעוי דרך, being the objects of God's wrath in 4Q405 fr. 23, 1:12.

Rituals, Repentance, and Internal Transformation

S. Pfann says that ritual immersions played a significant role in the religious practice of Jews in the Second Temple period.[54] It is therefore not surprising that among the various rituals at Qumran, immersion rituals were important cultic acts.[55] Pfann mentions that the major difference between the Qumran immersion rituals and those performed by their Jewish contemporaries was not so much the reason for the immersions or how they should be done but rather "the emphasis on the upright and humble condition of the heart and spirit during the immersion."[56] This does not mean, however, that repentance superseded the rituals. We need to see how this emphasis on *external* rituals was balanced by an equally strong emphasis on a corresponding *internal* attitude. From the outset, 1QS has frequent warnings against entering the covenant (and hence the community) insincerely and without repentance. 1QS 2:11-12a says:

11 ארור בגלולי לבו לעבור
12 הבא בברית הזה ומכשול עוונו ישים לפינו להסוג בו

11. Damned be anyone initiated with unrepentant heart to cross over and
12. who enters this covenant and places the obstacle of his sin before himself to stumble on it.[57]

As we saw earlier, repentance was central to entry into the covenant. Being a penitential community was integral to their self-identity, hence the cursing of those with an unrepentant heart. The above-

---

54. S. Pfann, "The Essene Yearly Renewal Ceremony and the Baptism of Repentance," in *The Provo International Conference on the Dead Sea Scrolls: Technical Innovations, New Texts, and Reformulated Issues,* ed. D. Parry and E. Ulrich (Leiden: Brill, 1999), 337–52 (337).
55. Archaeology makes it evident that these immersion rituals played an important role in the life of the community as proved by the numerous *miqva'ot* excavated at Khirbet Qumran.
56. Ibid., 338.
57. *DSSNT* 128. Literally: "cursed in the idols of his heart."

cited warning is again expressed in 1QS 2:25b–26a in relation to one whose commitment is insincere.

וכול המואס לבוא   25

[בברית א]ל ללכת בשרירות לבו לוא י[עבור בי]חד[58]   26

25.   And all who refuse to enter
26. [the covenant of Go]d so as to walk in the stubbornness of his heart shall not [enter the com]munity.

The larger context of the covenant-renewal ceremony implies that, outwardly, the individual was participating in the actual ceremony and thus outwardly appeared "to join" the covenant. The phrase "in the stubbornness of his heart" (בשרירות לבו) refers to a lack of repentance. Because of his insincerity, he was actually refusing to enter wholeheartedly, so in effect his entry was not really an entry at all: "[he]shall not enter the community" (לוא יעבור ביחד). The consequence of such behavior is described in no uncertain terms in 1QS 2:26:c—3:1. This text also confirms for us that he had already "participated" in the entry rites.

געלה   2:26

נפשו ביסורי דעת משפטי צדק לוא חזק למושב חיו ועם ישרים   3:1

לוא יתחשב

2:26.   His soul hates
3:1. the disciplines of knowledge of just judgments. He has not the strength to turn his life[59] and will not be reckoned with the upright ones.

The lack of repentance expressed as "stubbornness of his heart" (בשרירות לבו) in 1QS 2:26 is now expressed in terms of one's

58. Restoration of this lacuna based on E. Lohse, *Die Texte aus Qumran* (Munich: Kösel, 1971), 8.

59. *DSSNT*, 129: "He lacks the strength to repent." J. H. Charlesworth, *The Dead Sea Scrolls: Hebrew, Aramaic And Greek Texts with English Translations*, vol. 1, *The Rule of the Community and Related Documents*, PTSDSSP (Tübingen: Mohr Siebeck, 1994), 13: "he is unable to repent."

inability to turn: "he has not the strength to turn his life" (לוא חזק למושב חיו). This inability becomes the criterion for omission from the upright ones. Further, even if such a person does join the community, his repentance would not be considered genuine. As a result, such a person is further isolated by the other members through a rejection of his knowledge, energy, and wealth (1QS 3:2a). The reason for such treatment, which according to 1QS 3:1 was his lack of repentance, is even more explicitly stated in 1QS 3:2b–3a:

2   כיא בסאון רשע מחרשו וגואלים
3 בשובתו

2.   He plows in the mud of wickedness and there are stains
3. on his conversion.

This time lack of repentance is described in terms of continuing to plow in the "mud of wickedness" (בסאון רשע). Hence, insincere repentance was no repentance at all, as "there are stains on his conversion" (וגואלים בשובתו). J. Baumgarten argues that "conversion" (בשובתו) is not derived from שוב (as most scholars take it to be), suggesting instead שיבא, meaning "splinter" or "blade."[60] Based on this, he translates 1QS 3:3 thus: "for he ploughs in the mud of wickedness and the *blade of his plough* is besmirched by stains."[61] However, it seems more plausible to see בשובתו as deriving from שוב, as this is in keeping with the reference in 1QS 3:1 to שוב in terms of turning/repentance, wherein one does not have the strength to repent (לוא חזק למושב). Lack of sincere repentance nullifies any attempts to cleanse him, thereby invalidating the efficacy of rituals, especially purificatory ones. Therefore, merely performing the correct rituals is insufficient if he has not genuinely repented.

---

60. According to rabbinic sources, *b. Batra* 36b.
61. J. Baumgarten, "The meaning of 1QSerek III, 2–3," *RevQ* 6 (1967–1969): 287–88. However, he does not elaborate what is meant by "blade of his plough."

Whatever cultic act of cleansing he participated in would be of no avail.[62] However, the remedy to rectify this situation is then provided in 1QS 3:1-9. This large passage is best quoted in full:

3 ולוא יצדק במתור שרירות לבו וחושך יביט לדרכי אור בעין
תמימים

4 לוא יתחשב לוא יזכה בכפרים ולוא יטהר במי נדה ולוא יתקדש
בימים

5 ונהרות ולוא יטהר בכול מי רחץ טמא טמא יהיה כול יומי
מואסו במשפטי

6 אל לבלתי התיסר ביחד עצתו כיא ברוח עצת אמת אל דרכי איש
יכופרו כול

7 עוונותו להביט באור החיים וברוח קדושה ליחד באמתו יטהר
מכול

8 עוונותו וברוח יושר וענוה תכופר חטתו ובענות נפשו לכול חוקי
אל יטהר

9 בשרו להזות במי נדה ולהתקדש במי דוכי

3. He shall not be justified while he maintains the stubbornness of his heart since he regards as darkness paths of light. In the spring of the perfect

4. he shall not be counted. He will not become clean by acts of atonement, nor shall he be purified by the cleansing waters, nor shall he be made holy by seas

5. or rivers, nor shall he be purified by all the waters of ablution. Defiled, defiled, shall be all the days he spurns the decrees

6. of God so that he cannot be instructed within the community of his (God's) counsel. For it is by the spirit of the true counsel of God that are atoned the paths of man, all

7. his iniquities, so that he can look at the light of life. And it is by the spirit of holiness of the community, in its truth, that he is cleansed of all

8. his iniquities. And by the spirit of uprightness and of humility his sin is atoned. And by the compliance of his soul with all the laws of God

---

62. P. Guilbert when speaking of entry into the community says, "c'est l'insistance sur la necéssité d'une conversion intérieure. Sur laquelle l'auteur revient, après l'exposé du rituel, pour monter l'inefficacité des purifications, qui ne seraient pas accompagnées d'une véritable loyauté intérieure." P. Guilbert, "Le plan de la 'Règle de la Communauté,'" *RevQ* 1 (1959): 321–44 (328).

9. his flesh is cleansed by being sprinkled with cleansing water and being made holy with the waters of repentance.

This text has been the focus of much scholarly attention ever since its publication.[63] Its significance as a carefully thought-out repentance text is evident. Regarding this passage, E. Regev says: "Expiation and redemption within the covenant is attained through moral repentance and religious commitment to heavenly precepts, as well as a ritual bodily immersion in the 'waters of purification.'"[64] Regev's combination of the internal and external dimension of repentance gives expression to a much-neglected view. We will discuss this in more detail below. As this text immediately follows the section regarding insincere repentance (1QS 2:26—3:3a), in 3:1-9 we are confronted by eight verbs preceded by the negative particle לוא that together emphasize the absolute condemnation of participation in purificatory rituals without repentance.[65] Further, all of the acts of cleansing mentioned have to do with water rites.[66] Line 6b, which is in fact a causal clause, begins a new idea. According to the causal clause in 3:6 (introduced by an emphatic כיא), a shift occurs, from futility to hope: complete atonement and cleansing (or in short, the benefits of any ritual) are possible only through three "agents of cleansing" that produce a threefold result. These may be set forth as follows:

63. See my survey of literature in the introduction regarding attention given to this "lustration text."
64. E. Regev, "Abominated Temple and a Holy Community: The Formation of Notions of Purity and Impurity in Qumran," *DSD* 10, no. 2 (2003): 243–78 (273).
65. לוא יתחשב, לוא חזק, לוא יטהר, לוא יטהר, לוא יתקדש, לוא יזכה, לוא יתחשב, לוא יצדיק.
66. While the last three (מי רחץ, ימים ונהרות, מי נדה) explicitly refer to water rites, it is not so evident with the first two. עין תמימים, however, conveys the idea of "spring" or "fountain," thereby justifying its inclusion into this list of water-based rites. Based on the above references to water rites, כפורים too possibly alludes to water rites. Further evidence for this can be seen in its association with the verb יזכה, which clearly carries purificatory connotations.

Agent	Result
רוח עצת אמת אל	יכופרו כול עוונותו
רוח קדושה ליחד	יטהר מכול עוונותו
רוח יושר וענוה	תכופר חטתו

The text further implies that these three factors are in conjunction with each other and therefore are not to be separated. The recurrence of רוח followed by an abstract noun in each instance (יושר וענוה, קדושה, אמת), the three related agents (אל, יחד, איש [implied]), the three verbs of cleansing (יכופרו, יטהר, תכופר), and the common words for "sin" (עוונותו, חטתו) represent the close relation shared by the agents/result. Thus all three agents are necessary to bring about the required result, true cleansing. Further, the three "spirits" suggest that the driving forces that lead to atonement and cleansing are the role of God: "the spirit of the true counsel of God" (רוח עצת אמת אל); the role of the community: "the spirit of holiness of the community" (רוח קדושה ליחד); and the role of the individual: "the spirit of uprightness and of humility" (רוח יושר וענוה). The spirit of the true counsel of God initiates the process; the spirit of holiness of the community provides an appropriate arena for genuine change to occur; the spirit of uprightness and humility (of the individual) completes the process. [67]

The crux of this text, which underscores the need of something more than mere rituals, is found in 1QS 3:8b-9a, which makes this distinction between soul (נפש) and flesh (בשר).

---

67. O. Betz says, "Nicht das Wasser, sondern der Geist Gottes ist das Mittel, das den Menschen von allen verfehlungen frei macht." O. Betz, "Die Proselytentaufe der Qumransekte und die Taufe im Neuen Testament," *RevQ* 1 (1958): 213–34 (217). Similarly, Kvalaag notes, "the submission and humility of the human spirit makes atonement possible, but only God, by the spirit of holiness, can purify humans and purge them of all their iniquities." R. W. Kvalaag, "The Spirit in Human Beings in Some Qumran Non-Biblical Texts," in *Qumran between the Old and New Testaments*, ed. F. Cryer and T. Thomson, JSOTSup 290 (Sheffield: Sheffield Academic, 1990), 159–80 (172).

ובענות נפשו לכול חוקי אל   8

9 יטהר בשרו

8.   and by the humbling of his soul with all the laws of God

9. his flesh is cleansed

The "humbling of his soul" (ובענות נפשו), which is internal and moral, is set against "his flesh [being] cleansed"(יטהר בשרו), which is an external, physical, and ritual act. Thus true repentance is an internal, moral, and spiritual exercise that brings about an outward, physical, and ritual cleansing. This concept was not confined only to immersion rites but was evident in other cultic acts as well, such as the Day of Atonement ceremony. I will confine myself to a text from the *Temple Scroll* that exhibits cultic as well as repentance language. Given the community's insistence that external rituals be accompanied by a corresponding internal attitude (as seen above), it is plausible to assume that the ritual of atonement had strong repentance overtones, the former being validated by the latter. 11Q19 25:12b-16 provides instructions about the different types of animals used for different forms of atonement, thereby describing the "external" aspects of the ceremony. Interestingly, the immediately preceding text (11Q19 25:10b-12a) strongly emphasizes the "internal" aspects of the ceremony.

ובעשרה בחודש [blank]   10

11 הזה יום כפורים הוא ותענו בו את נפשותיכמה כי כול הנפש אשר

12 לוא תתענה בעצם היום הזה ונכרתה מעמיה

10.   [blank] And on the tenth of this month

11. is the Day of Atonement. On it you shall humble your souls, because all the souls that are

12. not humbled in strength on this very day will be expelled from its people.

The blank space in the middle of line 10 possibly marks a new paragraph that first of all states *when* the ceremony is to be observed: "on the tenth of this month" (ובעשרה בחודש הזה). Thus, before the external preparations (25:11-16), there is a crucial internal preparation (25:11-12). It is significant that the verb כנע is used twice. According to the sequence of thought, *because* it is the Day of Atonement, one needs to humble oneself.[68] The first reference to כנע focuses on the need to humble the soul (ותענו בו את נפשותיכמה), while the second usage of the verb (לוא תתענה) points to the consequence of *not* humbling the soul. Also, this humbling is not to be superfluous but sincere, literally, "in strength" (בעצם). Further, that the initial preparation is for the soul rather than the actual, external ritual is significant, as it provides another example of the need for an external ritual (Day of Atonement ceremony) to be accompanied by an appropriate internal response (repentance). In fact, the above text suggests that that the primary focus of the Day of Atonement is the "humbling of the soul."[69]

Based on what we have seen so far, there is sufficient evidence to show that, for the community, repentance and rituals were inseparably bound together. So striking was this approach to rituals that A. Leaney observes: "The sect is the first group within Judaism of whom we know who believed that moral failure (sin in our modern sense) incurred ritual defilement. They taught that to be cleansed

---

68. D. Volgger points out that these two sentences have a positive and negative emphasis, respectively. The fact that they are connected by כי shows that "the prescription to humble oneself on the tenth day of the seventh month is clearly underlined as a fundamental norm for the entire people of Israel." He further notes that this motif to "humble oneself" occurs again in 27:7 ("those who do not humble themselves"). From this, Volgger concludes that it links together the first (25:10-12) and final (27:7) section of the text about the Day of Atonement. D. Volgger, "The Day of Atonement according to the Temple Scroll," *Bib* 87 (2006): 251–59 (254).

69. J. Baumgarten says that the characterization of the Yom Kippur as a time for repentance and divine mercy is conventional. J. Baumgarten, "Yom Kippur in the Qumran Scrolls and Second Temple Sources," *DSD* 6 (1999): 184–91 (187).

from sin demanded both repentance and ritual purification."[70] The community saw their understanding of rituals as the fulfillment of a prophetic command. The prophets alluded to moral cleansing through ritual purity. Ezekiel prophesied the cleansing of Israel from moral impurity by the "sprinkling of clean water" (Ezek. 13:1; 36:25, 26; 37:23). Taking this idea yet further, C. Toews points out that at Qumran, moral purification was obtained through lustrations.

> Qumran satisfied the contemporary need for moral purification by applying the eschatological lustration to their present ritual of initiation. Their literal application of lustral imagery provides the earliest Second Temple evidence for a movement into praxis of the prophetic conception or [sic] moral purification.[71]

In furthering this "praxis," Toews stresses the importance of repentance in the whole procedure, speaking of the unacceptance of "counterfeit repentance" and they invalidity of the "pseudorepentant candidate." While she is right in emphasizing the importance of correct repentance, she appears to completely dismiss the ritual itself. It is clear that rituals needed to be coupled with genuine repentance that represented an internal transformation. Only then could the rituals achieve the required results of complete purification—both moral and ceremonial. The efficacy of any ritualistic washing was invalidated if unaccompanied by true repentance.

In all of the above sections, we saw that there is definitely an emphasis on ritual at Qumran. Apart from this, there are texts that explicitly draw attention to the internal attitude that is to accompany these rituals. Since these texts appear to deny the efficacy of external

---

70. Leaney, *Rule of Qumran*, 139. However, M. Himmelfarb is skeptical of this conflation of the categories of impurity and sin. For her, the 1QS text "uses the terminology of impurity in a poetic or evocative way." M. Himmelfarb, "Impurity and Sin in 4QD, 1QS and 4Q521," *DSD* 8, no. 1 (2001): 9–37 (37).

71. She observes that the language of ritual purity such as "to purify," "to cleanse," "impurity" is used of moral purity. C. Toews, "Moral Purification in 1QS," *BBR* 13, no. 1 (2003): 71–96 (90).

rituals if not accompanied by internal repentance, scholars rightly see this identification of moral purity with ritual purity as very important to the Qumran community. In fact, M. Knibb speaks of the "right behaviour and the correct inward disposition"[72] that is needed to enter the community. When scholars emphasize that external rituals had to be accompanied by an internal attitude of repentance, they almost stress this latter, internal dimension over and above the external, cultic act. However, we should note that although only when accompanied by repentance did the rituals have any efficacy at all, *repentance by itself was not usually a substitute or replacement for the external ritual at Qumran*. The two were inseparably linked together. This aspect unfortunately is not emphasized enough.[73] G. Vermes accurately assesses the situation when he says, "While the Scrolls clearly state the necessity of inward devotion, they lay substantial stress, as does Pharisaic and rabbinic orthodoxy, on matters relating to ritual purity of cultic origin."[74] Herein lies a distinctively Qumranic understanding of repentance: just as rituals need to be accompanied by repentance, *repentance needs to be accompanied by rituals*. In the Hebrew Bible, there are times when the external ritual is of no avail. The internal dimension is highlighted over and above the external. Despite my argument that the Qumran community was a penitential community, at no point do the scrolls indicate that it was only a correct inward state that ultimately mattered. At Qumran, the inward and the outward always went hand in hand. Rituals at Qumran served as an inseparable vehicle for repentance; they provided an appropriate framework within which repentance could function. Just as it is fair

---

72. M. Knibb, *The Qumran Community* (Cambridge: Cambridge University Press, 1987), 93.

73. Klawans mentions that "moral repentance must involve ritual purification in order to be fully effective." His aim, however, is to prove the relationship between impurity and immorality at Qumran, so he does not stress the necessity of both ritual and repentance per se. J. Klawans, "The Impurity of Immorality in Ancient Judaism," *JJS* 48 (1997): 1–16 (9).

74. G. Vermes, *The Religion of Jesus the Jew* (London: SCM, 1993).

to say of the community that if the rituals were not accompanied by true repentance then they were of no avail, the converse too was has to be considered: if there were no rituals, repentance could not be appropriately expressed and manifested. Both rituals and repentance dominated the lives of the community members. This enabled them to remain penitent.

Conclusion

We have seen in this chapter that at Qumran rituals played an important role. However, we have also seen that at every point these cultic acts needed to be accompanied by genuine repentance for them to be valid, and vice versa. We saw that this was evident in the confessional nature of many of the liturgical hymns and prayers. When we looked particularly at prescriptions pertaining to water rites, or even to the Day of Atonement ceremony, we noticed that their importance was not confined to a purely "ritualistic" act. Rather, for complete purification, the cleansing of the flesh through ritual had to be accompanied by a cleansing/humbling of the soul through repentance. For the community, repentance that attained moral purity (and inward cleansing) was inseparable from and balanced by ritual purity (and outward cleansing). This in turn allowed one to remain penitent.

This present chapter showed that once inside the separate, penitential community, ongoing repentance was manifested through daily cultic acts and rituals. Based on the findings of this chapter, we need to return again to our working definition, which sees repentance as "the radical turning away from anything that hinders one's whole-hearted devotion to God and the corresponding turning to God in love and obedience." As we have done in the preceding chapters, we now ask again, From *what* did they turn away? We saw in the texts examined that it was a *turning away from* evil (4Q437 fr. 4, 3-6; 4Q171 2:2-4); sin (1QS 1:24,25; 4Q505 fr. 1, 2-3; 1QH 8:13; 22:14; 4Q504 fr. 4, 5-7; 11Q5 19:13-15; 4Q400 fr. 1, 16); wickedness (1QS 5:14); an evil heart (4Q*Barkhi Nafshi*); stiffness of neck (4Q436 fr. 1, 2:2); the path of the wicked (4Q174 1:14); an unrepentant heart (1QS 2:11, 26); guilty deeds (1QH 12:33-34); and stubbornness of heart (1QS 2:25b; 3:3). Their turning away from the aforementioned attitudes or actions was expressed liturgically.

The second part of my definition refers to a *wholehearted turning to God*. This was seen in their turning to God and his law (11Q19 59:9-10; 4Q171 2:2), and (re)turning to the community as a sign of repentance, especially after an offense (1QS 7:16-17, 20-21; 8:18, 22). They had to walk in God's ways (4Q436 fr. 1, 1:4-7); it was also evident in their participation in the life of the community (1QS 3:1).

When we considered the *language and images* used to express repentance within a cultic context, we saw it expressed through explicit or implicit confessions (1QS 1:24-25; CD 20:28-30; 4Q393 fr. 1–2, 2:4-7; 4Q504 fr. 4, 5-7; 11Q5 19:13-15); heart language that included a "circumcised" heart (4Q434 fr. 1, 1:14; 1QS 5:5; 1QpHab 11:13); and a "penitent" heart (4Q*Barkhi Nafshi*). We found references to a "humbled" soul (1QS 3:8-9; 11Q19 25:10-11) and perfection of way (4Q404 fr. 1, 122). In the penal section, repentance was spoken of in terms of returning (or not returning) to the community (1QS 7:16-17, 20-21; 8:18, 22). In general, repentance was also expressed by linking it with actual rituals themselves, such as immersion rites (1QS 3:1-13) and the Day of Atonement ceremony (11Q19 25:10-11).

Based on the above understanding of repentance, we arrive at the following result: all external rituals had to be accompanied by a corresponding internal attitude. This attitude was repentance: ritual and repentance became inseparable. The ritual was futile without repentance. However, significantly, while repentance gave confessions, prayers, and rituals their efficacy, at Qumran, *repentance was never a substitute for external cultic acts*. The two had to be coupled together if either was to be of any benefit. Repentance was manifested in the external cultic act. The cultic act provided the framework within which repentance could occur in the daily life of the members of the community. Furthermore, whether it was through the frequent daily immersions[75] or daily/festival prayers or the Day of Atonement ceremony, we saw that all of these cultic acts were efficacious only when accompanied by repentance. Based on the frequency with which these rites were performed, we may plausibly assume that a penitential attitude was constantly necessary. Against this background, R. Kugler accurately says of these cultic acts at Qumran: "Ritual at Qumran was hegemonic, making every aspect of their experience religious."[76] Further, the interconnectedness of rituals and repentance at Qumran reminds us that, for the community, repentance was never a substitute for rituals; neither were rituals a substitute for repentance.[77] The one was an integral part of the other. Rituals were vehicles for repentance. Not only that, they provided a daily means though which (daily) repentance could be expressed. Their concern for repentance found expression in their emphasis on rituals, *and the locus for this was the temple-like context provided by the community itself*. This makes the penitential cultic acts

---

75. We have literary evidence (e.g., 1QS 3:3-12), archaeological evidence (the numerous *miqva'ot*), and also evidence from an ancient witness (e.g., Josephus, *J.W.* 2.128–130).

76. R. Kugler, "Making All Experience Religious: The Hegemony of Ritual at Qumran," *JSJ* 33, no. 2 (2002): 131–52 (152). E. Regev even more explicitly makes this connection when he says that "expiation and redemption is attained through moral repentance and religious commitment to the heavenly precepts, *as well as ritual bodily immersion* in the waters of purification." E. Regev, "Abominated Temple and a Holy Community: The Formation of the Notions of Purity and Impurity in Qumran," *DSD* 10, no. 2 (2003): 243–78 (273).

77. Hägerland implies the latter when speaks about "a set of symbolic actions which first-century Jews would normally perform as an integral part of repenting." Hägerland, "Jesus and the Rites of Repentance," 171.

of the Qumran community distinctive from other responses to the temple. At Qumran, the virtual-temple context provided by the very existence of the community is central.

Hence, in the light of our definition, for the Qumran community, repentance was turning away from wickedness and a turning to God *through rituals*. Thus we may conclude that repentance was a radical and spatial separation from those factors that hindered one's devotion to God. It also consisted of a corresponding turning to God in love and obedience. They were predestined to do so and constantly sought to remain penitent. This was accomplished through ritual and cultic acts performed within a virtual temple-like context. While these rituals were part and parcel of their daily life, the Qumran worldview was characterized by intense eschatological expectation. Thus we need to see how their covenantal, predestinarian, and cultic emphases that we have explored in the preceding chapters ultimately fit into their eschatological understanding. This will be the focus of the next chapter.

7

Repentance and Eschatology

We have seen that repentance was first of all a radical and spatial separation from wickedness and adherence to the community and covenant. This was possible because God had predestined it thus. The now separate, predestined community stayed penitent through daily rituals that had to be accompanied by genuine repentance. Since the community's perception of the world was eschatologically charged, we must place the above picture of repentance into an eschatological framework.

"Eschatology concerns mainly 'the last days' (אחרון קץ ,אחרית הימים) and what follows 'at the end of days.'"[1] This period would culminate with a final war against the forces of Belial. There would be a final judgment in which the wicked and the righteous would receive what they deserved. After this, wickedness and injustice

---

1. É. Puech, "Messianism, Resurrection and Eschatology at Qumran and in the New Testament," in *The Community of the Renewed Covenant*, ed. E. Ulrich and J. VanderKam (Notre Dame: Notre Dame University Press, 1994), 235–56 (235).

would be wiped out forever and an age of righteousness would follow.[2] J. J. Collins asserts: "The scrolls present a diverse corpus of eschatological doctrines which were formulated and maintained side by side within a highly compact community."[3] This diversity of eschatological strands in the scrolls leads P. R. Davies to challenge the impact of eschatology on the community.[4] For him, the "remarkably diverse variety of eschatological teachings creates something of a paradox."[5] Davies comments that the Qumran community apparently "failed to commit themselves even to articulate, a coherent or systematic description of the eschaton for which they so fervently held themselves in readiness."[6] Davies's observation regarding the lack of "a coherent or systematic description of the eschaton" and H. Stegemann's comment regarding an absence of "unity of doctrine" in matters of eschatology is untenable. In the rest of this chapter, I will show that the community's understanding of repentance demonstrates a coherent understanding of the eschaton. Thus it is hoped that this discussion will provide further evidence for the importance of a "coherent" eschatology at Qumran.

The importance of the relation between repentance and eschatology in the scrolls has rarely been considered. Outlining the general eschatological Qumran worldview will help to show that the

2. Although the above eschatological factors are important, I am not examining Qumran eschatology per se; rather, I am concerned with understanding *repentance* within an eschatological context.

3. J. J. Collins, "Patterns of Eschatology at Qumran" in *Traditions and Transformation: Turning Points in Biblical Faith*, ed. B. Halpern and J. Levenson (Winona Lake, IN: Eisenbrauns, 1981), 351–75 (351).

4. He questions the view that "eschatological expectation is thought to have exercised a definitive influence on its [the community's] formation, organization and teaching." P. R. Davies, "Eschatology at Qumran," *JBL* 104, no. 1 (1985): 39–55 (39).

5. Ibid.

6. Ibid. Like Davies, H. Stegemann says, "'Unity of doctrine' prevailed among the Essenes, it is true, in the organizational, legal, and ethical spheres, but not in the areas of messianism and eschatology." H. Stegemann, *The Library of Qumran: On the Essenes, Qumran, John the Baptist, and Jesus* (Grand Rapids: Eerdmans, 1998), 209.

community was aware of living on the threshold of the eschaton, a period in which life in the present was a reflection of and preparation for the future. Texts such as 4QMMT, 11Q19m 1QSa abd 4Q215 exhibit repentance language while at the same time fitting into this worldview. Selected texts from three biblical interpretations (4Q171, 4Q174, and 11Q13) consciously place repentance within an eschatological context. We note the significance of the phrase אחרית הימים and its bearing on eschatological repentance language in the texts examined. After this, we will be in a better position to consider how the community's eschatological worldview shaped their thinking on repentance and, more importantly, how their eschatological outlook was shaped by their understanding of repentance: By the end of the chapter we will show that at Qumran repentance alone could bring about the totality of the promised eschatological age.

The Eschatological Worldview at Qumran

L. Schiffman comments that from the earliest stages of Qumran research it was known that "the documents of the Qumran sect place great emphasis on eschatology."[7] The community believed they were living in an "interim period," the intersection of the final period of history and the dawn of the eschatological age. The community structured their present existence to mirror what they anticipated in the future. B. Nitzan aptly describes their response to this scenario.

> According to the evidence of Qumran literature, it was the community's aim to realize the eschatological repentance expected in the historiographic and prophetic biblical books. In this respect, the way of

---

7. L. H. Schiffman, *The Eschatological Community of the Dead Sea Scrolls*, SBLMS 38 (Atlanta: Scholars Press, 1989), 6. C. Evans and P. Flint observe that "the eschatological ideas present in the Dead Sea Scrolls shed welcome light on our understanding of eschatology around the turn of the Common Era.", introduction to *Eschatology, Messianism, and the Dead Sea Scrolls*, 9.

life recommended for the members of the Community was considered a way of repentance.[8]

According to Nitzan's premise, the community's understanding of eschatology shaped their understanding of repentance and was bound up with their understanding of Scripture. In the following sections, I will demonstrate this, thereby fulfilling my purpose of highlighting the coherence of eschatological thought at Qumran.

The Anticipated Eschatological Return to God

In most of the literature of the Second Temple period, the old order would soon come to an end. History was moving steadily to its consummation. The eschaton would be a time of great blessings if indeed one had lived appropriately and had "turned" back to God. We see this reflected in several texts. For example, the *Sibylline Oracles* are dominated by eschatology, which for the Jewish oracles are mainly concerned with the advent of a glorious kingdom and the transformation of the earth.[9] In *Jubilees*, God reveals to Moses on Mt. Sinai the blatant wickedness (1.7, 9, 12) and idolatry (1.9b, 11), which will result in captivity and exile (1.13). This will cause them to repent: "and afterward they will turn to me from among the nations with all their heart and with all their soul and with all their might" (1.15a). This repentance would lead to blessing and restoration: "When they seek me with all their heart and with all their soul, I shall reveal to them an abundance of peace in righteousness" (1.15c). The blessing is clearly *conditional*, dependant on repentance. This repentance is reemphasized a little later, this time in relation to a transformation of the heart. God says that after they acknowledge their sins, "they

8. Nitzan, "Repentance in the Dead Sea Scrolls,":146. Similarly, Vermes says that "they foresaw their community as fulfilling the prophetic expectations of the salvation of the righteous." Vermes, *Qumran in Perspective* (London: SCM, 1994), 163.
9. Collins, "Sibylline Oracles," in *OTP* 1:323.

will return to me in all uprightness and with all of [their] heart and soul. I will cut of the foreskin of their heart and the foreskin of the heart of their descendants" (1.23a).[10] The lasting nature of this repentance is stressed: "I shall purify them so that they will not turn away from following me *from that day and forever*" (1:23c [emphasis added]). Thus very early on in *Jubilees*, repentance is introduced as having the ability to reestablish Israel's relationship with God. *Jubilees* reemphasizes that a period of widespread wickedness (23.16-21) would result in captivity (23.22). This is followed by a time of repentance: "And in those days, children will begin to search the law, and to search the commandments and to return to the way of righteousness" (23.26). Thus, while apostasy is responsible for God's punishment, the return of God's favor requires repentance—a return to the "path of righteousness." Repentance brings about the following result: "the days will begin to increase and grow longer" (23.27a). After Abraham, human life becomes "increasingly shorter" due to sin. "When repentance takes place human life will be restored to its former longevity."[11] In other words, *Jubilees* offers us a significant example of the importance of eschatology and equally the importance of repentance as the appropriate response to imminent eschatological age.

Another example of this can be found in the *Testament of the Twelve Patriarchs*. Generally, there is normally an exhortation by the patriarch to an eschatological repentance in the lives of his sons' descendents.[12] For example, in the *Testament of Judah*, the patriarch tells of the rise of wickedness (23.1–3), which would lead to destruction of the temple and exile (23.3c). This unfortunate situation

---

10. Circumcision of the descendents' heart is reminiscent of Deut. 30:6.
11. Nickelsburg, *Jewish Literature*, 77. There also appears to be a thematic parallel between ch. 1 and ch. 23. In both chapters, we observe the following model of repentance: wickedness-punishment-repentance- restoration/blessings.
12. This second, general exhortation to a future repentance does not occur in *T. Reu.* and *T. Sim.*

will continue, he tells his sons, "until you return to the Lord in integrity of heart, penitent and living according to all the Lord's commands" (23.5a). Such repentance will lead to restoration (23.5b). Hence, repentance involves a return to the Lord, a penitential life, and results in blessings. Further, this repentance is eschatological. Its importance is seen in the fact that it can change the destiny of Israel and restore Israel's estranged relationship with God.

While the eschaton was generally seen as a period in the future, in many instances the new order had already begun to dawn. This was especially true of the Qumran community. The eschaton was not in the distance future, as it appears to be in some Second Temple texts. As a result, "they lived on the verge of the *eschaton,* with one foot, as it were, in the present age and one foot in the future age."[13] We will explore below the "present" and "future" dimensions of repentance in relation to eschatology.

Present Repentance and Eschatology

From the very beginning, the Essenes were conscious of living in the אחרית הימים.[14] The community's aim to realize the biblical demand for eschatological repentance (see Deut. 4:25-31; 30:1-10; Jer. 31:17-19, 30-33; Ezek. 36:24-28) that was expected in the אחרית הימים is expressed in 4QMMT C 13-22.[15]

---

13. Schiffman speaks of the "immediacy of the eschaton." Schiffman, *Eschatological Community*, 7.

14. A. Steudel, "אחרית הימים in the Texts from Qumran," *RevQ* 16 (1993): 225–46 (241). Her definition of the phrase is helpful: "אחרית הימים does not mean the time of salvation, it also does not mean a 'punctual end' of history, nor does it mean 'future.' Rather, what is meant by the term אחרית הימים is a limited period of time, that is the last of a series of divinely pre-planned periods into which history is divided. This last period of time directly before the time of salvation covers aspects of the past, as well as aspects of the present time and of the future" (231). See also Steudel, *Der Midrasch zur Eschatologie aur der Qumrangemeinde (4QmidrEschat a and b)* (Leiden: Brill, 1994), 163.

15. Text: E. Qimron and J. Strugnell, "MMT," in *Qumran Cave 4. V. Miqsat Ma'ase Ha-Torah,* DJD 10 (Oxford: Clarendon, 1994); reconstruction and translation of line 21b–22a is based on F. García Martínez, "4QMMT in a Qumran Context," in *Reading 4QMMT: New Perspectives on Qumran Law and History* (Atlanta: Scholars Press, 1996), 15–27 (18–19).

והיא כי 13

14 [יבו]א עליך [כול הדברים] האלה באחרי[ת] הימים הרכה

15 [וה]קללא [והשיבות]ה אל ל[בב]ך ושבתה אלו בכל לבבך

16 [ובכו]ל נפש]ך   באחרי[ת   [ ] [ ]וח[

17 [כתוב בספר מושה ובספרי הנביאים שיבואו   של]

18 [הבר]כו]ת ש[בא]ו[ו ב] [ ] [בימי שלומוה בן דויד ואף הקללות

19 [ש]באוו בי[מי יר]ובעם בן נבט ועד גל[ו]ת ירושלם וצדקיה מלך

יהוד[ה]

20 [ש]יב]י[אם ב]   [ואנחנו מכירים שבאו מקצת הדברכות

והקללות

21 שכתוב בס[פר מו]שה וזה הוא אחרית הימים שישובו בישר[אל]

22 לת[ורה   [ ] ולוא ישובו אחו[ר   [

13. and it shall come to pass, when

14. [all] these [things be]fall you" at the en[d] of days, the blessings

15. [and the] curses, "[then you will take] it to hea[rt] and you will return to him with all your heart

16. [and with a]ll [your] soul," [at the en]d [of time, so that you may live]

17. [it is written in the book of] Moses [and in the books of the prophets] that there will come . . .

18. [the bl]essi[ngs that] have (already) befal[len] . . .] in the days of Solomon the son of David. And the curses

19. [that] have (already) befall[en] from the d[ays of Jer]oboam the son of Nebat and up to the time when Jerusalem and Zedekiah King of Juda[h went into cap]tivity[16]

20. [that] he will brin[g] them [. . .]. And we know that some of the blessings and the curses have (already) been fulfilled,

21. as it is written in the bo[ok of Mo]ses. And this is the end of days when they will return to Isra[el]

22. To the l[aw . . .] and not depar[t from] . . .

First of all, our text begins with a citation from Deut. 30:1-2 (C 13-16),[17] which speaks of an eschatological return to God. This

---

16. Collins mentions that this refers to the blessings experienced under David and Solomon and the "curses" experienced from the time of Jeroboam to the Babylonian exile. Thus the "fulfillment" referred to in the text is not itself part of the end days. Collins, "The Expectation of the End in the Dead Sea Scrolls" in *Eschatology, Messianism, and the Dead Sea Scrolls*, 74–90 (80).

thereby provides the context in which C 21 is to be understood—for the community, the current period was indeed the end time: "and this is the end of days" (וזה הוא אחרית הימים). Second, the events predicted to occur in the end of days were already beginning to unfold. This is emphasized in lines 20b and 21: "And we know that some of the blessings and the curses have (already) been fulfilled, as it is written in the bo[ok of Mo]ses" (ואנחנו מכירים שבאו מקצת הדברכות והקללות שכתוב בס[פר מו]שה). Third, in such a situation, the only appropriate response is repentance: "when they will return in Israel to the law" (ישובו בישראל לתורה). The translation of the *editio princeps* ("when they will return to Israel forever") does not make sense. Rather, as F. García Martínez observes, although sometimes prepositions can be interchanged (here, from ב to ל, as implied in E. Qimron's translation: "to Israel"), the locative use "seems unjustified due to the use of the *lamed* again in the same sentence."[18] Consequently, the reconstruction of לתורה ("to the law") rather than לתמיד ("forever") is more plausible. This finds support in other occurrences "turning to the law" (4Q171 fr. 1–2, 2:2–3; 1QS 5:8; CD 15:9, 12; 16:1, 4). Thus he translates: "when they return *in* Israel to the Law." We can validate this reading when we consider the penitential overtones conveyed by the imagery of "returning to the law." Thus, for the community, the אחרית הימים was the time of spiritual return when those in Israel eventually return to the law.[19] This is in keeping with the preceding (spiritual) use of

---

17. In speaking of this transference of the phrase אחרית הימים from Deut. 31:29 into Deut. 30:1, G. Brooke comments that this particular phrase "seems to operate with some fluidity in scriptural quotations." He points out that it is added to a quotation of Deut. 25:19 in 4Q252 4:2; in Greek, it is added to Joel 2:28-32 when cited in Acts 2:17-21. G. Brooke, "The Explicit Presentation of Scripture in 4QMMT," in *Legal Texts and Legal Issues*, ed. M. Bernstein, F. García Martínez, and J. Kampen (Leiden: Brill, 1997), 69–88 (77).
18. García Martínez, "4QMMT in a Qumran Context," 18.
19. See Eisenman and Wise's translation: "when (those) in Isra[e]l are to return to the La[w of God."]. R. Eisenman and M. Wise, *The Dead Sea Scrolls Uncovered* (Shaftesbury: Elements 1992), 199–200.

the verb שוב in C 15. Although שוב in C 22, "they will not depart"
(ולוא ישובו אחור), does not have an explicitly spiritual meaning, it
is best understood in the light of the (spiritual) שוב of the preceding
line, once they return/repent, they will not turn away. Fourth, line
20 states that up to now, only some blessings have been realized:
"And we know that some of the blessings … have (already) been
fulfilled" (ואנחנו מכירים שבאו מקצת הדברכות), thereby implying
that such a repentance (as expressed in C 21) would realize the
promised blessings in totality. F. Watson says of this text:

> The passages from Deuteronomy enable the author to present the
> postexilic present as a moment of unique opportunity, offering the
> possibility of a definitive turning away from a past dominated by
> disobedience and the consequent reality of the divine curse. The
> addressee finds himself in a position of immense privilege and
> responsibility; his reaction to the letter will determine whether or not he
> is to play a leading role in Israel's final turning back to God.[20]

Watson's description of "the post-exilic present as a moment of
unique opportunity" is helpful. It confirms the importance of present
action (repentance) for the future ("Israel's final turning back to
God"). The responsibility on the part of the recipients is expressed
thus in 4QMMT C26-30:

26 ואף אנחנו כתבנו אליך
27 מקצת מעשי התורה שחשבנו לטוב לך ולעמך שר[א]ינו
28 עמך ערמה ומעד תורה הבן בכל אלה ובקש מלפנו שיתקן
29 את עצתך והרחיק ממך מחשבת רעה ועצת בליעל
30 בשל שתשמח באחרית העת במצאך מקצת דברינו כן

26.　　　　　　　　　　We have indeed written you
　27. some precepts of the Torah according to our decision, for your
welfare and the welfare of your people. For we have see (that)

---

20. F. Watson, "Constructing an Antithesis: Pauline and other Perspectives on Divine and human
Agency," in *Divine and Human Agency*, 99–116 (105).

28. You have wisdom and knowledge of the Torah. Consider all these things and ask him that he strengthen

29. your will and remove from you the plans of evil and the devices of Belial

30. so that you may rejoice at the end of time, finding that some of our practices are correct.

Thus, in the context of repentance, the *awaited* repentance (C 28b-29) of those outside the sending group (in the future) is a reflection of the *attained* repentance of a core group (in the present). Thus repentance in the present has been instrumental in heralding a part of the promised blessings.

Because the community believed that the eschatological age had already partially begun to irrupt, they saw the present as a time of preparation: "Their life was dedicated to preparing for that new age by living as if it had already come."[21] A text that expresses this idea is 4Q215a. It speaks of the present as the period of wickedness, then speaks of a future "time of righteousness."[22] In 4Q215a fr. 1, 3b-4a,[23] the present era of wickedness is contrasted with the coming era of peace in which there will be a transformation of humanity according to God's will. Further, an elect group has a key role at the culmination of the present age.[24]

---

21. Schiffman, *Eschatological Community*, 7. Similarly, J. Carmignac speaks of the constancy of the community's faithfulness: "soit pendant la pé riode de l'impiéte, soit pendant la période de la justice, les fils du Sadoq resterant toujours fid èles à Dieu." J. Carmignac, "La notion d'eschatologie dans la bible et à Qumrân," *RevQ* 7 (1969): 17–31 (26).

22. E. Chazon and M. Stone in their *editio princeps* say that the language of 4Q215a creates "a strong sense of 'heightened eschatology.'" E. Chazon and M. Stone, "Time of Righteous," in *Qumran Cave 4. XXVI*, ed. S. Pfann, et al., DJD 36 (Oxford: Clarendon, 2000), 174. However, they also note that the eschatological expectations of this composition share many themes with biblical end-of-days' prophecies and with extrabiblical eschatological predictions.

23. Text: Chazon and Stone, "Time of Righteousness."

24. T. Elgvin, "The Eschatological Hope of 4Qtime of Righteousness," *Wisdom and Apocalypticism in the Dead Sea Scrolls and in the Biblical Tradition*, ed. F. García Martínez (Leuven: Leuven University Press, 2003), 94.

ויצרופו בם לבחירי צדק וימח כול פשעם 3

4 בעבור חס[ד]יו כיא שלם קצהרשע[25] וכול עורלה ת[עבו]ר [כיא]

5 באה עת הצדק

3.   And they shall refine by them the elect of righteousness, and all their sins

4. will be obliterated on account of His mer[c]ies. For the period of wickedness is complete, and all unrighteousness shall [pass awa]y [For]

5. the time of righteousness is coming.

The text continues to speak of the advent of an age of peace (fr. 1, 6) and the dominion of goodness (fr. 1, 10).[26] T. Elgvin comments: "Through the trials an elect group is being refined and emerges as God's בחירי צדק."[27] That these refining afflictions are related to repentance can be deduced from the opening lines (4Q215a fr. 1, 2:2). Though fragmentary and lacking in verbs, what remains is significant.

2 [   ] [י]א לב אדם ו[ ] עולה [ ] ב[ ] [כור] עוני[י

2. [ ] human heart [ ] unrighteousness [ ] furnace [of afflic]tion.

Given the poor state of this line's preservation, we may tentatively assume that the object of refining alluded to in line 3 (בם יצרופו) is the human heart (לב אדם) since deceit (עלוה) will be purged from it. This assumption (of suggesting לב as the object of יצרופו) is based

---

25. קץ הרשע is written as one word (קצהרשע).

26. Chazon says, "The 'time of righteousness' is an era of religious perfection, social harmony, and wellbeing. It is characterized by the absence of all unrighteousness, a diffusion of knowledge on earth, and universal recognition and worship of God." E. Chazon, "A Case of Mistaken Identity: *Testament of Naphtali* (4Q215) and *Time of Righteousness* (4Q215a)," in *The Provo International Conference on the Dead Sea Scrolls: Technical Innovations, New Texts, and Reformulated Issues*, ed. D. Parry and E. Ulrich (Leiden: Brill, 1999), 110–23.

27. Elgvin, "Eschatological Hope," 92. This phrase בחירי צדק is conceptually similar to the phrase די[ונ צדק (4Q403 fr. 1, 16, 25, 27). Chazon cautions that while the community's "elect of righteousness" saw themselves as being tested and purified (1QS 1:18; 1QH 2:13; 5:16), "the refining of the righteous is by no means a strictly Qumranic concept, as can readily be seen from such biblical and apocryphal texts such as Ps 66:10-1; Isa 48:10; Zech 13:9; Dan 11:21-12:10; *Judith* 8:25-27; *Sir.* 2:1-6 and 33:1)." Chazon, "A Case of Mistaken Identity," 118.

on a conceptually similar idea expressed in 4Q416 fr. 3, 3:13b, which contains the exhortation: "refine your heart" (צרוף לבכה). Further, this idea is entirely consistent with other imagery concerning the heart that metaphorically alludes to repentance, such as circumcision of the heart and humbling the heart. This line of thought is taken up again in 4Q215a fr. 1, 12, where the group is described in the following terms:[28]

אנ[שי ענוה]   נבחנו במחש[ב]ת קדוש[ו 12

12. Tested by [His] holy pl[a]n are [the elect of truth,] the men of humility.

If the end result of the refinement of the heart (through repentance) is the creation of the elect of righteousness (בחירי צדק), these men are the "men of humility" (אנשי ענוה)—those who humbled their heart through repentance by submitting to the refining afflictions during the period of wickedness. The phrase "his holy plan" (במחשבת קדושו) could refer to God's eschatological plan, hidden from men in general but revealed to the elect.[29] Thus, on the threshold of the time of righteousness and age of peace, the hearts of a group of men are made penitent, refined by afflictions. This enables them to become the elect of righteousness, the nucleus of renewed humanity.[30] Repentance, spoken of here in the language of refinement (of the heart), is instrumental in securing the appropriate state of righteousness for the age to come.[31]

28. Text: Elgvin, "Eschatological Hope."
29. Ibid. This is based on a related text, 4QMysteries, where מחשבה is paralleled by רז: "He decides] every mystery and preordains every plan" (4Q299 3:11), 93.
30. Schiffman says that "the resulting eschatological community would reflect the perfection of the present community at Qumran." Schiffman, *Reclaiming the Dead Sea Scrolls*, 329.
31. 4Q285 too speaks of the age to come and deals with some of the actions that should be taken "at the time when wickedness will be defeated." One of these actions is (future) repentance. B. Nitzan, "Benedictions and Instructions for the Eschatological Community," *RevQ* 16 (1993): 77–90. Regarding the reconstruction of line 7: עון בי[, Nitzan suggests the following

To sum up, 4Q215a provides further evidence where repentance in the present has bearings on the promised blessings of the eschatological age.

Future Repentance and Eschatology

While the two texts above described how repentance in the present affected the future age, there are texts that focus purely on a future repentance. Although I have used two texts from the *Temple Scroll*, I acknowledge that several scholars do not see this scroll as an eschatological work, and rightly so.[32] However, I have included the following texts form 11Q19 in this section because they represent an eschatological scenario within the literary context of Israel's action following the exile.[33]

The first part of column 59 describes the curses of a disobedient people. Israel has become idolatrous (59:3) and undergo suffering,

---

reconstruction: שׁ[בי עון] (or עו[ז]בי עון). It would then read: "those who repented of sin (שׁ[בי עון]) will return (ושׁובו)." When line 2 is read alongside the restored line 7, those who had been excluded "from the midst of the congregation" (line 2) will be "repenters of sin and will return." P. S. Alexander confirms that the fragment "certainly closes with a note of repentance. Perhaps the repentance is that of the sons of light who, though not so wicked as to be classified as sons of darkness, have nevertheless done wrong, and must be punished and must repent." P. S. Alexander, "A Reconstruction and Reading of 4Q285," *RevQ* 75 (2000): 333–48 (346).

32. G. Brooke challenges: "Is the scroll . . . a blueprint for a future Temple, and for an Israel to be reconstituted? Or is it a vision of how things *should have been*?" *The Complete World of the Dead Sea Scrolls*, 160. S. White Crawford says: "The Temple Scroll presents and ideal plan, but one meant to be undertaken by humans in historical time; it is not eschatological." S. White Crawford, *The Temple Scroll and Related Texts* (Sheffield: Sheffield Academic, 2000), 28. M. Wise, however, accentuates what he believes to be the eschatological significance of this document when he says that it was "intended as an eschatological law for the land, a new Deut[eronomy]." M. Wise, *A Critical Study of the Temple Scroll from Qumran Cave 11* (Chicago: Oriental Institute of the University of Chicago, 1990), 200.

33. In using this document, we must be aware that our repentance texts are basically restatements of the biblical conception of eschatological repentance. Further, we will do well to keep Stegemann's caution in mind: he stresses that nobody cited it as an authority and its existence is not mentioned in any of the works written at Qumran. Because of this, he cautions that "there is nothing concrete to indicate how members of the group took some profit from it, or to show how they valued it. We can only speculate on these topics." H. Stegemann, "The Literary Composition of the Temple Scroll and Its Status at Qumran," in *Temple Scroll Studies*, ed. G. Brooke, JSPSup 7 (Sheffield: JSOT Press, 1989), 123–48 (143–44).

desolation (59:2, 4-5), and rejection by God. 11Q19 59:6b-7 therefore says:

6   וקראו ולוא אשמע וזעקו ולוא אענה

7 אותמה מפני רוע מעלליהמה

6.   [and] they shall call but I shall not listen, they shall shout and I shall not reply

7. to them because of the evil of their deeds.

This "calling" (קרא) and "shouting" (זעק) carries overtones of repentance. At first glance, this text implies that because of their wickedness, unfaithfulness to the covenant and rejection of law (59:8b-9a), there is no mercy, thereby precluding the possibility for repentance. However, 59:9b-10a suggests that after a while, possibly when *genuine* repentance takes place, there is hope and salvation for those same people:

9   אחר ישובו

10 אלי בכול לבבמה ובכול נפשמה ככול דברי התורה

9.   afterward they shall return

10. to me with all their heart and with all their soul in agreement with all the words of this law.

In line 9, "afterward" (אחר) is a pivotal word since it signifies a later period in which repentance (וישובו) took place on the part of the ones referred to in 59:6-7 (whose cries are not heard). Therefore, אחר belies a different attitude (a genuinely penitent one). Rather than merely crying out to God for help and salvation in a time of need and as an act of desperation (11Q19 59:6-7), they now *wholeheartedly* feel the need to turn to him: "with all their heart and with all their soul" (בכול לבבמה ובכול נפשמה). Thus in 11Q19 59:9b, they consciously repent rather than repent as a last resort. The message is clear: repentance brings blessings.[34] Because of this repentance, God saves and redeems them (59:11).

Another text that alludes to a future repentance is 1QSa 1:1-3.[35] In fact, the present and the future appear to be harmonized.

1 וזה הסרך לכול עדת ישראל באחרית הימים בהספ[ם ליחד להתה]לך

2 על פי משפט בני צדוק הכוהנים ואנושי בריתם אשר ס]רו מלכת בד]רך

3 העם המה אנושי עצתו אשר שמרו בריתו בתוך רשעה לכ [פר בעד האר]ץ

1. And this is the rule for all of the congregation of Israel in the end of days: When they assem[ble as a community to wa]lk

2. according to the regulation of the Sons of Zadok, the priests, and the men of their covenant who have [turned away from walking in the w]ay

3. of the people. These are the men of his counsel who have kept their covenant with him amid the evil to a[tone for the lan]d.

The extent of the application of this composition is set forth in the opening lines: "And this is the rule for all of the congregation of Israel" (וזה הסרך לכול עדת ישראל). It has a temporal dimension to it in which a yet unfulfilled period is envisaged: "in the end of days" (באחרית הימים). In this future period, the present leaders of the community, namely, the Zadokite priests, will continue to lead this eschatological community. The distinguishing mark of these priests and the men of their covenant is the fact that they have repented from evil (ס]רו מלכת בד[רך העם). D. Green comments that "'walking in the way of the people' as per a sectarian mindset was identical to 'walking in the way of wickedness' (1QS 5:10; CD 8:9)."[36] The

---

34. This latter aspect is based on texts such as 5:15b; Deut. 4:29b; 30:2b; Hos. 3:5a. Wise, *A Critical Study*, 230.
35. Text: Schiffman, *Eschatological Community*.
36. D. Green, "Halakah at Qumran: The Use of the √ הלך in the Dead Sea Scrolls," *RevQ* 86 (2005): 235–69 (247).

phrase "walking in the way of the people" seems to be the opposite of "walking in the way of God."[37]

Since the following discussion is based on a restored lacuna (ס[רו מלכת בד]רך) we need to establish that this reconstruction is tenable. The text is damaged just following the ד. In the piece that fits in after the tear, we are able to discern the ר and ך of דרך. This restoration is generally widely accepted by most scholars. Lohse has: "die sich abgewend[t haben vom Wandel auf] dem Weg";[38] Vermes: "who have turned aside from the way of";[39] Knibb: "who have turn[ed aside from walking in] the way";[40] Charlesworth: "who have tu[rned away from walking in the] way";[41] García Martínez and Tigchelaar: "who have turn[ed away from the] path of";[42] Hence, this restoration enjoys scholarly consensus. The basis for it is found in other texts that allude to the same idea of "turning from the way (of the people)."[43]

To return to our text, Schiffman observes that "the Zadokites and the members of the sect are seen as having foresworn the improper conduct of the rest of the people."[44] This group is further described thus: "these are the men of his counsel who have kept their covenant with him amid the evil" (המה אנושי עצתו אשר שמרו בריתו בתוך רשעה). The sentence begins with "these" (המה), suggesting that it is the same group in focus (the priests and those with them). This core group is a penitential group, men who have repented—"they have turned" (סרו)—and who have stayed penitent. This is seen in their

---

37. Green, "Halakah at Qumran," 247.
38. E. Lohse, *Die Texte aus Qumran. Hebräisch und Deutsch* (Munich: Kasel, 1971), 47.
39. G. Vermes, *The Dead Sea Scrolls in English*, rev. ed. (London: Penguin, 2004), 100.
40. Knibb, *The Qumran Community*, 146.
41. Charlesworth, *The Dead Sea Scrolls: Hebrew, Aramaic And Greek Texts with English Translations*, 111.
42. *DSSSE* 101.
43. CD 8:4-5a; 19:2a; 11Q13 2:24; 4Q174 1:14, 15. These examples are terminologically and conceptually similar in their use of סור (alluding to repentance), and their references to דרך העם preceded by the preposition מ- (alluding to the object from which one turns) further add plausibility to the restoration of 1QSa 1:3.
44. Schiffman, *Eschatological Community*, 12.

ability to remain faithful to the covenant, thereby remaining "turned" from evil.

This group of penitents will have a tremendous impact on the rest of Israel in the end of days, namely, in bringing about a transformation of Israel. "The entire community of Israel is to be identical with the sect in the end of days."[45] The way in which this transition and expansion from a small group into the whole of Israel occurs is noteworthy: the future (large) group referred to in line 1:"for all the congregation of Israel" (לכול עדת ישראל) is in fact a reflection of the core group of priests whose repentance in the present is described thus in line 2b: "[those who] turned away from walking in the way of the people" (סרו מלכת בדרך העם). Further, העם are those from whose ways the community turned away through repentance. If they (העם) are to eventually be described in line 1 as "all the congregation of Israel in the end of days" (כול עדת ישראל באחהרית הימים), that is, in the future, and incorporated into the community, nothing short of complete repentance on the part of this group (העם) will bring this about, since it was repentance that put the core group in their privileged position in the first place. This expanded community in the end of days (consisting of all Israel) is constituted primarily through repentance. Schiffman comments, "As the sect finally overcomes its enemies and is seen to be victorious, the righteous of Israel who turn to God and adopt the sectarian way of life will also be included in the sect."[46] E. P. Sanders observes that the community always held open the possibility of repentance to their fellow Israelites: "The community believed that eschatological Israel would be formed by the conversion of the rest of Israel to the way of the sect."[47] Neither Schiffman's nor Sanders's

45. Ibid. See also CD 4:2b–4: "The priests are the penitents of Israel [שבי ישראל] who left the land of Judah. . . . And the sons of Zadok [בני צדוק] are the chosen of Israel, the men of renown, who stand to serve at the end of days [אחרית הימים]."
46. Schiffman, *Eschatological Community*, 68.

remarks are entirely accurate. Schiffman subtly qualifies the extent of those who can repent when he speaks of "the *righteous* of Israel who *turn to God*" (emphasis added). This is most likely due to the fact that there are very few texts apart from 1QSa 1:1 that speak of the repentance of *all* Israel (CD 15:5; 16:1), hence his attempt to qualify "all Israel." Schiffman's above qualification of "Israel" is significant since it implicitly acknowledges the absence of this idea of the repentance of all Israel. Further, the lack of attestation of this concept in other scrolls allows us to conclude that it represented a very early theological position of the community that was later abandoned. This view would then refute Sanders's premise of the community "always holding open" the possibility for repentance. In all probability, this may have been a temporarily held view, or at the most, a minority position. To return to our texts, it speaks of the future repentance of all Israel, at the same time that (future) repentance cannot be separated from the present repentance of a core group of Zadokite priests.

To summarize, there are texts that speak of the bearing that repentance in the present has on the future age. Thus the way of life recommended for the members of the community was considered a "way of repentance."[48] There are also those texts that speak of a future repentance. While the former category of repentance pertains to a small group, the latter is indicative of the repentance of all Israel. (However, this motif does not receive much attention in the scrolls.)

Eschatology and Penitential Interpretations of Scripture

If the community's eschatological worldview was shaped by their understanding of the biblical text, then it is reasonable to assume

---

47. Sanders, *Paul and Palestinian Judaism*, 247.
48. Nitzan, "Repentance in the Dead Sea Scrolls," 146. The eschatological community would be structured as a reflection of the present community. Schiffman, *Eschatological Community*, 68.

that at least some of the pesharim would provide evidence for this. The eschatological emphasis of the pesharim demonstrates that the members of the community perceived that the end was close at hand and the significance of the biblical prophets for the אחרית הימים was never given up by them.[49]

Our discussion of the following texts intends to show that one of the ways the Bible was read at Qumran was to emphasize the importance of repentance specifically within an eschatological context. Despite the presence of a sort of agenda, we would do well to keep in mind G. Brooke's caution that the scribes of the Second Temple period "implicitly respected the plain meaning of the authoritative texts, with which they were dealing."[50]

4Q171 2:2-4

This text has enough allusions to the future era of righteousness to discern its basic eschatological context.[51] These include the references to the time when "there will not be found on earth any [wi]cked man" (2:7), or the promise concerning the penitents of the desert: "and to them [the penitents of the desert] will be all Man's inheritance, and to their seed forever" (3:1b-2a). There are also present in 4Q171 adequate references to the present as a time of testing and the future as a time of righteous blessing and deliverance for us to discern the eschatological overtones of this text.[52] Our

---

49. Steudel, "אחרית הימים," 242. In many instances, the actual pesher concerning the phrase אחרית הימים is too fragmentary or nonexistent to discern any context (e.g., 4Q163 fr. 23, 2:19 or 4Q164 fr. 1, 7).

50. As opposed to the assumption that biblical interpretation at Qumran was primarily or exclusively concerned with the atomistic interpretation of the prophets such as unfilled blessings and curses. G. Brooke, "Reading the Plain Meaning of Scripture in the Dead Sea Scrolls," in *Jewish Ways of Reading the Bible*, ed. G. Brooke, JSSSup 11 (Oxford: Oxford University Press, 2000), 67–90 (70).

51. Text: J. Allegro, ed., *Qumran Cave 4.1*, DJD 5 (Oxford: Clarendon, 1966).

52. These eschatological references justify our inclusion of 4Q171 in the present chapter.

immediate concern, however, is with what this scroll says about repentance within this eschatological context.

In column 2, the commentary on the text of Psalm 37 begins with the following citation of Ps. 37:8-9: "Curb anger and control temper and do not get irritated—it only leads to evil. For those doing evil will be cut off." The interpretation follows:

2   פשרו על כול <u>השבים</u>

3 לתורה אשר לוא ימאנו <u>לשוב</u> מרעתם כוא כול הממרים

4   <u>לשוב</u> מעונם יכרתו

    2.   Its interpretation concerns all who turn back

    3. to the law, who do not refuse to repent from their wickedness, for all those who rebel

    4. from repenting of their iniquity will be cut off.

In the above text, the verb שוב occurs three times (underlined for emphasis), each time alluding to repentance, though in different ways. The first occurrence concerns "all the returners to the law" (כול השבים לתורה). This group of people is further described by the second occurrence of שוב as those "who do not refuse to repent from their wickedness" (לוא ימאנו לשוב מרעתם). This sentence is an elaborate way of speaking about those who *do repent*. Their repentance was associated with their return to the law. Further evidence for this may be derived from 1QS, where the most basic criterion to join the community is to "keep oneself at a distance from all evil" (1QS 1:4b) since in doing so one is able to "return to the law of Moses" (1QS 5:8).[53] Thus returning to the law in 4Q171, 2:2-3 is definitely related to repentance. Also, the subject of the relative clause in line 3: "who do not refuse to repent" (אשר לוא ימאנו לשוב) is clearly "all who turn back" (כול השבים) of line 2. This

---

53. See the discussion in chapter 3 where "separating" and "turning away" from evil are accompanied by "turning to" the law. The latter then is manifestation of the former.

verbal similarity (לשוב and השבים) emphasizes that lines 2 and 3 are focusing on the same penitential group. The third occurrence of שוב which is in line 3b-4a indicates the fate of those who do not return to the law and who do not repent: "those who rebel to turn from their iniquity" (כול הממרים לשוב מעונם): "they will be cut off" (יכרתו).

There is an interesting contrast of ideas and concepts. In line 2b-3a, "the returners to the law" (השבים לתורה), alluding to those who repent, are contrasted in line 3b with "the resisters to turn" (הממרים לשוב), alluding to those who do not repent. While the first two uses of שוב are used to speak of repentance, the third use refers to a lack of repentance.[54] Thus we may conclude that repentance is crucial to the overall eschatological theme in this pesher.[55]

4Q174 1:14-17

The eschatological emphasis of 4Q174[56] hardly needs to be established since this dimension has been the subject of intense study.[57] Our concern with this text is confined to the first part of the second unit (4Q174 1:14-17).[58]

---

54. Possibly alluding to those who had the opportunity to repent but did not, as in the case of those who "return to the law" but insincerely; cf. 1QS 3:1.

55. To the above-mentioned references to repentance in 4Q171 can be added the occurrence of the epithet "penitents of the desert" (שבי המדבר) in 4Q171 3:1 and "penitents of Israel" (שבי ישראל) in 4Q171 4:34. Fr. 11 refers to those "who turn [לשוב] together to the law."

56. Text: Allegro, *Qumran Cave 4*, 5.

57. See particularly Steudel, *Der Midrasch zur Eschatologie*; and G. Brooke, *Exegesis at Qumran: 4QFlorelegium in Its Jewish Context*, JSOTSup 29 (Sheffield: JSOT Press, 1985). We see here a frequent recurrence of the phrase אחרית הימים. G. Brooke speaks of the "sense of futurity" in this phrase while at the same time "embracing something of the eschatological and historical self-understanding of the community." Brooke, *Exegesis at Qumran*, 176.

58. Brooke observes that the start of the second unit is "defined by the paragraphing of the manuscript, by formulary introduction and by the change in content of the scriptural citations from 2 Samuel 7 to Psalm 1." Brooke, *Exegesis at Qumran*, 144. He also points out that although Psalms 1 and 2 were known as belonging together, they were considered at Qumran as two distinct parts of a whole." Ibid., 147.

14 מדרש מאשרי האיש אשר לוא הלך בעצת רשעים פשר
הדב]ר ...[סרי מדרך
15 אשר כתוב בספר ישעיה הנביא לאחרית [ה]ימים ויהי כחזקת
[היד ויסירנו מלכת בדרך]
16 העם הזה והמה אשר כתוב עליהמה בספר יחזקאל הנביא אשר
לו]א יטטאו עוד]
17 [בג]ל[ו]ליהמה המה בני צדוק וא[נ]שי עצת[מ]ה רו]...[י
אחריהמה לעצת היחד

14. Midrash of "Happy is the man that does not walk in the counsel of the wicked." The interpretation of this pass[age . . .] those who turn aside from the way of [. . .]

15. As it is written in the book of Isaiah the prophet concerning the last days, "And it was with a strong [hand that he turned me aside from walking in the way of]

16. this people. And they are the ones of whom it was written in the book of Ezekiel the prophet, ["They shall] no[t defile themselves any more

17. with] their [i]d[o]ls"—they are the sons of Zadok and the m[e]n of the[ir] counsel, [. . .] after them to the counsel of the community.

The use of Psalm 1 as part of this "eschatological midrash" is significant when one considers its emphasis on repentance. In line 14, regarding "the man who does not walk in the counsel of the wicked," the commentary runs as follows: "the interpretation of this wor[d...] those who turn aside from the way" (פשר ... הדב]ר [סרי מדרך). That "those who turn aside from the way" refers to a group that have repented is obvious from the context. However, the text is damaged at the point that describes the object from which one turns, so we need to consider the various possible reconstructions. While the *editio princeps* has רשעים, Brooke's reading of חטאים is more logical since it is in keeping with Psalm 1.[59] This interpretation is followed by more scriptural citations that further emphasize the

59. Brooke argues: "If the first lines of the psalms are quoted with the intention that the rest of them is to be understood, then the restoration would be better as חטאים from Ps 1:2, used there in a phrase with דרך." Ibid., 115.

initial focus on those who have repented and turned away from the path of the wicked. The argument follows on from Ps. 1:1 because immediately following the פשר of this verse is this text from Isa. 8:11, which displays conceptual and verbal similarity to the pesher in line 14. The introductory formula referring to Isaiah's prophecy "concerning the last days" (לאחרית הימים) is significant since this provides an eschatological setting for the citation that follows in lines 15c-16a: "And it was with a strong [hand that he turned me aside from walking on the way of this people" (ויהי כחזקת [היד ויסירנו מלכת בדרך] העם הזה). The citation is introduced by the phrase "as it is written" (אשר כתוב). Here, אשר refers back to line 14, the interpretation of Ps. 1:1. Thus verbal and conceptual similarity expressed through the use of the verb סור in line 15 becomes the main point of contact between the Isaiah text and the Psalms citation.[60] Instead of a *qal* imperfect third person singular first person singular suffix: ויסרני ("and he turned me aside"), Brooke's reading of a *hip'il* imperfect third person singular first person plural suffix: ויסירנו ("and he will cause us to turn away") is preferable based on 1QIsaᵃ. Further, the first person plural suffix "gives greater sense to the plural identification in the *pesher* that follows."[61] Although by itself Isa. 8:11 alludes to repentance, the introductory formula added to this text (לאחרית הימים) is suggestive of a conscious attempt to link repentance and eschatology.

The idea of this eschatological repentance is furthered with the help of a partial citation from Ezekiel (44:10), which is introduced in the following way in line 16: "and they are (those of) whom it is was written concerning them" (הזה והמה אשר כתוב עליהמה). Isaiah 8:11 is linked to the Ezekiel text by הזה והמה. This connecting

---

60. Specifically seen in the conceptual parallel with "turners from the way" (סרי מדרך) in Ps. 1:1, and "and he will turn me from walking in the way of . . ." (ויסרני מלכת בדרך) in Isa. 8:11. Terminological similarity is underlined.

61. Ibid., 116.

device encompasses even more since it would now include Ps 1:1. and its interpretation together with Isa. 8:11. Thus המה of Ezek. 44:10 refers right back to the סרי הדרך or penitents. Of these it is said in lines 16c-17a: "They should not defile themselves anymore with their idols" (לו]א יטטאו עוד] בג]ל[ו]ליהמה). The final interpretation in line 17 throws some light on the identity of the group in question: "They are the sons of Zadok and the men of their counsel, [. . .] after them to the counsel of the community" (המה בני צדוק וא]נ[שי עצת[מ]ה רו[...]י אחריהמה לעצת היחד). Regarding the lacuna in line 17, (י[...]רו), Brooke reads the second letter as ח instead of ו. Further, based on the final letter י, he takes it to be a participle. Since the first two letters are ר and ח he arrives at רחק (hence רחקי).[62] Thus he says, "In partial fulfilment of 1QS 1:4 the Sons of Zadok and the men of their counsel have kept far from all evil."[63] Further, this reference to the בני צדוק is climactic. Apart from marking the end of the midrash on Psalm 1, it also draws to a conclusion all that has been said about repentance: there is a thread that holds together סרי הדרך (line 14/Ps. 1:1), יסירנו (line 15/ Isa. 8:11), המה (line 16a/introduction formula to citation) אשר לו]א יטטאו (line 16b/Ezek. 44:10) and finally המה (line 17), which now refers to בני צדוק. The penitents are therefore described thus: "they are the sons of Zadok and the m[e]n of the[ir] counsel" (בני צדוק וא]נ[שי עצת[מ]ה). Hence, after setting an eschatological context for the biblical texts cited, this part of the midrash speaks of the repentance of a specific group, described as the sons of Zadok, who separated from evil and whom God turned aside from the way of the people.

---

62. We saw in ch. 4 that רחק is often used to speak to speak of repentance as a "separation" from evil. See the introductory injunction in 1QS 1:4a: לרחוק מכול רע.

63. Brooke, *Exegesis at Qumran*, 119.

11Q13 2:2-6

11Q13 introduces to us another dimension of repentance within an eschatological context,[64] namely, repentance mediated through a divine agent. Further, this document provides us with interesting information concerning the eschatology of the Qumran community.[65] Our concern with the heavenly figure of Melchizedek is his salvific role at the end of days, particularly in the area of repentance. Column 2 opens with a focus on the festival of Jubilee, citing the injunction in Lev. 25:13 to "return" to one's property and family (11Q13 2:2). This is then coupled with Deut. 15:2, which speaks about "remission of debts" (11Q13 2:3). Both these texts from the Hebrew Scriptures allude to material and financial issues since in the Leviticus text the "return" is to one's property and in the Deuteronomy text, the "remission" pertains to monetary issues. It is significant that our text takes these material/monetary concepts and transfers into them a spiritual content in its interpretation. Here is the relevant text from 11Q13 2:4-6:

4 פשרו לא[חרית הימים על השבויים אשר [היו מתאבלים כול יומי ממשלת בליעל] אשר

5 הכריתמה מן בני השמ[י]ם ומנחלת מלכי צדק כ]   [והמה בני גורל מלכי צדק אשר

6 ישיבבמה אליהמה וקרא להמה דרור לעזוב להמה [משא] כול עוונותיהמה

4. [The interpretation of it for the e]nd of days concerns the captives who [were in mourning all the days of the dominion of Belial][66] who

---

64. Text: F. García Martínez, E. Tigchelaar, and A. van der Woude, eds., "11QMelchizedek," in *Qumran Cave 11. II. (11Q2–18, 11Q20–31)*, DJD 23 (Oxford: Clarendon, 1998).

65. M. de Jonge and A. S. van der Woude, "11QMelchizedek and the New Testament," *NTS* 12 (1965): 301–26 (304).

66. Kobleski's reading of line 4 as mentioning the "captivity of Belial" is consistent with the references to Belial in 2:13, 22, and 25. P. J. Kobelski, *Melchizedek and Mechireša'*, CBQMS 10 (Washington, DC: Catholic Biblical Association of America, 1981).

5. cut them off from the sons of heav[e]n[67] and from the inheritance of Melchizedek [ ] But they are the chil[dren of the lot of Melchiz]edek who

6. will bring them back, and proclaim liberty to them, relieving them [of the burden] of all their iniquities.

2:4 refers to a group presently in the clutches of Belial but who will ultimately be delivered by Melchizedek. Line 6 mentions the verb שוב as in "(who) will bring them back" (ישיבמה). Notably, the text cited (Lev. 25:13) has תשובו in the *qal* (second person singular), whereas in its pesher in 11Q13 2:2c the verb has been converted into the *hip'il* of ישיבמה (third person plural third person masculine plural suffix). We know from the previous line that Melchizedek is the subject of the verb ישיב. P. J. Kobelski suggests that the pronominal suffix (מה-) added to the *hip'il* form of שיב probably refers to השבויים ("captives" in 11Q13 2:2).

Apart from the change of form, a change in meaning has taken place as well; there is a shift from a material/economic reading to a spiritual one. However, Kobelski does not emphasize the spiritual overtones of the verb ישיבמה. The connection with "relieving them of the burden of their sins" (לעזוב להמה [משא] כול עוונתיהמה) later in the line justifies us taking this to be an allusion to repentance. Nitzan notes this spiritualized reading when she says of Melchizedek's role of saving the captives who were captured to the way of wickedness by Belial: "the full meaning . . . of saving these captives is

67. Most of the words at the beginning of line 5 are very faint and some hardly distinguishable, and so their reconstruction is very tenuous. However, in the light of an alternative reading found in the *editio princeps* we may reconstruct: "whose teachers have been hidden and kept secret." García Martínez, Tigchelaar, and van der Woude, "11QMelchizedek," 226–27. Kobelski's reading is more plausible because it is consistent with the overall imagery and other references to Belial in 2:13, 22, and 25, where he is control of the captives. Further, this reference to the "hidden teachers" introduces into the overall context a concept that makes no significant contribution to and finds no support elsewhere in the general flow of the text. On the other hand, CD 4:15 states that Israel was "captured" by the nets of Belial, thus lending support to Kobleski's reading.

not physical, but relieving them [of the burden] of all their iniquities at the time of eschatological expiation, on the 'D[ay of Atone]ment' at '[the en]d of the tenth [ju]bilee.'"[68] Melchizedek then becomes the agent who facilitates repentance since he causes them to repent (ישיבמה).[69] The fact that this group is his—"these are the sons of the lot of Melchizedek" (והמה בני גורל מלכי צדק)—serves as a motivational factor for Melchizedek's actions.

Kobelski suggests that the association of Melchizedek with the verb שוב "makes it probable that Melchizedek plays an instrumental role in the fulfilment of the return associated with the jubilee year mentioned in the citation of Lev 25:13."[70] Since all this is to occur at the end of the tenth Jubilee (2:7), which is in fact in the end of days (2:4), this spiritual reading of the verb ישיבמה ties in neatly with the eschatological "return" spoken of in texts such as Deut. 30:2 and Lev. 26:39-42.

The mediatory role of Melchizedek in this text is obvious. This stems from the priestly role associated with Melchizedek: because of its importance in the biblical tradition about him, it is impossible to separate from him here.[71] This text introduces an eschatological agent who is instrumental in bringing about a spiritual return (repentance) and enabling those of his lot to turn from the way of the people.

To sum up, from our examination of repentance language in 4Q171, 4Q174, and 11Q13, we can conclude that the community's

---

68. B. Nitzan, "Eschatological Motives in Qumran Literature: The Messianic Concept," in *Eschatology in the Bible and in Jewish and Christian Tradition*, ed. H. G. Reventlow, JSOTSup 243 (Sheffield: Sheffield Academic Press, 1997), 132–51 (149–50).

69. In 2:24, there is a reference to "those who turn aside [הסרים] from walking [in the w]ay of the people," which parallels those referred to in 2:6.

70. Kobelski, *Melchizedek and Mechireša'*, 57.

71. Ibid. Puech notes that this priestly function derives from Gen. 14:18 and Ps. 110:4. He says that in 11Q13, the central figure is clearly considered as the high priest of the heavenly liturgy of the Day of Atonement since he executes divine judgments and makes definitive expiation, which is seen in his divine pardon of the sins committed by those of his lot. É. Puech, "Notes sur le Manuscrit de XIQMelkîsèdeq," *RevQ* 12 (1987): 483–513 (512).

understanding of eschatological repentance was sometimes interwoven with their understanding of biblical texts.

Conclusion

I noted earlier that some scholars are of the opinion that there is a lack of coherence regarding eschatological issues in content. Nevertheless, while the content of eschatology at Qumran might be varied, there is certainly a coherent and underlying pattern, which may be stated as follows: Through an act of radical repentance and separation from surrounding wickedness, the Qumran community believed this initial act of repentance inaugurated the eschatological age. For the age to occur in its totality, this *penitential* community provided the appropriate example needed to initiate the eschatological "return to God." The return to God by all Israel marked the culmination of the eschatological blessings, then *repentance alone led to the fruition of the eschatological age*. The start of the eschatological age was due to the repentance of a small group; the totality of the eschatological age would be because of the repentance of the majority. This suggests that the community's understanding of eschatology was characterized by repentance. Not very many have ever examined the relation between repentance and eschatology. In so doing, we become aware of the underlying coherence of the basic eschatological understanding at Qumran.

Another significant feature that we noticed is the influence of Scripture on the community's eschatological understanding of repentance. Some texts (Deut. 15:2; Lev. 25:13; Ps. 37:8-9; Ps. 1:1; Isa. 8:11) that in themselves are not "repentance texts," are *given* repentance interpretations. While Brooke notes that those dealing with biblical texts at Qumran would have been concerned about the "plain" meaning of the text, he also says that the text transmitters were concerned with continuing to present something of that meaning *"whilst obviously having interpretative concerns of their own."*[72] Based on our discussion above, I noted that the phrase אחרית הימים is significant to our understanding of repentance,[73] suggesting that repentance language was often consciously associated with the content of אחרית הימים.

Regarding the emphasis on repentance we have seen in the preceding chapters, we can now conclude that the above picture of repentance was the result of their eschatological worldview, which in fact necessitated such a kind of penitential response, in order for the complete eschatological age to dawn.

Based on the observations of this chapter, we need to return to our working definition, which sees repentance as "the radical turning away from anything that hinders one's whole-hearted devotion to God and the corresponding turning to God in love and obedience." As in the preceding chapters, we now ask again, *From what* did they radically turn away? We saw in the texts examined that, consistent with the earlier chapters, repentance continued to be a *turning away from* evil (1QSa 1:3; 4Q174 1:16); the plans of evil (4QMMT C 29); sin (4QMMT C 7-8); the burden of iniquities (11Q13 2:24); wickedness (4Q171 1:2; 4Q174 1:14); the way of the people (4Q174 1:14; 11Q13 2:24); Belial and his dominion (11Q13 2:24); the devices of Belial (4QMMT C 19); and incorrect halakah and impurities (4QMMT C 7-8).

---

72. Brooke, "Reading the Plain Meaning of Scripture in the Dead Sea Scrolls, 77 (emphasis added).
73. Apart from its occurrence as a phrase, 11Q19 59:9b-10 has only אחר (after) but is clearly ideological similar to אחרית הימים . Similarly, 4QMMT C 30 has אחרית העת ("end of time"). It must be noted that while there are other instances where the phrase occurs within an eschatological context, in the scrolls, the phrase occurs thirty-three times in Hebrew texts. To this number can be added those occurrences where it is fragmentarily preserved and could be reconstructed. Steudel, "אחרית הימים ," 227. However, these occurrences are devoid of repentance language.

The second part of our definition refers to a *wholehearted turning to God*. In the texts we examined, this was seen primarily in their turning to God and his law (4QMMT C 12-13; 11Q19 59:9-10; 4Q171 2:2) and in their participation in the life of the community (1QSa 1:1-3). In one text (4Q285), it was seen in "returning to the community."

When we consider the *language and images* used to express repentance within an eschatological context, we see that it largely remained within the language of the prophetic and historiographic biblical books. Most commonly used was the image of (re)turning (1QSa 1:2; 4Q171 2:2-4; 4Q174 1:14-16; 4Q285; 4QMMT C 25; 11Q19 59:9). We saw language of "separation'" (4QMMT C7), "refining of the heart" (4Q215a), "being restored" to God, and "being relieved" from sin/the captivity of Belial through the agency of a divine being (11Q13 2:6).

We also encountered the following *result*: repentance in the present was first of all in obedience to the prophetic call for repentance in the last days. Hence, repentance secured the blessings promised in the last days. The community knew that their repentance up to then had already caused the future to at least partially irrupt into the present. According to texts such as 1QSa 1:1-3 and 4QMMT C 30, their repentance would serve as an example for the rest of Israel. Further, the community's sustained repentance would lead to an era of righteousness and salvation (4Q215a). Hence, it is not incorrect to say that their eschatological worldview *necessitated* an attitude of repentance. To take it a step further, if there was no repentance, then the promised eschatological age could not break in in all its totality. In other words, repentance was necessary to realize the promised eschatological age. Thus, while the eschatological worldview at

Qumran certainly shaped their thinking on repentance and *demanded* repentance, their eschatology was *dependent* on their repentance.

Our expanded definition of repentance based on the preceding chapters sees it as a radical and spatial separation from those factors that hindered one's devotion to God. It consisted of a corresponding turning to God by turning to the community and its law in love ad obedience. They were predestined to do so and constantly sought to remain penitent. This was manifested through ritual and cultic acts. This repentance alone made the eschatological age a reality.

Conclusion

As we attempt to locate repentance at Qumran within the wider context of their religious experience, we realize that the Qumran community, like any other religious movement, implies an organized attempt to introduce change in religion.[1] The community conformed to certain generalizations regarding religious movements. M. Nye talks of religious movements attracting attention for propagating ideas or practices that are said to be more specialized or esoteric than those of longer-established religious groups.[2] With regard to the Qumran community, this aspect can be related to the repentance-as-separation motif, with the aim of joining the community with its distinctive interpretation of the law and its unique understanding of the covenant of repentance and the role of those who were part of this community and covenant. Nye also states that there is a tendency for new religious movements to allow laypeople to participate more fully in their activities than is common in many older religious organizations.[3] This does not really apply to the Qumran community since the priestly nature of the members of the community is a

---

1. M. Nye, *Religion: The Basics* (London: Routledge, 2003), x. He notes: "This is normally accompanied by strain and conflict between religious movements and their competitors or opponents."
2. Ibid., xiii–xiv.
3. Ibid., xiii–xiv.

widely accepted scholarly view. Nye also observes that participants are encouraged to translate their spirituality into practical, everyday action. We saw this demonstrated through the emphasis on rituals at Qumran, which in turn was an expression of their predestined penitential state. Smart too states that religions tends to express itself through rituals and that even the simplest form of religious service involves ritual, "in the sense of some form of outer behaviour coordinated to an inner intention to make contact with, or participate in, the invisible world."[4]

All in all, when considering religious experience at Qumran with its penitential emphasis, we return to N. Smart's *experiential* dimension of religion, which postulates that experience of the divine is fundamental to any religious experience. This "quest for, contact with or participation in the world is that personal religion involves the hope of, realization of, experience of that world."[5] Whether personal (as Smart notes) or corporate (as in the case of the Qumran community—or any religious group for that matter), this experiential dimension is central to the validity of the religious encounter. For the Qumran community, this experience was undergirded by repentance, as we have seen in the previous chapters. In fact, their penitential, religious experience exhibits most—if not all—of the dimensions of religion Smart talks about. We see the presence of the *mythological* dimension, which accentuates the importance of historical events of religious significance in a tradition and the reenactment of a highly important event that once occurred in a particular community.[6] At Qumran, entry into to the community through the annual covenant-renewal ceremony was of great

---

4. Smart, *The Religious Experience of Mankind*, 16. He also grounds these rituals in history when he notes that the "meaning of ritual cannot be understood without reference to the environment of belief in which it is performed" (17).

5. Ibid., 21.

6. Ibid., 18.

importance for new members as well as for existing ones and served as a reenactment through which the experience of the founding members of the community became a shared experience with subsequent members.

Religious experience at Qumran clearly had a *doctrinal* aspect to it, doctrines that gave systematization, clarity, and intellectual power to what is revealed through the mythological and symbolic language of religious faith and ritual.[7] While the term *doctrine* is certainly anachronistic to the scrolls, there is evidence of the existence of "doctrines" at Qumran. The systematization of the beliefs of the Qumran community are ever present, and in some instances (see ch. 6), there is a definite penitential underpinning to the systematization of religion.

The strict disciplinary system operative in the daily life of the community as well as some elements of the *Rules* reflect a code of ethics that controlled the community. This is true to the *ethical* dimension that Smart talks of.[8] Relevant to our purposes, we saw that repentance was closely knit to this aspect.

This conformity to both Smart's dimensions of religion and Nye's general characteristics of religious movements is significant to our attempt to understand the role and function of repentance within the religious experience of the community. It indicates that the Qumran community is not merely a fictitious, literary phenomenon. Insofar as it is possible to establish the historicity of the community, we are dealing with the experiences and practices of a real religious movement in Second Temple Judaism. Smart, when highlighting the social dimension of religion, points out that "religions are not just a system of belief: they are also organizations . . . [and] have a communal and social significance."[9] The importance of this social

7. Ibid., 19.
8. Ibid., 19.

dimension is that it indicates the way in which men's lives are shaped by these claims and the way in which religious organizations operate.[10] Every aspect of the Qumran community's religious experience that we examined occurred within the context of an existing community.

I noted at the early on in this study that in the early decades of scrolls scholarship, when attempts were being made to provide a comprehensive picture of the community's beliefs, "repentance" was given very little attention. Nearly seventy years on, this situation has not changed much. Scholars acknowledge the importance of repentance, although largely in passing. Few studies provide a detailed investigation into the concept of repentance in the scrolls. Through our detailed investigation of repentance at Qumran, it is hoped that this book has contributed to Qumran scholarship in two ways: it has addressed a significant lacuna in the secondary literature, and it has attempted to establish the importance of repentance at Qumran. Lack of attention given to repentance motifs in the scrolls could result in an impoverished understanding of Qumran soteriology. An enhanced understanding of repentance in the scrolls can be used to reconstruct its function within the community's religious experience. We remind ourselves of the start of our journey.

We embarked on a journey into the religious world of the Qumran community and their scrolls, documents that both reflected and influenced their religious experience. We can broadly describe the "calling points" on this journey—places we stopped to get a better understanding of various aspects of religious experience related to repentance—as covenant, predestination, cult, and eschatology. Fundamental to understanding these areas was our community-

9. See ch. 2 above. Ibid. He adds that "the religious and ethical ideals are adapted to existing social conditions and attitudes" (20).
10. Ibid., 20.

centered analysis of the material. That is to say, none of the areas we examined or the penitential implications we drew out could be separated from the very existence of the community itself; they all derived their meaning and content from the religious experience of the community as a whole. P. Garnet notes that one of the functions of the community is to "provide a concrete opportunity for repentance."[11] The words of B. Nitzan aptly summarize where we are so far.

> In the Qumran community, repentance became the most important obligation of its members. The covenant of their obligation was defined as a ברית תשובה, "a covenant of repentance," and self-designations of its members include שבי פשע, "those who repent"; שבי המדבר, "the penitents of the desert"; השבים לתורה, "those who return to the Torah"; and שבי ישראל, "the penitents of Israel." Their specific outlook with regard to repentance, as reflected in their halakic interpretation of the Torah, influenced their polemical stance toward other Jewish circles that did not accept their regulations. In addition, the deterministic outlook held by the community strengthened its members during the afflictions caused by those who objected to their specific observance of the Torah, by which they defined their covenant with god.[12]

In the earliest and formative stages of the community's existence, we see a small group of individuals withdrawing from mainstream religion and creating an alternative community in the wilderness. We saw from texts such as 4QMMT that at this point in time, the door to reconciliation with the "rest of Israel" was left open, and attempts were made to offer the hand of fellowship to those whom the community perceived to be in error. This accounts for the "us-them"/"we-you" language we encounter in 4QMMT (C26-30).

11. This is in connection with the core group making atonement for the land and for those who are part of the community (cf. 1QS 8:1-3). Garnet, *Salvation and Atonement in the Qumran Scrolls*, 111.
12. Nitzan "Traditional and Atypical Motifs in Penitential Prayers from Qumran," in *Seeking the Favor of God*, 187.

The act of repentance of the small group was seen as beneficial to themselves and hence was offered to the "larger" group. It is possible to speculate on this invitation: attempts at reconciliation indicate that the rigid predestination we see at work in later texts was not present at this stage. It is unlikely that physiognomy played a major role in determining the authenticity of new members. Repentance, which for the core, founding group was the major criterion for joining, was possibly available to all at this stage of the community's existence. While there is no concrete evidence to support this, this "open" invitation to the community could well represent an earlier stage in the thought process of the community, before the identity markers that determined who could repent and who couldn't were still fluid.

However, this initial 'openness' changed as time went by and the community became more exclusive in its outlook. The act of penitential separation demonstrated by the core, founding group became the pattern for subsequent members of the community. As we saw in chapter 3, one joined the community through an act of separation. Further, joining the community in this manner also meant subscribing to the "correct" interpretation of the law of Moses, a reading of the law by the core, founding community. This distinctive reading of the law became the basis of the community's distinctiveness in subsequent times. We saw in chapter 3, this reading was clearly a penitential interpretation of the law that ultimately put its adherents on course to realize and bring about the eschatological age. In other words, life in the community with all that it entailed as initially defined by a core, founding group and that was shaped into a more rigid structure (with prescribed rituals and an elaborate disciplinary system) as time went by became in itself the controlling agent for its adherents. In all the preceding chapters, I have constantly highlighted the importance of repentance in the daily life of the community. We can conclude that repentance was controlled by the community. That is to say, Qumran's distinctive understanding of repentance lay in the fact that it was thoroughly community based. Joining this penitential community meant being subsumed into the community's understanding of repentance. There could be no alternative way of expressing one's repentance. The implications of this to the religious experience of the Qumran community was, we observed, community-controlled religious experience. How one repented, what one did to express this repentance, the benefits one achieved through repentance in this particular way, were all community-defined.

In this we begin to see a distinct thread emerging that sets apart the role and function of repentance at Qumran—it was a repentance that was intricately interwoven into the self-identity of the Qumran community. Repentance forms the parameters of existence within the community: repentance was required at the point of entry and at the end, to realize the eschatological age. It was certainly required *between* these two "points"—the strong emphasis on the penitential life evidences this. I noted that there is a lack of scholarly consensus as to whether this whole process was completed and rigidly fixed and controlled by predestination (reducing the members of the community to robotic automatons, thus robbing their repentance of any experiential element) or whether the community's understanding of predestination was flexible enough to allow for human experience, thus enhancing their penitence. Regardless of whether this situation is resolved, the importance of repentance at every level of the community's existence cannot be denied, no matter which camp scholars might be inclined to support in the divine-human-agency debate.

Before we isolate the functions of repentance at Qumran, we need to revisit for the last time the working definition of repentance that we have interacted with at each calling point: "the radical turning away from anything which hinders one's whole-hearted devotion to God and the corresponding turning to God in love and obedience." We can now modify and expand this definition so as to incorporate the cumulative evidence provided by each of our chapters. Thus we might conclude that for the Qumran community, repentance was the radical turning away from anything that hindered one's wholehearted devotion to God. It was predestined and spatially manifested by separation and a by a corresponding turning to God, the community, and its law. One thereby "stayed turned" in love and obedience through daily rituals, thus ensuring the advent of the eschatological age.

Repentance within religious experience at Qumran can be subsumed into all aspects of the "penitential life" that we encountered at every stage of the community's existence. It is fair to say that the Second Temple Judaism of the time demonstrated an emphasis on maintaining a penitential life. For example, in the *Testaments of the Twelve Patriarch*, the patriarchs exhort their children to choose the good way, emphasizing universal virtues such as piety and self-control.[13] Joseph exhorts his descendants "to pursue self-control" through "fasting and humility of heart" (*T. Jos.* 10.2), obviously referring to the manifestation of repentance in everyday life. In *Jubilees*, the Israelites and their descendants are circumcised (*Jub.* 1.23a) so that "they will not turn away from following me [the Lord] from that day and for ever" (*Jub.* 1.23c). There is a reference to repentance (circumcision) as well as the fact of *staying* penitent ("from that day and forever"). This should not be surprising since repentance, which involved "turning to God," obviously meant living thereafter in an appropriate manner. However, certain distinctive features about the Qumran emphasis on this penitential

---

13. Other virtues such as uprightness, honesty, generosity, compassion, and hard work are also expressed. H. C. Kee, "Testaments of the Twelve Patriarchs," in *OTP* 1:779.

life undergirded their religious experience. Only at Qumran was it so interrelated to the predestinarian issue: if repentance was predestined, so was the penitential life. For the Qumran community, attainment of and continuance in the penitential life was of fundamental importance since it was a manifestation of their separation/repentance; it also allowed them to remain in the community and conform to its laws; it was the appropriate way to live in the eschatological age since the totality of this age could irrupt only if such a penitential life was maintained. Hence in the scrolls, a penitential life was not merely a means to salvation: it was almost equated with salvation itself. It brought members of the community into the presence of the angels and thus into the presence of God himself. The locus for this quasi-divine, temple-like status was the community.[14] Again, this has to be set within the context of predestination and the other eschatological implications of their separated, penitential state. To demonstrate this, we are now ready to collate and summarize the findings of the preceding chapters.

As I highlight the functions of repentance, it should be borne in mind that there are some repentance themes present within contemporaneous non-Qumran literature, but equally, some themes are particularly reshaped by, emphasized by, or even distinctive to the Qumran understanding of repentance: repentance enabled them to become/join a separate community; it enabled them to remain in this separate covenantal community; it enabled them to maintain their predestined, penitential state, and thereby fulfill the requirements of the eschatological age. We can now look at these aspects in detail.

---

14. Interestingly, my position is not incompatible with D. Lambert, who is generally not in favor of attributing repentance to the Qumran community. Lambert says that in the case of the notion of divine creation, the community saw "an actual transformation of human nature, a rendering of human beings into something quasi-divine, angel-like, that may indeed possess an immortal sort of existence." D. Lambert "Was the Qumran Community a Penitential Movement?," 511.

Repentance Led to the Formation of the Community

A fundamental function of repentance was that it marked the desire to turn away from the surrounding wickedness and therefore separate from the rest of Israel (4QMMT C 7-8). Such repentance expressed by separation led to the formation of a new entity (1QS 8:12-14). This penitential separation was at the heart of the community's identity and existence. They could see themselves as a "community" with clearly delineated boundaries only because they had separated from the surrounding wickedness of the rest of Israel. The "repentance-as-separation" motif becomes a powerful boundary marker to determine who is and who is not a member of the community. The germinal group that later became a full-blown "community" was born out of an act of repentance (expressed by withdrawal to the desert). The wilderness therefore became the manifestation of repentance as well as the locus for repentance. The very existence of the community can be attributed to its spatially manifested repentance (1QS 5:1). There is no evidence of any other community that *voluntarily* became an organized entity displaying absolute separatism. Although the community did this so as not to compromise its beliefs, it was not because of external threat and fear.[15] The Qumran community demanded a radical and spatial absolute separation that was well organized and hierarchical. Furthermore, this separation was the most basic criterion for entrance into the community and for participation in the community of the renewed covenant.

Repentance Ensured a "Return to the Law"

If repentance manifested by withdrawal represented the turning-*away* aspect, then acceptance of the law of Moses in its

---

15. As in the case of *T. Mos.* 9 and 1 Macc. 2:29-38.

sectarian interpretation represented the turning-*toward* aspect: one (re)turned to the sectarian law of Moses (1QS 5:8; CD 15:9, 12; 16:2, 5). Their spatial physical separation was accentuated by their distinctive understanding of the law of Moses, known only to the members of the community. The theme of repentance, the return to a way of life in accordance with God's covenant with Israel, is nearly ubiquitous in first-century Judaism.[16] While the "object" to which one turned was undoubtedly God, in the scrolls we see that this "(re)turning" had a threefold emphasis: first, it was a return to the law as interpreted by the Zadokite leadership of the community. Second, this distinctive interpretation of the law underscored the community's status as a separate entity and hence emphasized its distinctiveness; thus, to turn to the law was to turn to the community. Third, one turned to the covenant because joining the community enabled one to be included in the covenant. The only way to become part of the renewed covenant was to become part of the community. T. Hägerland says: "To enter the community is, from a Qumran point of view, to return to the true Mosaic covenant. Those outside the community are apostates, sinners; a formulaic penitential prayer is necessary for anyone who wants to repent and re-enter the covenant.[17]

In other words, the proper and correct interpretation of the law was accessible only to the community, thus emphasizing the importance of the community as a whole. Thus, at Qumran, joining the covenant meant acceptance of a new alliance and participation in a new entity, namely, the community. The corollary to this is that repentance (as defined in the above terms) could not happen apart from the community. One turned to the community since it provided the locus in which the sectarian law functioned. Separation

16. Hägerland, "Jesus and the Rites of Repentance," 168.
17. Ibid., 172.

from wickedness was not advocated so that one could exist in a vacuum; rather, this separation/turning away from wickedness was followed by "turning to" the community. At Qumran, repentance was community-defined. Repentance for the community was not only a turning away from wickedness but also a corresponding turning to the sectarian law of Moses, community, and covenant.

Repentance Was Predestined and Undergirded a Life of Penitence

At Qumran, one repents only because one is predestined to so do. M. Bockmuehl describes this situation thus: "Although the sons of light *freely choose* to belong to the covenant and thus be saved, the very fact that they do so is itself an expression of the overruling grace of God, whose sovereign design disposes over both the saved and the damned."[18] This predestined repentance leads to an emphasis on an ongoing penitential life. M. Abegg notes the need for a "penitential life" when he says, "To be consistent with the corpus of Qumran literature, repentance must precede doing; otherwise there was no true benefit for the recipient or for Israel (C 31-32)."[19] R. S. Arnold's denial of this emphasis is striking. In examining the annual covenant-renewal ceremony and the role of repentance at this juncture in daily life at Qumran, he reduces repentance to "an essential requirement of potential initiates" and asserts: "Inside the *Yahad*, since the members were expected to maintain a life of perfection, the need for repentance was also essentially obviated."[20] Again, apart from the bulk of evidence from other scrolls that emphasize the need to stay penitent once inside the community, I have argued that within 1QS

18. M. Bockmuehl, "1QS and Salvation at Qumran," in *Justification and Variegated Nomism* 397.
19. Abegg, "4QMMT C 27, 31 and 'Works Righteousness,'" *DSD* 6, no. 2 (1999): 139–47 (144).
20. R. Arnold, "Repentance and the Qumran Covenant Ceremony," (paper for penitential prayer in Second Temple Judaism Consultation, SBL National Conference, November 2004), 14.

itself, the penal code could be divided into offenses for which repentance was possible and those for which it was not (see below).

I noted that there is an emphasis on the penitential life even in our non-Qumran material. In this context, we need to see how the Qumran emphasis on this penitential life was distinctive. First, only at Qumran was it related to the predestinarian issue: if repentance was predestined, so was the penitential life; second, it was intricately bound up with rituals. Performance of rituals ensured the maintenance of a penitential life, which in turn ensured continuance in the community. Unlike other Second Temple literature where a similar motif occurs, the scrolls indicate no place as such for this penitential life to enhance *individual* spirituality; rather, it cemented one's place in the community. Ongoing repentance gave the community its penitential identity. Remaining penitent also enabled them to remain in the community and to remain in the renewed covenant and, eventually, to bring about the eschatological age. At Qumran, repentance was not a one-time event but was always coupled with the need to stay penitent. As G. Boccacinni describes it:

> Human beings are saved because they are righteous, but they are righteous because they have been chosen. What they are does not depend on what they have done or will do. On the contrary, what they have done and will do depends on what they are and what they are is totally out of human control, because it has been predestined by God.[21]

The extent to which this aspect was emphasized and the content that was put into it far surpassed this motif in the other sources we looked at.

21. Boccacinni, *Beyond the Essene Hypothesis*, 64.

Repentance Was Daily Expressed through Rituals

A fourth function of repentance within the religious experience of the community was the efficaciousness it lent to daily rituals and to cultic acts of worship. S. Pfann observes that an appropriate inner attitude (namely, repentance) "was required *any time* an immersion took place."[22] While accompanying rituals were important and even prescribed in the penitential expression of the religious of the Second Temple world, there are instances, especially in the Hebrew bible, where it is unambiguously stated that the internal attitude is more important than the external act, thereby implying that if the internal attitude is "correct," then in the final analysis, the external act is dispensable. Not so at Qumran. Repentance as such did not occur apart from the ritual and cultic acts associated with it—a development even on the Hebrew Scripture and texts that highlighted the internal aspect over and against the external aspect of religion (and hence repentance). Repentance was never a substitute for rituals; neither were rituals a substitute for repentance. The one was an integral part of the other. Rituals were vehicles for repentance; as R. Kugler observes: "Ritual at Qumran was hegemonic, making every aspect of their experience religious."[23]

The distinctiveness about this is that they provided a daily means though which repentance could continually be expressed, which was in fact a manifestation of their predestined penitential state. Furthermore, all this happened within the community. The community then provides the temple-like context for these cultic acts

---

22. Pfann, "The Essene Yearly Renewal Ceremony and the Baptism of Repentance," in *The Provo International Conference on the Dead Sea Scrolls* 338 (emphasis added).

23. Kugler, "Making All Experience Religious152. E. Regev even more explicitly makes this connection when he says that "expiation and redemption is attained through moral repentance and religious commitment to the heavenly precepts, *as well as ritual bodily immersion* in the waters of purification." Regev, "Abominated Temple and a Holy Community" 273 (emphasis added).

to be performed. The withdrawal of the community to the desert needs to be juxtaposed with the impurity of the temple (caused by the wickedness of the Jerusalem priests). This was a major factor for their separation; the community perceived the current temple to be polluted, and their disassociation from the temple was a "turning away from" wickedness, an act of repentance. This situation would have undoubtedly influenced their thinking about the penitential life: in the absence of the prescribed ways of demonstrating a restored relationship with God through temple-related acts,[24] it is understandable that they took pains to demonstrate (and emphasize) the need for a penitential life precisely because of their disassociation from the temple. This becomes a unique factor at Qumran—the locus for all religious expression and cultic acts was the community itself.

Repentance Was a Determining Factor in the Disciplinary Procedures of the Community

Repentance functioned prominently in the disciplinary procedures of the community. In the penal code of the community (1QS 6:24—7:25), two types of disciplinary action could be meted out to errant members. The first type was a temporary expulsion (of varying length based on the nature of the offense), while the second type was a permanent expulsion. The first type, temporary expulsion, presupposed a subsequent reinstatement. We can conclude from this that genuine repentance enabled one to be reinstated (CD 10:2-3). Such a "return" would necessarily be dual-layered: a mental turning and acknowledgment of one's error as well as a physical (re)turn

---

24. This might be the case with works like Tobit and Judith, in which acts of piety represent a penitential life. Life during the exile makes up the literary setting of these documents. Therefore, for Tobit and Judith too, the absence of temple-based means of expressing religiosity resulted in an emphasis on alternative acts of piety. Likewise, in *Sib. Or.* 4.8, 27, Collins describes this rejection of temple cults as one of the "distinctive doctrines" of oracle 4. J. J. Collins, "Sibylline Oracles," in *OTP* 1:383.

to the community. The second type, however, involved absolute banishment from the community, for which offenses repentance was not allowed. Therefore, we may divide the disciplinary procedures listed in 1QS into those that allowed repentance and those that did not. In the light of this, another function of repentance was to serve as a key factor that could enable restoration of fellowship and reinstatement in the community.

Repentance Shaped the Eschatological Thinking of the Community

A final function of repentance can be seen in its influence on the community's eschatological worldview. We saw in chapter 7 that in the eschatological worldview of the community, the phrase אחרית הימים is often linked with repentance language, thereby indicating that for the community, repentance and eschatology were closely related. According to F. García Martínez, "The members of the Qumran community lived in an atmosphere of excessive eschatology."[25] The Qumran community saw themselves as living in "the final period of history." The present had not quite come to an end, and the future had already (although partially) irrupted (4QMMT C 20-21). Since they saw themselves as the divinely chosen remnant, they believed that it was their task to realize the eschatological repentance demanded by the prophetic and historical books of the Bible and thereby to enable the eschatological age to arrive in its totality. Only an ongoing penitential life would bring about this age in all its completeness.

The fact that the eschatological age was characterized by repentance explains the emphasis that the community placed on a daily penitential life. Repentance in the present, in other words,

25. J. Barrera, "The Essenes of Qumran: Between Legalism and Apocalyptic," in *The People of the Dead Sea Scrolls: Their Writings, Beliefs and Practices*, 73.

had eschatological implications: the community's repentance up to now had already caused the future age to partially irrupt into the present. So if there was no ongoing repentance, then the promised eschatological age could not break in in all its totality. In other words, a vital function of repentance was that it would bring about a realization of the promised eschatological age. On the one hand, the community's eschatological worldview necessitated a penitential response; on the other hand, their eschatology was dependent on their repentance: without a continuous penitential life in the present, the blessings of the future age would not be realized. Thus the scrolls bear witness to a key feature of eschatological piety within the community: the conscious association of repentance with eschatology. According to the non-Qumran material, the advent of the eschatological age would have dawned anyway, regardless of whether repentance was necessary. At Qumran, repentance in fact enabled the eschatological age to come in its totality; in other words, at Qumran, eschatology was dependent on the community's repentance. Thus, for G. Vermes, "Qumran eschatological piety can be summed up as faith and perseverance: in due course 'all the ages of God reach their appointed end.'"[26]

The function of repentance for the community has been a neglected feature in scrolls scholarship, especially in studies on the beliefs of the community. This is unfortunate because as we have now seen, repentance was the very basis of the community's existence and a factor that shaped the community's very self-identity. Initially, one core group—possibly the founders of the community—saw their act of separation from surrounding wickedness as causing the dawn of the eschatological age. This became the pattern and norm for

26. G. Vermes, "Eschatological World View in The Dead Sea Scrolls and in the New Testament" in *Emanuel: Studies in Hebrew Bible, Septuagint and Dead Sea Scrolls in Honour of Emanuel Tov*, ed. S. Paul, R. Kraft, L. Schiffman, and W. Fields (Leiden: Brill, 2003), 479–94 (486).

subsequent adherents of the community. The combined repentance of all the members of the community had the effect of enabling the eschatological age to irrupt in its totality. As a result, the community itself became at every stage the very locus for repentance. This is central to understanding the Qumran community as an important *penitential movement* in Second Temple Judaism. It definitively impinges on the community's worldview of covenant, election, cult, and eschatology. In fact, all these worldviews can be subsumed into a single and comprehensive one: *the penitential worldview*. This penitential worldview dominated and permeated all levels of the community's existence and in effect their religious experience. It was necessary for separation, entry, and continuing in the community, participating in the renewed covenant and also making sense of the end/salvation. It was the very basis of their self-identity. Since withdrawal to the desert was the expression of their repentance as well as the locus for it, this separate, penitential community living on the isolated shores of the Dead Sea is appropriately described by the epithet "penitents of the desert" (שבי המדבר).

It is evident that repentance played a very significant role in the lives of the members of the Qumran community. This made their religious experience a predominantly "penitential" one in a way that gave it a distinctive feel. While my analysis of repentance throughout this book has been largely text-based, it could therefore face the criticism of being merely a literary construct; it could be argued that there is no concrete evidence if repentance as described actually happened on a daily basis. That said, it is not implausible to conclude that most of the repentance texts surveyed here are indeed evidence of some corresponding practice at Qumran. Those who joined the community and read these texts would have easily been brought into something of that type of religious experience, which their enactment would have engendered. Their religious experience expressed through their repentance was not unrealistic; it was rather a religious experience expressed by a life conformed to God's will within a clear, penitential framework.

Bibliography

Texts and Translations

Abegg, M., P. Flint, and E. Ulrich. *The Dead Sea Scrolls Bible. The Oldest Known Bible Translated for the First Time into English.* New York: HarperCollins, 1999.

Abegg, M., J. Bowley, and E. Cook. *The Dead Sea Scrolls Concordance.* 2 vols. Leiden: Brill, 2003.

Allegro, J., ed. *Qumran Cave 4.1.* DJD 5. Oxford: Clarendon, 1966.

Barthélemy, D., and J. T. Milik, eds. *Qumran Cave I.* DJD 1. Oxford: Clarendon, 1955.

Baumgarten, J., et al., eds. *Qumran Cave 4. XIII. The Damascus Document (4Q266–273).* DJD 18. Oxford: Clarendon, 1996.

Black, M., ed. *Apocalypsis Henochi Graece.* Leiden: Brill, 1970.

Charles, R. H., ed. *The Apocrypha and Pseudepigrapha of the Old Testament.* 2 vols. Oxford: Clarendon, 1913.

Charlesworth, J. H., ed. *The Dead Sea Scrolls: Hebrew, Aramaic And Greek Texts with English Translations.* Vol. 1, *The Rule of the Community and Related Documents.* PTSDSSP. Tübingen: Mohr-Siebeck, 1994.

———, ed. *The Dead Sea Scrolls: Hebrew, Aramaic And Greek Texts With English Translations.* Vol.4A, *Pseudepigraphic and Non-Masoretic Psalms and Prayers.* PTSDSSP. Tübingen: Mohr-Siebeck, 1998.

————, ed. *The Old Testament Pseudepigrapha*. Vol. 1, *Apocalyptic Literature and Testaments*. London: Darton, Longman & Todd, 1983.

————, ed. *The Old Testament Pseudepigrapha*. Vol. 2, *Expansions of the "Old Testament" and Legends, Wisdom and Philosophical Literature, Prayers, Psalms, and Odes, Fragments of Lost Judeo-Hellenistic Works*. London: Darton, Longman & Todd, 1985.

Charlesworth, J. H., and C. A. Newsom, eds. *The Dead Sea Scrolls: Hebrew, Aramaic and Greek Texts with English Translations*. Vol.4B, *Angelic Liturgy: Songs of the Sabbath Sacrifice*. PTSDSSP. Tübingen: Mohr-Siebeck, 1999.

Chazon, E., et al., eds. *Qumran Cave 4. XX. Poetical and Liturgical Texts, Part 2*. DJD 29. Oxford: Clarendon, 1999.

Eshel, E., H. Eshel, C. Newsom, B. Nitzan, E. Schuller, and A. Yardeni, eds. *Qumran Cave 4. VI. Poetical and Liturgical Texts, Part 1*. DJD 11. Oxford: Clarendon, 1998.

García Martínez, F., E. Tigchelaar, and A. van der Woude, eds. *Qumran Cave 11. II. (11Q2–18, 11Q20–31)*. DJD 23. Oxford: Clarendon, 1998.

García Martínez, F., and E. Tigchelaar, eds. *The Dead Sea Scrolls: Study Edition*. 2 vols. Leiden: Brill, 1997–1998.

Knibb, M., ed. *The Ethiopic Book of Enoch: A New Edition in the Light of the Aramaic Dead Sea Fragments*. 2 vols. Oxford: Clarendon, 1978.

Kobelski, P. J. *Melchizedek and Mechireša'*. CBQMS 10. Washington, DC: Catholic Biblical Association of America, 1981.

Lohse, E. *Die Texte Aus Qumran. Hebräisch und Deutsch*. Munich: Kasel, 1971.

Nitzan, B., et al., eds. *Qumran Cave 4. XX Poetical And Liturgical Texts, Part 2*. DJD 29. Oxford: Clarendon, 1999.

Philonenko, M. *Joseph et Aséneth*. Leiden: Brill, 1968.

Pfann, S., et al., eds. *Qumran Cave 4. XXVI*. DJD 36. Oxford: Clarendon, 2000.

Qimron, E., and J. Strugnell, eds. *Qumran Cave 4. V. Miqsat Ma'ase Ha-Torah*. DJD 10. Oxford: Clarendon, 1994.

Schechter, S. *Documents Of Jewish Sectaries I: Fragments of a Zadokite Work*. Cambridge: Cambridge University Press, 1910.

Schiffman, L., and J. C. VanderKam, eds. *Encyclopaedia of the Dead Sea Scrolls*. 2 vols. Oxford: Oxford University Press, 2000.

Tov. E. et al., eds. *Texts from the Judean Desert: Indices and an Introduction to the DJD Series*. Oxford: Clarendon, 2002.

Tromp, J. *The Assumption of Moses. A Critical Edition with Commentary*. Leiden: Brill, 1993.

Wise, M., M. Abegg, and E. Cook, eds. *The Dead Sea Scrolls: A New Translation*. San Francisco: HarperSanFrancisco, 1999.

Secondary Sources

Abegg, M. "4QMMT C 27, 31 and 'Works Righteousness.'" *DSD* 6, no. 2 (1999): 139–47.

———. "The Covenant of the Qumran Sectarians." In *The Concept of the Covenant in the Second Temple Period*, edited by S. Porter and J. de Roo, 81–92. Leiden: Brill, 2003.

Alexander, P. S. "The Redaction History of *Serek ha-Yahad*." *RevQ* (1996): 437–56.

———. "'Wrestling against Wickedness in High Places': Magic in the Worldview of the Qumran Community." In *The Scrolls and the Scriptures: Qumran after Fifty Years*, edited by S. Porter and C. Evans, 318–37. JSPSup 26. Sheffield: Sheffield Academic, 1997.

———. "A Reconstruction and Reading of 4Q285." *RevQ* 75 (2000): 333–48.

———. "Predestination and Freewill in the Theology of the Dead Sea Scrolls." In *Divine and Human Agency in Paul and His Cultural Environment*, edited by J. M. G. Barlay and S. Gathercole, 27–49. LNTS 335. London: T&T Clark, 2006.

Altman, A., ed. *Biblical Motifs: Origins and Transformations*. Cambridge, MA: Harvard University Press, 1966.

Arnold, R. "Repentance and the Qumran Covenant Ceremony." A Paper for Penitential Prayer in Second Temple Judaism Consultation, SBL National Conference, November 2004.

Attridge, H. "Historiography." In *Jewish Writings of the Second Temple Period*, edited by M. Stone, 157–84. Assen: Van Gorcum, 1984.

Avery-Peck, A. J., J. Neusner, and B. Chilton, eds. *Judaism in Late Antiquity*. Part 5, vols. 1 and 2, *The Judaism of Qumran: A Systematic Reading of the Dead Sea Scrolls*. Leiden: Brill, 2001.

Baillet, M. "Un Recueil Liturgique de Qumrân, Grotte 4: 'Les Parôles Des Luminaires.'" *RB* 68 (1961): 195–250.

Bardtke, H. "Considérations sur les cantiques de Qumrân." *RB* 63 (1955): 220–33.

———. *Bibel und Qumran*. Berlin: Evangelische Haupt, 1966.

Barthélemy, D. "La sainteté selon la communauté de Qumrân et selon l'évangile." In *La secte de Qumrân et les origines du Christianisme*, edited by J. Van Der Ploeg et al., 203–16. Leuvan: Desclée de Brouwer, 1959.

Bauckham, R. *The Fate of the Dead: Studies on the Jewish and Christian Apocalypses*. Leiden: Brill, 1998.

Baumgarten, A. "Who Cares and What Does it Matter: Qumran and the Essenes Once Again!" *DSD* 11, no. 2 (2004): 174–90.

Baumgarten, J. "The Meaning of 1QSerek III, 2-3." *RevQ* 6 (1967–1969): 287–88.

———. *Studies in Qumran Law*. Leiden: Brill, 1977.

———. "The Damascus Document Reconsidered." In *The Dead Sea Scrolls at Fifty*, edited by R. Kugler and E. Schuller, 149–50. Atlanta: Scholars Press, 1999.

Beall, T. S. *Josephus' Description of the Essenes Illustrated by the Dead Sea Scrolls*. Cambridge: Cambridge University Press, 1988.

Beckford, J. E., ed. *New Religious Movements and Solution and Rapid Social Change*. London: Sage, 1986.

Becker, J. *Die Anfänge des Christentmus*. Stuttgart: Kohlhammer, 1987.

Belleville, L. L. *Reflections of Glory: Paul's Polemical Use of the Moses-Doxa Tradition in 2 Corinthian 3:1-18*. JSNTSup. Sheffield: JSOT Press, 1991.

Bernstein, M., F. García Martínez, and J. Kampen, eds. *Legal Texts and Legal Issues: Proceedings of the Second Meetings of the International Organization for Qumran Studies, Cambridge 1995*. Leiden: Brill, 1997.

———. "Pseudepigraphy in the Qumran Scrolls: Categories and Functions." In *Pseudepigrahpic Perspectives: The Apocrypha and Pseudepigrapha in the Light of the Dead Sea Scrolls*, edited by E. Chazon and M. Stone, 1–26. STDJ 31. Leiden: Brill, 1999.

Betz, O. "Die Proselytentaufe der Qumransekte und die Taufe im Neuen Testament." *RevQ* 1 (1958): 213–34.

Block, D. *The Book of Ezekiel. Chs 1-24*. NICOT. Grand Rapids: Eerdmans, 1997.

Boccaccini, G. *Beyond the Essene Hypothesis: The Parting of Ways between Qumran and Enochic Judaism*. Grand Rapids: Eerdmans, 1998.

Bockmuehl, M. *Revelation and Mystery*. Tübingen: Mohr Siebeck, 1990.

———. "Redaction and Ideology in the Rule of the Community." *RevQ* 72 (1998): 541–60.

———. "1QS and Salvation at Qumran." In *Justification and Variegated Nomism*. Vol. 1, *The Complexities of Second Temple Judaism*, edited by D. A. Carson, P. O'Brien, and M. Seifrid, 381–414. WUNT. Tübingen: Mohr Siebeck, 2001.

Boda, M. J, D. Falk, and R. A. Werline, eds. *Seeking the Favor of God*. Vol. 2, *The Development of Penitential Prayer in Second Temple Judaism*. Atlanta: SBL, 2007.

Box, G. H., and W. O. E. Oesterley. "Sirach." In *The Apocrypha and Pseudepigrapha of the Old Testament*. Vol. 1, *Apocrypha*, edited by R. Charles, 268–517. Oxford: Clarendon, 1913.

Brandenburger, E. "Himmelfahrt Moses." In *Apokalypsen*, edited by E. Brandenburger, U. Müller, and A. Klijn, 59–84. *JSHRZ* 5.2. Gütersloh: Gütersloher Verlaghaus; Gerd Mohn, 1976.

Brooke, G. *Exegesis at Qumran. 4QFloreligium in Its Jewish Context*. JSOTSup. 29. Sheffield: JSOT Press, 1985.

———, ed. *Temple Scroll Studies*. Sheffield: JSOT Press, 1989.

———. "Isaiah 40:3 and the Wilderness Community." In *New Qumran Texts and Studies*, edited by G. Brooke and F. García Martínez. Leiden: Brill, 1994.

———. "The Explicit Presentation of Scripture in 4QMMT." In *Legal Texts and Legal Issues: Proceedings of the Second Meetings of the International Organization for Qumran Studies, Cambridge 1995*, edited by M. Bernstein, F. García Martínez, and J. Kampen, 67–88. Leiden: Brill, 1997.

———. Review of G. S. Oemega, *Der Gesalbte und sein Volk*. DSD 4 (1997): 367.

———. "'The Canon within the Canon' at Qumran and in the New Testament." In *The Scrolls and the Scriptures: Qumran Fifty Years After*, edited by S. Porter and C. Evans,242–66. JSPSup. 26. Sheffield: Sheffield Academic, 1997.

———. "Body Parts in the *Barkhi Nafshi* and the Qualification for Membership of the Worshipping Community." In *Sapiential, Liturgical and Poetical Texts from Qumran: Proceedings of the Third Meeting of the International Organization for Qumran Studies, Published in Memory of Maurice Baillet*, edited by D. Falk, F. García Martínez, and E. Schuller, 80–94. Leiden: Brill, 2000.

———. "*E Pluribus Unum:* Textual Variety and Definitive Interpretation in the Qumran Scrolls." In *The Dead Sea Scrolls in their Historical Context*, edited by T. Lim, 107–19. Edinburgh: T&T Clark, 2000.

————. "Reading the Plain Meaning of Scripture in the Dead Sea Scrolls." In *Jewish Ways of Reading the Bible*, edited by G. Brooke, 67–90. JSSSup 11. Oxford: Oxford University Press, 2000.

————, ed. *Jewish Ways of Reading the Bible*. JSSSup 11. Oxford: Oxford University Press, 2000.

————. *Qumran and the Jewish Jesus*. Cambridge: Grove, 2005.

————. *The Dead Sea Scrolls and the New Testament*. London: SPCK, 2005.

Brooke, G., and F. García Martínez, eds. *New Qumran Texts and Studies*. Leiden: Brill, 1994.

Brooke, G., and L. Schiffman, "The Past: On the History of Dead Sea Scrolls Research." In R. Kugler and E. Schuller, eds. *The Dead Sea Scrolls at Fifty*. Atlanta: Scholars, 1999, 9-20.

Broshi, M. "The Archaeology of Qumran—A Reconsideration." In *The Dead Sea Scrolls: Forty Years Of Research*, edited by D. Dimant and U. Rappaport, 103–15. STDJ. Leiden: Brill, 1993.

Brownlee, W. H. "The Wicked Priest, the Man of Lies, and the Righteous Teacher—The Problem of Identity." *JQR* 73, no. 1 (1982): 1–37.

Bruce, F. F. "Qumrân and Early Christianity." *NTS* 2 (1956): 176–90.

Buis, P., and J. Leclercq. *Le Deutéronome*. Paris: Gabalda, 1963.

Burrows, M. *The Dead Sea Scrolls*. London: Secker & Worburg, 1956.

————. *More Light on the Dead Sea Scrolls: New Scrolls and New Interpretations*. New York: Viking, 1958.

Cairns, I. *Deuteronomy: Word and Presence*. Grand Rapids: Eerdmans, 1992.

Callaway, P. R. *The History of the Qumran Community: An Investigation*. Sheffield: Sheffield Academic, 1988.

Carmignac, J. "La Notion D'Eschatologie dans la Bible et À Qumrân." *RevQ* 7 (1969): 17–31.

Carson, D. A. *Divine Sovereignty and Human Responsibility: Biblical Perspectives in Tension*. Atlanta: John Knox, 1981.

Carson, D. A., P. O'Brien, and M. Seifrid, eds. *Justification and Variegated Nomism*. Vol. 1, *The Complexities of Second Temple Judaism*. Tübingen: Mohr Siebeck, 2001.

Chamberlain, J. V. "Toward a Qumran Soteriology." *NovT* 3 (1959): 305–13.

Charlesworth, J. H. *The Pseudepigrapha and Modern Research*. Missoula, MT: Scholars Press, 1976.

———, ed. *The Old Testament Pseudepigrapha*. Vol. 2, *Expansions of the "Old Testament" and Legends, Wisdom and Philosophical Literature, Prayers, Psalms, and Odes, Fragments of Lost Judeo-Hellenistic Works*. London: Darton, Longman & Todd, 1985.

———. "Prayer of Manasseh." In *The Old Testament Pseudepigrapha*. Vol. 2, *Expansions of the "Old Testament" and Legends, Wisdom and Philosophical Literature, Prayers, Psalms, and Odes, Fragments of Lost Judeo-Hellenistic Works*, ed. J. H. Charlesworth, 625–37. London: Darton, Longman & Todd, 1985.

———. *Jesus Within Judaism*. London: SPCK, 1989.

———. *The Pesharim and Qumran History: Chaos or Consensus?* Grand Rapids: Eerdmans, 2002.

Chazon, E. "Is *Divrei Ha-Me'orot* a Sectarian Prayer?" In *The Dead Sea Scrolls: Forty Years Of Research*, edited by D. Dimant and U. Rappaport, 3–17. Leiden: Brill, 1993.

———. "Prayers from Qumran and Their Historical Implications." *DSD* 1 (1994): 265–84.

———. "A Case of Mistaken Identity: *Testament of Naphtali* (4Q215) and *Time of Righteousness* (4Q215a)." In *The Provo International Conference on the Dead Sea Scrolls: Technical Innovations, New Texts, and Reformulated Issues*, edited by D. Parry and E. Ulrich, 110–23. Leiden: Brill, 1999.

Chazon, E., and M. Stone, eds. *Pseudepigrahpic Perspectives: The Apocrypha and Pseudepigrapha in the Light of the Dead Sea Scrolls*. STDJ 31. Leiden: Brill, 1999.

Chilton, B. "Jesus and the Repentance of E. P. Sanders." *TynBul* 39 (1988): 1–18.

Chilton, B., and J. Neusner. *Judaism in the New Testament: Practices and Beliefs.* London: Routledge, 1995.

Christiansen, J. *The Covenant in Judaism and Paul: A Study of Ritual Boundaries as Identity Markers.* Leiden: Brill, 1995.

Cohen, S. D. J. *From the Maccabees to the Mishnah.* Philadelphia: Westminster, 1987.

Collins, J. J. "Patterns of Eschatology at Qumran." In *Traditions in Transformation: Turning Points in Biblical Faith*, edited by B. Halpern, and J. Levenson, 351–75. Winona Lake, IN: Eisenbrauns, 1981.

———. "Forms of Community in the Dead Sea Scrolls." In *Emmanuel: Studies in Hebrew Bible, Septuagint and Dead Sea Scrolls in Honour of Emmanuel Tov*, edited by S. Paul, R. Kraft, L. Schiffman, and W. Fields, 97–111. Leiden: Brill, 2003.

Condra, E. *Salvation for the Righteous Revealed: Jesus Amid Covenantal and Messianic Expectations in Second Temple Judaism.* Leiden: Brill, 2002.

Craigie, P. C., P. Kelley, and J. Drinkard. *Jeremiah 1–25.* WBC 26. Dallas: Word, 1991.

Crawford, S. W. "Not According to Rule: Women, the Dead Sea Scrolls and Qumran." In *Emanuel: Studies in Hebrew Bible, Septuagint and Dead Sea Scrolls in Honour of Emanuel Tov*, edited by S. Paul, R. Kraft, L. Schiffman, and W. Fields, 127–50. Leiden: Brill, 2003.

Cross, F. M. *The Ancient Library of Qumrân and Modern Biblical Studies.* London: Duckworth, 1958.

———. "The Development of Jewish Scripts." In *The Bible and the Ancient Near East: Essays in Honour of W. F. Albright*, edited by G. E. Wright, 133–202. London: Routledge & Kegan Paul, 1961.

Cryer, F. H., and T. Thompson, eds. *Qumran Between the Old and New Testaments.* Sheffield: Sheffield Academic, 1998.

Danker, F. *II Corinthians*. ACNT. Minneapolis: Augsburg Fortress, 1989.

Davies, P. R. *Behind the Essenes: History and Ideology in the Dead Sea Scrolls.* Atlanta: Scholars, 1987.

———. *The Damascus Covenant*. Sheffield: JSOT Press, 1983.

———. "Eschatology at Qumran." *JBL* 104, no. 1 (1985): 39–55.

———. *Sects and Scrolls: Essays on Qumran and Related Topics*. Atlanta: Scholars, 1996.

Davies, P. R., G. Brooke, and P. Callaway. *The Complete World of the Dead Sea Scrolls*. London: Thames & Hudson, 2002.

Davila, J. *Liturgical Works*. Eerdmans Commentaries on the Dead Sea Scrolls. Grand Rapids: Eerdmans, 2000.

Deasley, A. *The Shape of Qumran Theology*. Carlisle, UK: Paternoster, 2000.

De Jonge, M., ed. *Outside the Old Testament*. Cambridge: Cambridge University Press, 1985.

De Jonge, M., and A. S. van der Woude. "11QMelchizedek and the New Testament." *NTS* 12 (1965): 301–26.

Delcor, M. "Recherches sur un Horoscope en Langue Hébraïque provenant de Qumrân." *RevQ* 5 (1964–1966): 521–42.

———, ed. *Qumran. Sa piété, sa théologie et son milieu*. Paris: Gembloux, 1978.

Denis, A.-M. *Introduction Aux Pseudépigraphes Grecs D'Ancien Testament*. Leiden: Brill, 1970.

———. *Introduction à la littérature religieuse judéo-hellénistique*. Vols. 1 and 2. Turnhout: Brepols, 2000.

Dillard, R. *2 Chronicles*. WBC 15. Dallas: Word, 1987.

Dimant, D. "Qumran Sectarian Literature." In *Jewish Writings of the Second Temple Period*, edited by M. Stone, 483–550. Assen: Van Gorcum, 1984.

———. "The Library of Qumran: Its Content and Character." In *The Dead Sea Scrolls: Forty Years Of Research*, edited by D. Dimant and U. Rappaport, 170–76. Leiden: Brill, 1992.

————. "The Qumran Manuscripts: Content and Significance." In *Time to Prepare the Way in the Wilderness*, edited by D. Dimant and L. Schiffman, 23–58. Leiden: Brill, 1995.

Dimant, D., and U. Rappaport, eds. *The Dead Sea Scrolls: Forty Years Of Research*. Leiden: Brill, 1992.

Deasley, A. *The Shape of Qumran Theology*. Carlisle, UK: Paternoster, 2000.

De Lange, N. *An Introduction To Judaism*. Cambridge: Cambridge University Press, 2000.

DeSilva, D. A. *Introducing the Apocrypha*. Grand Rapids: Baker Academic, 2002.

De Vaux, R. *The Archaeology of Qumran*. London: Oxford University Press, 1973.

Dombkowski, D. "The Qumran Community and 1Q Hodayot: A Reassessment." *RevQ* 39 (1981): 323–64.

Driver, G. R. *The Judean Scrolls: The Problem and a Solution*. New York: Schocken, 1965.

Dupont-Sommer, A. *The Essene Writings From Qumran*. Oxford: Basil Blackwell, 1961.

Eckey, W. *Die Apostelgeschichte. Der Weg des Evangeliums von Jerusalem nach Rom*. Volume 1: Acts of the Apostles 1,1–15,35. Vluyn: Neukirchener, 2000.

Egger-Wenzel, R., and I. Krammer, eds. *Der Einzelne und seine Gemeinschaft bei Ben Sira*. Berlin: de Gruyter, 1998.

Elgvin, T. "The Eschatological Hope of 4QTime of Righteousness." In *Wisdom and Apocalypticism in the Dead Sea Scrolls and in the Biblical Tradition*, edited by F. García Martínez, 89–102. Leuven: Leuven University Press, 2003.

Elliott, M. A. *The Survivors of Israel: A Reconsideration of the Theology of Pre-Christian Judaism*. Grand Rapids: Eerdmans, 2000.

Emerton, J., ed. *Congress Volume: Vienna 1980*. VTSup 32. Leiden: Brill, 1982.

Ego, B., A. Lange, and P. Pilhofer, eds. *Gemeinde ohne Tempel*. Tübingen: Mohr Siebeck, 1999.

Evans, C. *Saint Luke*. London: SCM, 1990.

———. "Covenant in the Qumran Literature." In *The Concept of the Covenant in the Second Temple Period*, edited by S. Porter and J. de Roo, 55–80. Leiden: Brill, 2003.

Evans, C., and P. Flint, eds. *Eschatology, Messianism, and the Dead Sea Scrolls*. Grand Rapids: Eerdmans, 1997.

Fabry, H. J. "Die Wurzel שוב in der Qumranliteratur." In *Qumran. Sa piété, sa théologie et son milieu*, edited by M. Delcor, 285–93. Paris: Gembloux, 1978.

Falk, D. "4Q393: A Communal Confession." *JJS* 45 (1994): 184–207.

———. *Daily, Sabbath, and Festival Prayers in the Dead Sea Scrolls*. Leiden: Brill, 1998.

———. "Qumran Prayers Texts and the Temple." In *Sapiential, Liturgical and Poetical Texts from Qumran: Proceedings of the Third Meeting of the International Organization for Qumran studies Published in Memory of Maurice Baillet*, edited by D. Falk, F. García-Martínez, and E. Schuller, 106–26. Leiden: Brill, 2000.

Falk, D., F. García Martínez, and E. Schuller, eds. *Sapiential, Liturgical and Poetical Texts from Qumran: Proceedings of the Third Meeting of the International Organization for Qumran Studies, Published in Memory of Maurice Baillet*. Leiden: Brill, 2000.

Fisdel, S. *The Dead Sea Scrolls: Understanding the Spiritual Message*. Northvale, NJ: Aronson, 1998.

Fitzgerald, A. "*MTNDBYM* in 1QS." *CBQ* 36 (1974): 495–502.

Fitzmyer, J. A. *To Advance the Gospel: New Testament Studies*. Grand Rapids: Eerdmans, 1998.

———. *The Semitic Background of the New Testament.* Grand Rapids: Eerdmans, 1997.

———. *The Dead Sea Scrolls and Christian Origins.* Grand Rapids: Eerdmans, 2000.

Flint, P. W., ed. *The Bible at Qumran: Text, Shape and Interpretation.* Grand Rapids: Eerdmans, 2001.

Flint, P. W., and J. VanderKam, eds. *The Dead Sea Scrolls after Fifty Years.* 2 Vols. Leiden: Brill, 1999.

Flusser, D. *The Spiritual History of the Dead Sea Sect.* Tel Aviv: MOD, 1989.

Forkman, G. *The Limits of the Religious Community.* Lund: CWK Gleerup, 1972.

Fraade, S. D. "To Whom It May Concern: 4QMMT and Its Addressee(s)." *RevQ* 19 (2000): 507–27.

Gaventa, B. R. *First and Second Thessalonians.* IBC. Louisville: John Knox, 1998.

García Martínez, F., and A. Van der Woude. "A 'Groningen' Hypothesis of Qumran Origins and Early History." *RevQ* 14 (1990): 521–42.

———. *Qumran and Apocalyptic: Studies on the Aramaic Texts from Qumran.* Leiden: Brill, 1992.

———. *Wisdom and Apocalypticism in the Dead Sea Scrolls and in the Biblical Tradition.* Leuven: Leuven University Press, 2003,

———. "Apocryphal, Pseudepigraphical, and Para-Biblical Texts from Qumran." *RevQ* 83 (2004): 365–77.

García Martínez, F., and J. Barrera, eds. *The People of the Dead Sea Scrolls: Their Writings, Beliefs and Practices.* Leiden: Brill, 1995.

Garnet, P. *Salvation and Atonement in the Qumran Scrolls.* Tübingen: Mohr Siebeck, 1977.

Gathercole, S. J. *Where Is Boasting? Early Jewish Soteriology and Paul's Response in Romans 1–5.* Grand Rapids: Eerdmans, 2002.

Georgi, D. *Weisheit Salomos*. *JSHRZ*. III.4. Gütersloh: Gütersloher Verlaghaus; Gerd Mohn, 1981.

Golb, N. *Who Wrote the Scrolls? The Search for the Secret of Qumran*. London: Michael O'Mara, 1995.

Goodblatt, D., A. Pinnick, and D. Schwartz, eds. *Historical Perspectives: From the Hasmoneans to Bar Kokhba in the Light of the Dead Sea Scrolls*. Leiden: Brill, 2001.

Goppelt, L. *The Theology of the New Testament*. 2 vols. Grand Rapids: Eerdmans, 1981–1982.

Grabbe, L. *Judaism from Cyrus to Hadrian*. Vol. 2, *The Roman Period*. Minneapolis: Fortress, 1992.

Greenleaf-Pedley, K. "The Library at Qumran." *RevQ* 2 (1959/1960): 21–41.

Guilbert, P. "Le Plan de la 'Règle de la Comunauté.'" *RevQ* 1 (1959): 321–44.

Gunkel, H. *Die Psalmen*. Göttingen: Vandenhoeck & Ruprecht, 1968.

Hägerland, T. "Jesus and the Rites of Repentance." *NTS* 52 (2006): 166–187.

Haenchen, E. *The Acts of the Apostles: A Commentary*. Translated by R. McL. Wilson. Oxford: Blackwell, 1971.

Haight, R. *Christian Community in History*. Vol. 1, *Historical Ecclesiology*. New York: Continuum, 2004.

Halpern, B., and J. Levenson, eds. *Traditions in Transformation. Turning Points in Biblical Faith*. Winona Lake, IN: Eisenbrauns, 1981.

Hare, D. "Lives of the Prophets." In *The Old Testament Pseudepigrapha*. Vol. 2, *Expansions of the "Old Testament" and Legends, Wisdom and Philosophical Literature, Prayers, Psalms, and Odes, Fragments of Lost Judeo-Hellenistic Works*, edited by J. H. Charlesworth, 379–99. London: Darton, Longman & Todd, 1985.

Harrington, D. *Invitation to the Apocrypha*. Grand Rapids: Eerdmans 1999.

———. "Pseudo-Philo." In *The Old Testament Pseudepigrapha*. Vol. 2, *Expansions of the "Old Testament" and Legends, Wisdom and Philosophical Literature, Prayers, Psalms, and Odes, Fragments of Lost Judeo-Hellenistic*

Works, edited by J. H. Charlesworth, 297–377. London: Darton, Longman & Todd, 1985.

Harris, J. G. "The Covenant Concept among the Qumran Sectaries." *EvQ* 39.2 (1967): 86–92.

Hartley, J. *Leviticus*. WBC 4. Dallas: Word, 1992.

Heger, P. "Did Prayer replace Sacrifice at Qumran?." *RevQ* 86 (2005): 213–33.

Hempel, C. "The Earthly Essene Nucleus of 1QSa." *DSD* 3 (1996): 253–69.

———. *The Laws Of The Damascus Document*. Leiden: Brill, 1998.

———. *The Damascus Texts*. Sheffield: Sheffield Academic, 2000.

Hengel, M. "Qumran and Hellenism." In *Religion in the Dead Sea Scrolls*, edited by J. J. Collins and R. Kugler, 46–56. Grand Rapids: Eerdmans, 2000.

Hillers, D. *Lamentations*. AB. Garden City, NY: Doubleday, 1972.

Himmelfarb, M. "Impurity and Sin in 4QD, 1QS and 4Q521." *DSD* 8, no. 1 (2001): 9–37.

Høgenhausen, J. "Rhetorical Devices in 4QMMT." *DSD* 10, no. 2 (2003): 187–204.

Hollander, H. W. "The Testaments of the Twelve Patriarchs." In *Outside the Old Testament*, edited by M. De Jonge, 71–91. Cambridge: Cambridge University Press, 1985.

Holmes, S. "The Wisdom of Solomon." In *The Apocrypha and Pseudepigrapha of the Old Testament*. Vol. 1, *Apocrypha*, edited by R. Charles. Oxford: Clarendon, 1913.

Holm-Nielsen, S. *Hodayot: Psalms from Qumran*. Aarhus: Universitetsforlaget, 1960.

Horgan, M. P. *Pesharim: Qumran Interpretations of Biblical Books*. Washington, DC: Catholic Biblical Association of America, 1979.

Hughes, P. E. *A Commentary on the Epistle to the Hebrews*. Grand Rapids: Eerdmans, 1977.

Humbert, J.-B. "L'espace sacré à Qumrân." *RB* 101 (1994): 161–214.

Hyatt, J. P. "The View of Man in the Qumran 'Hodayot.'" *NTS* 2 (1956): 276–84.

Isaac, E. "1 Enoch." In *The Old Testament Pseudepigrapha*. Vol. 1, *Apocalyptic Literature and Testaments*, edited by J. H. Charlesworth, 5–89. London: Darton, Longman & Todd, 1983.

Iwry, S. "Was There a Migration to Damascus? The Problem of שבי ישראל." *Eretz-Israel* 9 (1969): 80–88.

Johnson, M. D. "Life of Adam and Eve." In *The Old Testament Pseudepigrapha*. Vol. 2, *Expansions of the "Old Testament" and Legends, Wisdom and Philosophical Literature, Prayers, Psalms, and Odes, Fragments of Lost Judeo-Hellenistic Works*, edited by J. H. Charlesworth, 249–95. London: Darton, Longman & Todd, 1985.

Kalimi, I. "The Book of Esther and the Dead Sea Scrolls' Community." *ThZ* 60 (2004): 101–6.

Kampen, J., and M. Bernstein, eds. *Reading 4QMMT: New Perspectives on Qumran Law and History*. Atlanta: Scholars Press, 1996.

Kapelrud, A. S. "Der Bund in den Qumran-Schriften." In *Bibel und Qumran*, edited by H. Bardtke, 137–49. Berlin: Evangelische Haupt, 1966.

Kee, H. C. "Testaments of the Twelve Patriarchs." In *The Old Testament Pseudepigrapha*. Vol. 1, *Apocalyptic Literature and Testaments*, edited by J. H. Charlesworth, 775–828. London: Darton, Longman & Todd, 1983.

Keener, C. S. *A Commentary on the Gospel of Matthew*. Grand Rapids: Eerdmans, 1999.

Kimbrough, S. "The Ethic of the Qumran Community." *RevQ* 6 (1969): 483–89.

Klawans, J. "The Impurity of Immorality in Ancient Judaism." *JJS* 48 (1997): 1–16.

Knibb, M. "Martyrdom and Ascension of Isaiah." In *The Old Testament Pseudepigrapha*. Vol. 2, *Expansions of the "Old Testament" and Legends,*

Wisdom and Philosophical Literature, Prayers, Psalms, and Odes, Fragments of Lost Judeo-Hellenistic Works, edited by J. H. Charlesworth, 143–76. London: Darton, Longman & Todd, 1985.

———. "The Ethiopic Book of Enoch." In *Outside the Old Testament*, edited by M. De Jonge, 26–55. Cambridge: Cambridge University Press, 1985.

———. *The Qumran Community*. Cambridge: Cambridge University Press, 1987.

Krašovec, J. "Sources of Confession of Sin in 1QS 1:24-26 and CD 20: 28-30." In *The Dead Sea Scrolls: Fifty Years After the Discovery*, edited by L. Schiffman, E. Tov, and J. VanderKam, 306–21. Jerusalem: Israel Exploration Society, 2000.

Kroft, R. "Pliny on Essenes, Pliny on Jews." *DSD* 8, no. 3 (2001): 255–61.

Kugler, R. "Rewriting Rubrics: Sacrifice and the Religion of Qumran." In *Religion in the Dead Sea Scrolls*, edited by J. J. Collins and R. A. Kugler, 90–112. Grand Rapids: Eerdmans, 2000.

———. "Making All Experience Religious: The Hegemony of Ritual at Qumran." *JSJ* 33, no. 2 (2002): 131–52.

———. "Hearing 4Q225: A Case Study for Reconstructing the Religious Imagery of the Qumran Community." *DSD* 10, no. 1 (2003): 81–103.

Kugler, R., and E. M. Schuller, eds. *The Dead Sea Scrolls at Fifty*. Atlanta: Scholars Press, 1999.

Lambert, D. "Was the Qumran Community a Penitential Movement?" In *The Oxford Handbook of the Dead Sea Scrolls*, edited by T. Lim and J. J. Collins, 501–13. Oxford: Oxford University Press, 2012.

Lange, A. *Weisheit und Prädestination: Weisheitliche Urordnung und Prädestination in den Textfunden von Qumran*. Leiden: Brill, 1995.

———. "Wisdom and Predestination in the Dead Sea Scrolls." *DSD* 2 (1995): 340–54.

La Sor, W. *The Dead Sea Scrolls and the New Testament*. Grand Rapids: Eerdmans, 1972.

Leaney, A. R. C. *The Jewish and Christian World 200 bc to ad 200.* Cambridge: Cambridge University Press, 1984.

———. *The Rule of Qumran and Its Meaning.* London: SCM, 1966.

Légasse, S. "Les Pauvres en éspirit et les 'voluntaires' de Qumran." *NTS* 8 (1961/1962): 336–45.

Laperrousaz, E.-M. *Qoumrân. L'établishment essénien des bords de la mer morte.Histoire et archéologie du site.* Paris: Picard, 1976.

Le Déaut, R. "Le Thème De la Circoncision de Coeur (Dt. XXX, 6; Jer. IV, 4) dans les versions anciennes (LXX et Targum) et à Qumrân." In *Congress Volume: Vienna 1980*, edited by J. Emerton, 178–205. VTSup 32. Leiden: Brill, 1982.

Lim, T. H. *The Dead Sea Scrolls in their Historical Context.* Edinburgh: T&T Clark, 2000.

———. *Pesharim.* Sheffield: Sheffield Academic, 2002.

Löhr, H. *Umkehr und Sünde im Hebräerbrief.* Berlin: de Gruyter, 1994.

Lüdemann, G. *Das frühe Christentum nach den Traditionen der Apostelgeschichte. Ein Kommentar.* Göttingen: Vandenhoeck & Ruprecht, 1987.

Magness, J. *The Archaeology Of Qumran and the Dead Sea Scrolls.* Grand Rapids: Eerdmans, 2002.

Maier, G. *Mensch und freier Wille.* Tübingen: Mohr Siebeck, 1971.

Maier, J. *The Temple Scroll: An Introduction, Translation and Commentary.* Sheffield: JSOT Press, 1985.

———. "The Judaic System of the Dead Sea Scrolls." In *Judaism in Late Antiquity.* Part 2, *Historical Synthesis*, edited by J. Neusner, 84–108. Leiden: Brill, 1995.

Maier, J., and K. Schubert, K. *Die Qumran-Essener. Texte der Schriftrollen und Lebensbild der Gemeinde.* Munich: Ernst Reinhardt, 1973.

Mansoor, M. *The Thanksgiving Psalms.* Leiden: Brill, 1961.

Merrill, E. H. *Qumran and Predestination: A Theological Study of the Thanksgiving Psalms.* Leiden: Brill, 1975.

Metso, S. *The Textual Development of the Qumran Community Rule*. Leiden: Brill, 1997.

Metzger, B. "The Apocrypha and Pseudepigrapha." In *The Expositor's Bible Commentary*. Vol. 1, *Introductory Articles*, edited by T. E. Gaebelin, 161–78. Grand Rapids: Zondervan, 1979.

Milgrom, J. "Repentance." In *Encyclopedia Judaica*, 14:[AQ: Please provide page numbers.]. Jerusalem: Keter, 1974.

Moore, C. A. *Tobit*. AB 40A. Garden City, NY: Doubleday, 1996.

Mueller, J. *The Five Fragments of the* Apocryphon of Ezekiel*: A Critical Study*. JSPSS. Sheffield: Sheffield Academic Press, 1994.

Mueller, J., and S. E. Robinson, "Apocryphon of Ezekiel." In *The Old Testament Pseudepigrapha*. Vol. 1, *Apocalyptic Literature and Testaments*, edited by J. H. Charlesworth, 487–95. London: Darton, Longman & Todd, 1983.

Muraoka, T. "Notae Qumranicae Philologicae." *RevQ* 17 (1996): 573–83.

Murphy, R. E. "*Yeser* in the Qumran Literature." *Biblica* 39 (1958): 334–44.

———. "Sin, Repentance, and Forgiveness in Sirach." In *Der Einzelne und Seine Gemeinschaft bei Ben Sira*, edited by R. Egger-Wenzel and I. Krammer, 261–69. Berlin: de Gruyter, 1998.

Murphy-O'Connor, J. "An Essene Missionary Document? CD II,4-VI,1." *RB* 77 (1970): 201–29.

Najman, H. "Towards a Study of the Uses of the Concept of Wilderness in Ancient Judaism." *DSD* 13, no. 1 (2006): 99–113.

Nave, G. D. *The Role and Function of Repentance in Luke-Acts*. Atlanta: Scholars Press, 2002.

Negoïtsa, A. "Did the Essenes Survive the 66–71 War?." *RevQ* 6 (1969): 517–30.

Neusner, J., ed. *Judaism in Late Antiquity*. Part 2, *Historical Synthesis*. Leiden: Brill, 1995.

Newsom, C. "'Sectually Explicit' Literature from Qumran." In *The Hebrew Bible and Its Interpreters*, edited by W. Propp, B. Halpern, and D. N. Freeman, 167–87. Winona Lake, IN: Eisenbrauns, 1990.

Newton, M. *The Concept of Purity at Qumran and in the Letters of Paul.* Cambridge: Cambridge University Press, 1985.

Nickelsburg G. W. E. *Jewish Literature between the Bible and the Mishnah.* London: SCM, 1981.

———. "Currents in Qumran Scholarship: The Interplay of Data and Agendas, and Methodology." In *The Dead Sea Scrolls at Fifty*, edited by R. Kugler and E. M. Schuller, 79–99. Atlanta: Scholars Press, 1999.

Nitzan, B. "Benedictions and Instructions for the Eschatological Community." *RevQ* 16 (1993): 77–90.

———. "Repentance in the Dead Sea Scrolls." In *The Dead Sea Scrolls after Fifty Years*, edited by P. Flint and J. VanderKam, 2:145–70. Leiden: Brill, 1999.

———. "The Concept of the Covenant in Qumran Literature." In *Historical Perspectives: From the Hasmoneans to Bar Kokhba in the Light of the Dead Sea Scrolls*, edited by D. Goodblatt, A. Pinnick, and D. Schwartz, 85–104. Leiden: Brill, 2001.

———. "Traditional and Atypical Motifs in Penitential Prayers from Qumran." In *Seeking the Favor of God.* Vol. 2, *The Development of Penitential Prayer in Second Temple Judaism*, edited by M. J. Boda, D. Falk, and R. A. Werline, 187–208. Atlanta: Society of Biblical Literature, 2007.

Noth, M. *Leviticus.* OTL. London: SCM, 1965.

Nye, M. *Religion: The Basics.* London: Routledge, 2003.

Oegema, G. *Apokalypsen.* JSHRZ 6.1,5. Gütersloh: Gerd Mohn, 2001.

Parry, D., and E. Ulrich, eds. *The Provo International Conference on the Dead Sea Scrolls: Technical Innovations, New Texts, and Reformulated Issues.* Leiden: Brill, 1999.

Parry, D., and S. Ricks. *Current Research and Technological Developments on the Dead Sea Scrolls*. Leiden: Brill, 1996.

Paul, S., R. Kraft, L. Schiffman, and W. Field, eds. *Emanuel: Studies in Hebrew Bible, Septuagint and Dead Sea Scrolls in Honour of Emanuel Tov*. Leiden: Brill, 2003.

Peterson, M., W. Hasker, B. Reichenbach, and D. Basinger. *Reason and Religious Belief: An Introduction to the Philosophy of Religion*. Oxford: Oxford University Press, 1991.

Puech, É. "Messianism, Resurrection and Eschatology at Qumran and in the New Testament." In *The Community of the Renewed Covenant*, edited by E. Ulrich and J. VanderKam, 235–56. Notre Dame: Notre Dame University Press, 1994.

———. "Notes sur le Manuscrit de XIQMelkîsédeq." *RevQ* 12 (1987): 483–513.

Pfann, S. "The Essene Yearly Renewal Ceremony and the Baptism of Repentance." In *The Provo International Conference on the Dead Sea Scrolls: Technical Innovations, New Texts, and Reformulated Issues*, edited by D. Parry and E. Ulrich, 337–52. Leiden: Brill, 1999.

Pohlmann, K.-F. *Ezechielstudien*. BZAW 202. Berlin: de Gruyter, 1992.

Popovic, P. "Physiognomic Knowledge in Qumran and Babylonia: Form, Interdisciplinarity, and Secrecy." *DSD* 13, no. 2 (2006): 150–76.

Porter, S., and J. de Roo, eds. *The Concept of the Covenant in the Second Temple Period*. Leiden: Brill, 2003.

Porter, S., and C. Evans, eds. *The Scrolls and the Scriptures: Qumran after Fifty Years*. Sheffield: Sheffield Academic, 1997.

Pouilly, J. *La Règle de la Communauté de Qumrân. Son Évolution Littéraire*. Paris: Gabala, 1976.

Preuss, H. D. *Deuteronomium*. Darmstadt: Wissenschafliche Buchgesellsschaft, 1982.

Priest, J. "The Testament of Moses." In *The Old Testament Pseudepigrapha*. Vol. 2, *Expansions of the "Old Testament" and Legends, Wisdom and Philosophical Literature, Prayers, Psalms, and Odes, Fragments of Lost Judeo-Hellenistic Works*, edited by J. H. Charlesworth, 919–34. London: Darton, Longman & Todd, 1985.

Rabenau, M. *Studien zum Buch Tobit*. BZAW 220. Berlin: de Gruyter, 1994.

Rad, G. von. *Deuteronomy. A Commentary*. OTL. Philadelphia; Westminster, 1966.

Ringgren, H. *The Faith of Qumran: Theology of the Dead Sea Scrolls*. Philadelphia: Fortress, 1963.

Roberts, B. J. "Qumran Scrolls and Essenes." *NTS* 3 (1956): 58–65.

Roth, C. Why the Qumran Sect Cannot Have Been Essenes." *RevQ* 1 (1959): 417–22.

———. "'Qumran and Masadah': A Final Clarification Regarding the Dead Sea Sect." *RevQ* 5 (1964): 81–88.

Russell, D. S. *The Old Testament Pseudepigrapha: Patriarchs and Prophets in Early Judaism*. London: SCM, 1987.

Sacchi, P. *The History of the Second Temple Period*. Sheffield: Sheffield University Press, 2000.

Sauer, G. *Jesus Sirach*. JSHRZ 3.5. Gütersloh: Gütersloher Verlaghaus; Gerd Mohn, 1981.

Sanders, E. P. *Paul And Palestinian Judaism: A Comparison of Patterns of Religion*. London: SCM, 1977.

———. "Jesus and the Sinners." *JSNT* 19 (1983): 5–36.

———. *Jewish Law from Jesus to the Mishnah*. London: SCM, 1990.

———. *Judaism: Practice And Belief, 63 b.c.e.–63 c.e.* London: SCM, 1992.

———. "The Dead Sea Sect and Other Jews: Commonalities, Overlaps and Differences." In *The Dead Sea Scrolls in their Historical Context*, edited by T. H. Lim, 7–43. T&T Clark: Edinburgh, 2000.

Sandmel, S. "Parallelomania." *JBL* 81 (1962): 1–13.

Schiffman, L. H. *The Halakhah at Qumran*. Leiden: Brill, 1975.

———. *The Eschatological Community of the Dead Sea Scrolls*. SBLMS 38. Atlanta: Scholars Press, 1989.

———. *Reclaiming the Dead Sea Scrolls: Their True Meaning for Judaism and Christianity*. Philadelphia: Jewish Publication Society, 1994.

———. "Utopia and Reality: Political Leadership and Organization in the Dead Sea Scrolls Community." In *Emmanuel: Studies in Hebrew Bible, Septuagint and Dead Sea Scrolls in Honour of Emmanuel Tov*, edited by S. Paul, R. Kraft, L. H. Schiffman, and W. Fields, 413–27. Leiden: Brill, 2003.

Schiffman, L. H., et al., eds., *The Dead Sea Scrolls: Fifty Years after Their Discovery*. Jerusalem: Israel Exploration Society, 2000.

Schuller, E. *Non-Canonical Psalms from Qumran: A Pseudepigraphic Collection*. HSM 28. Atlanta: Scholars Press, 1986.

———. "4Q380 and 4Q381: Non-Canonical Psalms from Qumran." In *The Dead Sea Scrolls: Forty Years of*, edited by D. Dimant and U. Rappaport, 90–99. Leiden: Brill, 1992.

Schürer, E. *The History of the Jewish People in the Age of Jesus Christ (175 bc–ad 135)*. Revised and edited by G. Vermes, F. Millar, and M. Black. Vol. 2. Edinburgh: T&T Clark, 1979.

Schwemer, A.-M. *Vitae Prophetarum*. JSHRZ 1.7. Gütersloh: Gütersloher Verlaghaus; Gerd Mohn, 1997.

Seely, D. R. "The 'Circumcised Heart' in 4Q434 *Barkhi Nafshi*." *RevQ* 17 (1992): 527–35.

———. "Implanting Pious Qualities as a Theme in the *Barkhi Nafshi* Hymns." In *The Dead Sea Scrolls: Fifty Years after Their Discovery*, edited by L. Schiffman, E. Tov, and J. VanderKam, 322–31. Jerusalem: Israel Exploration Society, 2000.

Shanks, H. *Understanding the Dead Sea Scrolls*. London: SPCK, 1993.

Shemesh, A. "The Origins of the Laws of Separatism: Qumran Literature and Rabbinic *Halacha*." *RevQ* 70 (1997): 207–39.

Skehan, P., and A. Di Lella. *The Wisdom of Ben Sira*. AB 39. Garden City, NY: Doubleday, 1987.

Sparks H. F. D., ed. *The Apocryphal Old Testament*. Oxford: Clarendon, 1984.

Stanton, G. N. *Jesus and Gospel*. Cambridge: Cambridge University Press, 2004.

Stegemann, H. *The Library of Qumran: On the Essenes, Qumran, John the Baptist, and Jesus*. Grand Rapids: Eerdmans, 1998.

———. "Qumran Challenges for the Next Century." In *The Dead Sea Scrolls: Fifty Years after Their Discovery*, edited by L. H. Schiffman, E. Tov, and J. VanderKam, 944–50. Jerusalem: Israel Exploration Society, 2000.

Stern, C., ed. *Gates of Repentance*. New York: Central Conference of American Rabbis, 1979.

Stockhausen, C. K. *Moses' Veil and the Glory of the New Covenant*. Rome: Editrice Pontificio Instituto Biblio, 1989.

Stone, M. E. *Scriptures, Sects and Visions*. Cleveland: Collins, 1980.

———, ed. *Jewish Writings of the Second Temple Period*. Philadelphia: Fortress, 1984.

———. "The Dead Sea Scrolls and the Pseudepigrapha." *DSD* 3, no. 3 (1996): 270–95.

Steudel, A. "אחרית הימים in the Texts from Qumran." *RevQ* 16 (1993): 225–46.

———. *Der Midrasch zur Eschatologie aur der Qumrangemeinde (4QmidrEschat a and b)*. Leiden: Brill, 1994.

Strugnell, J. "The Angelic Liturgy at Qumran—4Q Serek Shirot 'Olat Hasshabat." In *Congress Volume: Oxford 1959*, 318–45. VTSup 7. Leiden: Brill, 1960.

Sung, C.-H. *Vergebung der Sünden*. WUNT 5. Tübingen: Mohr Siebeck, 1993.

Sussmann, Y. "Appendix 1." In *Qumran Cave 4.5: Miqsat Ma'ase Ha-Torah*, edited by E. Qimron and J. Strugnell, 179–200. DJD 10. Oxford: Clarendon, 1994.

Sutcliffe, E. *The Monks of Qumran: The People of the Dead Sea Scrolls*. London: Burn & Oates, 1960.

———. "Hatred at Qumran." *RevQ* 2 (1959/1960): 345–55.

Talmon, S. "The 'Desert Motif' in the Bible and in the Qumran Literature." In *Biblical Motifs: Origins and Transformations*, edited by A. Altman, 31–63. Cambridge, MA: Harvard University Press, 1966.

———. *The World of Qumran from Within*. Jerusalem: Magness, 1989.

———. "The Community of the Renewed Covenant: Between Judaism and Christianity." In *The Community of the Renewed Covenant*, edited by E. Ulrich and J. C. VanderKam, 3–24. Notre Dame: Notre Dame University Press, 1994.

Taylor, J. E. *The Immerser: John the Baptist within Second Temple Judaism*. Grand Rapids: Eerdmans. 1997.

Tomasino, A. *Judaism before Jesus: The Events and Ideas That Shaped the New Testament World*. Downers Grove, IL: InterVarsity Press, 2003.

Tov, E. "The Orthography and Language of the Hebrew Scrolls Found at Qumran and the Origin of these Scrolls." *Textus* 13 (1986): 31–57.

———. "The Biblical Scrolls Found in the Judean Desert and their Contribution to Textual Criticism." *JJS* 39 (1988): 5–37.

Trever, J. C. *The Dead Sea Scrolls: A Personal Account*. Grand Rapids, Eerdmans, 1977.

Van Der Horst, P. W. "Pseudo-Phocylides." In *The Old Testament Pseudepigrapha*. Vol. 2, *Expansions of the "Old Testament" and Legends, Wisdom and Philosophical Literature, Prayers, Psalms, and Odes, Fragments of Lost Judeo-Hellenistic Works*, edited by J. H. Charlesworth, 565–82. London: Darton, Longman & Todd, 1985.

VanderKam, J. C. *An Introduction to Early Judaism*. Grand Rapids: Eerdmans, 2001.

———. *The Dead Sea Scrolls Today*. Grand Rapids: Eerdmans, 1994.

Van Der Ploeg, J. *The Excavations at Qumran: A Survey of the Judean Brotherhood and Its Ideas*. Translated by K. Smyth. London: Longmans, Green, 1958.

Van Der Ploeg, J., et al., eds. *La secte de Qumrân et les origines du Christianisme*. Leuvan: Desclée de Brouwer, 1959.

Van Der Woude, A. S. "Fifty Years of Qumran Research." In *The Dead Sea Scrolls after Fifty Years*, edited by P. Flint and J. VanderKam, 1–45. Leiden: Brill, 1998.

Vermes, G. "The Essenes and History." *JJS* 32 (1981): 18–31.

———. "The Oxford Forum for Qumran Research: Seminar on the Rule of War from Cave 4 (4Q285)." *JJS* 43 (1992): 85–94.

———. *The Religion of Jesus the Jew*. London: SCM, 1993.

———. "The So-Called King Jonathan Fragment (4Q448)." *JJS* 44 (1993): 294–300.

———. "The Present State of Dead Sea Scrolls Research." *JJS* 45 (1994): 101–10.

———. *An Introduction to the Complete Dead Sea Scrolls*. London: SCM, 1999.

———. *Jesus in His Jewish Context*. Minneapolis: Fortress Press, 2003.

Vogt, E. *Untersuchungen zum Buch Ezekiel*. Rome: Biblical Institute Press, 1981.

Volz, D. P. *Der Prophet Jeremia*. KZAT 10. Leipzig: A. Deichertsche, 1928.

Watson, F. *Paul and the Hermeneutics of Faith*. London: T&T Clark, 2004.

———. "Constructing an Antithesis: Paul and Other Jewish Perspectives on Divine Human Agency." In *Divine and Human Agency in Paul and his Cultural Environment*, edited by J. M. G. Barclay and S. Gathercole, 99–116. LNTS 335. London: T&T Clark, 2006.

Weinfeld, M. *The Organizational Pattern and the Penal Code of the Qumran Sect.* Fribourg: Éditions Universitaires, 1986.

———. "Grace after Meals in Qumran." *JBL* 111 (1992): 427–40.

Weingreen, J. *From Bible to Mishna: The Continuity of Tradition.* Manchester: Manchester University Press, 1976.

Whittaker, M. "Life of Adam in Eve." In *The Apocryphal Old Testament,* edited by H. D. F. Sparks, 141–68. Oxford: Clarendon, 1984.

Wilckens, U. *Die Missionsreden der Apostelgeschichte.* WMANT 5. Vluyn: Neukirchener, 1974.

Willitt J. "The Remnant of Israel in 4QpIsaiaha (4Q161) and the Dead Sea Scrolls." *JJS* 57, no. 1 (2006): 11–25.

Winston, D. *The Wisdom of Solomon.* AB 43. Garden City, NY: Doubleday, 1979.

Wintermute, O. S. "Apocalypse of Zephaniah." In *The Old Testament Pseudepigrapha.* Vol. 1, *Apocalyptic Literature and Testaments,* edited by J. H. Charlesworth, 497–507. London: Darton, Longman & Todd, 1983.

———. "Jubilees." In *The Old Testament Pseudepigrapha.* Vol. 2, *Expansions of the "Old Testament" and Legends, Wisdom and Philosophical Literature, Prayers, Psalms, and Odes, Fragments of Lost Judeo-Hellenistic Works,* edited by J. H. Charlesworth, 35–142. London: Darton, Longman & Todd, 1985.

Wise, M. O. *A Critical Study of the Temple Scroll from Qumran Cave 11.* Chicago: Oriental Institute of the University of Chicago, 1990.

Wright, R. B. "Psalms of Solomon." In *The Old Testament Pseudepigrapha.* Vol. 2, *Expansions of the "Old Testament" and Legends, Wisdom and Philosophical Literature, Prayers, Psalms, and Odes, Fragments of Lost Judeo-Hellenistic Works,* edited by J. H. Charlesworth, 639–70. London: Darton, Longman & Todd, 1985.

Yadin, Y. *The Scroll of the War of the Sons of Light Against the Sons of Darkness.* Oxford: Oxford University Press, 1962.

———. *The Temple Scroll; The Hidden Law of the Dead Sea Sect.* London: Weidenfeld and Nicolson, 1985.

Zenger, E. *Das Buch Judit. JSHRZ* 1.6. Gütersloh: Gütersloher Verlaghaus; Gerd Mohn, 1981.

Index of Authors

Index of Scriptures and Ancient Literature

CPSIA information can be obtained at www.ICGtesting.com
Printed in the USA
LVOW04s0053130115

422401LV00005B/8/P